THE SONG OF THE AGES

PART III: EDEN'S RETURN

NICK PADOVANI

The Song of the Ages Part III: Eden's Return
Copyright © 2021 by Nick Padovani
Published by Eyes Open Press
Visit us at www.eyesopenpress.com
Printed in the United States of America
ISBN-13: 978-0-9991806-8-6 (paperback)
ISBN-13: 978-0-9991806-9-3 (e-book)

All rights reserved solely by the author. No part of this book may reproduced in any form without the permission of the author.

Unless otherwise indicated, all Scripture quotations are taken from the *New American Standard Bible* (NASB). Copyright © 1960, 1962, 1968, 1971, 1972, 1973, 1975, 1977, 1995 by The Lockman Foundation. Used by permission. All rights reserved.

Scripture quotations taken from the *Amplified Bible, Classic Edition* (AMPC). Copyright © 1954, 1958, 1962, 1964, 1965, 1987 by The Lockman Foundation. Used by permission. All rights reserved.

Scripture quotations taken from *The Holy Bible,* English Standard Version (ESV). Copyright © 2001 by Crossway, a publishing ministry of Good News Publishers. Used by permission. All rights reserved.

Scripture quotations taken from the *King James Version* (KJV)—public domain. Rights in the Authorized Version in the United Kingdom are vested in the Crown. Reproduced by permission of the Crown's patentee, Cambridge University Press.

Scripture quotations taken from *The Knox Bible* (KNOX). Copyright © 1945, 2012 by Baronius Press. All rights reserved.

Scripture quotations taken from *The Message* (MSG). Copyright © 1993, 1994, 1995, 1996, 2000, 2001, 2002. Used by permission of NavPress Publishing Group. All rights reserved.

Scripture quotations taken from the *New International Version* (NIV). Copyright © 1973, 1978, 1984, 2011 by Biblica, Inc.™. Used by permission. All rights reserved.

Scripture quotations taken from the *New King James Version* (NKJV). Copyright © 1979, 1980, 1982 by Thomas Nelson, Inc. Used by permission. All rights reserved.

Scripture quotations taken from the *New Living Translation* (NLT). Copyright © 1996, 2004, 2015 by Tyndale House Foundation. Used by permission of Tyndale House Publishers Inc., Carol Stream, Illinois 60188. All rights reserved.

Scripture quotations marked TPT are taken from *The Passion Translation*, copyright © 2017. Used by permission of Broadstreet Publishing Group, LLC, Racine, Wisconsin, USA. All rights reserved.

Cover Design by Ariel Janho

Contents

Foreword   5

Before You Begin   7

1 Arrival   9
2 Maturing the Nations   21
3 The Song and the Apocalypse Pt. 1   37
4 The Song and the Apocalypse Pt. 2   47
5 The Heavenly Mission Base   59
6 A Mystery in the Field   71
7 Dismantling Shadows   83

Seventh Selah   **93**

8 A Door of Hope   95
9 Full Circle: Back to Jerusalem   111
10 Still Asleep (Reprise)   125
11 Waking the Harlot   143
12 Rising from the Wilderness   159
13 Like Thunder and Dawn   179
14 Whales, Deserts, and the Head of Creation   191

Eighth Selah   **205**

15 The Kiss of the Ages   207
16 The Royal Seal   227
17 Ring Within a Ring   251

The Song of the Ages: Part III

18	Transfiguration of the Cosmos Pt. 1	273
19	Transfiguration of the Cosmos Pt. 2	297
20	The Lake of Fire	321
21	The Cross Versus the Wand	343

Ninth Selah — *365*

22	Bringing the Song to the Nations	367
23	The Word of Her Testimony	383
24	Chief of the Mountains	393

Foreword

As an author, I know what it's like for God to sovereignly appoint and anoint a person to write a book that unveils revelation that goes beyond the mind's ability to comprehend by mere intellect alone. To undertake and tackle unveiling the wisdom of the wisest king who ever lived would most certainly have to be the call of God. After reading this amazing trilogy, I am convinced that Nick Padovani was called to do this.

Responding to the call of God is a *yes* that none of us take lightly. I've known Nick for many years now and I am consistently moved by the wisdom and humility by which he preaches, teaches, and writes. But I believe the reason Nick was graced to write about the Song of Songs has to do with something spoken of in psychology today as the metaphysical gaze.

That term speaks to a recognized countenance of people enraptured in delight at the glory of God, a spiritual awareness, and the joy of the fellowship of the saints. The idea is that there is a recognizable glow of love upon the face of those who have spent considerable time beholding the glory of the Lord. Nick Padovani shines, and you can see the light of the Spirit of God in his countenance and read it in his words. If somebody wants to write a book on the love of God and the joy of being the Bride, and the delight of covenant union, but they don't carry adoration upon their countenance, I probably won't care to read what they have written. But when Nick Padovani tells me he's written three

The Song of the Ages: Part III

volumes on the Song of Solomon, I want to read them all. I've seen his face, I've heard his voice, and Nick shines with an adoration for the presence of the Lord.

In *The Song of the Ages* trilogy, you'll discover the dance of faith and works, understand what true apostolic ministry is, discover the purposes of God for creation, find the new covenant in the Old Testament, and be ignited in awe and wonder as your attention and affection is drawn to the loving gaze of our risen Savior.

Thank you, Nick, for saying *yes* to the call.

Bill Vanderbush
Author and Speaker

Before You Begin

(An Opening Note)

This final journey through the Song of all Songs can easily stand on its own. You needn't read the past two volumes to receive the impact of this one. And yet, the previous expeditions through King Solomon's inspired poetry provide a solid foundation for what you're about to encounter. Reading this book alone would be similar to fast-forwarding to the most intense part of a song without allowing all the musical build-up to prepare your heart for the end. Either way, for those who are jumping in for the first time, or those who have been wading in the waters, here are some basic things to know as we prepare to get moving again.

The poetry and lyrics making up the Song of Songs are one giant parable—a symbolic story we've been unraveling like golden thread from a mysterious quilt of metaphors and signs. To do this, we've utilized an ancient manner of Bible interpretation called *sod*, the Hebrew word for *mystery*. Such was the method used by Jesus, the apostles, and many rabbinical leaders before them in their exposition of the Scriptures. It involves discovering the deeper and usually more allegorical meaning behind the sacred text. In the case of the Song, this deeper meaning is centered in one reality— the union between Christ and us, represented by *the Beloved and the Shulammite*. This simple message then leads to many other things,

The Song of the Ages: Part III

including heaven's great plan to restore the cosmos—a plan in which each of us have an important part to play.

The first chapter will catch you up on some of the things you may have missed or forgotten in the overall story of the Shulammite's travels. This will take you back into where we left off in the lyrics, beginning in Song of Songs 7:6. Through this, many notions about Christianity will be thoroughly re-examined, including subjects like evangelism, discipleship, missions, the end-times, and more. This is because the Song of Solomon is like a tuning fork that releases a pure sound in helping tune all the other instruments of theology. Like an architect's plumbline, it helps set the rest of the building in order. All the elements of the Christian faith come into proper harmony through the Song of the Ages. It is my hope that a more complete and refreshing vision of the faith will emerge out of this final journey through the Song's dramatic ending.

Not far into this book you will also see how the Song of Songs ties in with the Book of Revelation. As it goes on, *Eden's Return* might seem as much a commentary on John's Apocalypse as it is a study on Solomon's ballad. But actually, this whole thing was never meant to be a study of one particular book. It's really about unlocking the glorious message of union found throughout all of Scripture. The Song of Songs just happens to be our core text, with Revelation close behind it.

As you read, please understand that you are living in remarkable times. We are in the midst of the rising dawn, a new era in the manifestation of God's Kingdom on earth. As you read—hopefully with your heart as much as your mind—you will discover there are currents of wind that come off the melody hidden within this Song. If caught by a believing heart, these currents will carry you headfirst into that dawn. You will be part of the first-fruits of a new day, basking in the sun and calling the world homeward.

1
Arrival

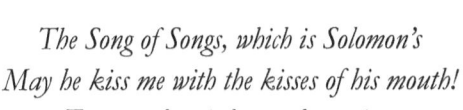

The Song of Songs, which is Solomon's
May he kiss me with the kisses of his mouth!
For your love is better than wine.
(Sgs. 1:2)

How beautiful is your love, my sister, my bride!
How much better is your love than wine...
(Sgs. 4:10)

How beautiful and how delightful you are,
My love, with all your charms!
(Sgs. 7:6)

For a long time, man has hunted desperately after the knowledge of his origin, scouring fossils and stars, caves and galaxies, in order to discover something of his starting place. Like a person interviewing old family members and searching through faded documents in hopes of learning about the blood in their veins, our entire race has gone through earth, sea, and sky with the same purpose. How surprising is it then, and how beautiful and strange, to discover the origin of our species was actually a *divine kiss?*

We were formed in the dust, yet we were never meant to remain a blend of chemical-infused earth. We were made by Love to bear the image of Love. This is why God leaned into man's earthly form and kissed him into being. The Maker drew near to Adam and breathed into his nostrils the spark of divine life, which became our true genesis. Even when we fell back into the dust, forsaking the One who had made us, creating fossils of war instead of legacies of love, we would yet be brought back to our true identity by another divine kiss from heaven.

In the coming of Christ, a fresh kiss of the Spirit was poured out upon all flesh. Heaven touched earth like falling rain pressings its lips against chapped soil. This rain proved that the seed of the Word, the image of Christ, was still present within God's lost children. Though dormant and cold, this hidden seed had only been waiting for the rains of the Spirit to awaken its inner fire—a fire of love that was meant to blossom with colorful heat and infinite passion.

The Shulammite

In the beginning of the Song of Songs, we discovered a young woman longing for this great kiss of the Spirit to awaken the flames within her. She was quite literally burnt out and thus seeking after a fresh ignition. Through an ensuing journey of love and revelation, this woman became the Shulammite Bride who rose confidently and humbly into her place as a restored child of God. We found that this woman represents each and every person who is in pursuit of their origin in God; who is reaching out for the "more" behind their existence.

We also found that thousands of years before fairytales like Sleeping Beauty were penned, a wise king from Israel had already

Arrival

captured their intrinsic storyline in the Song of all songs. Humankind is the true beauty who was put to sleep by the spell of religion and fear, now captive to a dreary forgetfulness and guarded by a dragon known as the accuser (Rev. 12:9-10). This is the message behind the Song of the Ages; one that goes on to declare how our great Prince came to dispel our fears and awaken us to true love. In His coming, Christ kissed all humanity and raised us up before the Father through His all-encompassing resurrection. Unfortunately, there are still many who choose to stay upon a bed of slumber. They reject the kiss of heaven and resist the Song of grace that would set their hearts free.

The Shulammite is obviously not in this category. She allowed her heart to open to God's love and found that it tasted better than the sweetest of wine. We found that this wine of God's love is intricately tied to the work of Jesus. In the Scriptures, wine represents the very blood of Christ. The night before His crucifixion, Jesus lifted up a cup of wine and said, "This is the blood of the covenant, which is poured out for many for forgiveness of sins" (Matt. 26:28). The wine of Jesus's grace, poured out on the cross, is the kiss that comes to our hearts and awakens us to our true and original existence. The Bride is the one who has learned to drink down this wine of grace, to receive its kiss, and to allow divine life to blossom within her. This has led to her rising and releasing her own kiss back to the Lord (Sgs. 4:10).

It goes without saying that God's sleeping beauty could not kiss the Prince back until He had first kissed her. Hence, "We love because He first loved us" (1 Jn. 4:19). In receiving the overflow of His grace, the Bride released the wine of her own love back to Christ. Halfway through the Song, we then saw the King enjoying her returning kiss and He too compared it to wine. All of this has been a picture of mankind coming into maturity, which is going to become a beautiful theme filling the pages ahead.

The Song of the Ages: Part III

Each one of us were made to grow up into love, to develop and flourish in the full expression of the image of God—who is Love itself. The Bride's journey has magnificently revealed these things, especially when her life uncovered the jaw-dropping truth that we captivate the heart of the Creator. We're the beauty that has held hostage the heart of the King, propelling Him to go through hell and high water to rescue each one of us. It turns out our beauty stems from the fact that the same wine of glory within God has been placed within us as well. We reflect God like a daughter can uniquely reflect her father; like the prodigal son still bore the DNA of his searching dad. This truth is the hidden seed and the pearl of great price for which Jesus sold everything to redeem.

The Great Climax

We now come to the closing scenes of this great Story and Song. A symphony has been rising with a crescendo that began quiet and unsure, yet grew into the most powerful chorus of awakened love. We've crossed a threshold in the music God is conducting through the ready pen of Solomon. The Song of the Lamb has built up toward a resolute ending and now, as musicians will sometimes say, we have "arrived." The rest of the Song is simply about enjoying this moment of arrival where all the pieces of the Song, its instruments and lyrics, its rhythm and story, come together in harmonious force. What now follows is where the kiss of God and the kiss of the mature Bride collide together into an overflowing energy of love. This overflow will touch those who are still "asleep"—the people of the world who are unaware or still resistant to the music that calls them home. The kiss will now come to their hearts as well.

> *And your mouth is like the best wine!*
> *It goes down smoothly for my beloved,*

Arrival

Flowing gently through the lips of those who fall asleep.
(Sgs. 7:9)

This Song has reminded us about grace and its overflowing effects. Real fruitfulness comes from the excess of joy and freedom. Religion, on the other hand, is about forcing these things to happen through fear and obligation. But true life can never be forced or demanded. It can only explode out of the power of a divine kiss. Religion creates life in the sterile lab of human works. Grace creates life within the infinite expanse of God's heart. And its fruit is a fiery bang that is bigger than the moment of creation.

Since we're now enjoying this divine surplus of grace, we'll take our time through these closing parts, even slowing down the music to really soak in the full climax of the Song. In many ways, this book will be more practical than the previous two volumes of *The Song of the Ages*. It will focus more on the explosive fruits that flow out of our faith in this beautiful Gospel ballad. In the first part of the Song, the Shulammite was discovering her identity, learning to rest in its truth even when she didn't outwardly experience it. In the next part, she was discovering her great calling and destiny, which of course goes hand in hand with her identity. But since we are so addicted to finding our identity in what we do, we took a lot of time before arriving at the "destiny" part.

Once the Bride understood who she was, she could more clearly embrace the incredible works she was called to do. In our previous study of the Song, we found that all of this is pointing to the fact that she is indeed the true city of light found in the book of Revelation. She is the city all mankind is longing for, and within her borders is the transforming Tree of life (Rev. 22:2). It's the leaves of her maturing life that bring healing to the brokenness of the nations—and the medicine within these leaves *is* the Song of the Ages.

The Song of the Ages: Part III

The Dance of Faith and Works

Let's be clear about something. Our life's purpose is undeniably simple. It is to know and enjoy God and receive the wine of His love. However, to know God is to love our brother (1 Jn. 4:7-8). True intimacy with our heavenly Bridegroom will always lead to birthing and raising up spiritual children. In other words, enjoying the Gospel leads to fruit-bearing, which involves getting our hands dirty and ministering to other children of God throughout the world by raising them up into this same ballad of truth. Another way of saying this is that when a person awakens to their sonship, it will naturally lead to divine responsibilities. Not the sterile obligations of religion, but the mature rising of a man or woman who knows that he or she is commissioned by their Father to minister in the courts of His Kingdom.

And so, all of this helps settle an age-old struggle throughout church history regarding faith and works. In this Song, the two find their balance like a spinning top upon the floor of God's Word. And perhaps a top is a good image, because these things are not meant to come together in a static doctrine where everything can be explained and categorized line by line (where we wrestle with questions like, "how much is too much grace," or "how much is too much work," and "what are the correct proportions between the two"). There is a *spin* to this thing. A dance that resembles the ebb and flow of water, which literally changes with wind and gravity.

Today, throughout the entire Body of Christ, there are movements that are looking afresh at the wonders of faith and grace. There is an awakening to the work of Christ and its effect upon this entire creation, whereby the cross has brought redemption to all things (Col. 1:20). This unmasks the amazing truth that the glory of God already fills this entire creation, including all the people within it. In these movements, there is a massive and appropriate

Arrival

amount of focus on *rest* and resisting the ever-present temptation to strive and struggle. On the flipside, there are many movements focused on the work that still needs to be done. Orphans that need to be cared for, widows that need to be cheered, and all sorts of people who need to hear and believe this wonderful Gospel. Unfortunately, these movements are sometimes in opposition to each other, sending warning signs within their camps of the dangers and heresies of the other side.

But herein lies the power of the mature Bride and the story being told of her throughout the Song. The Shulammite has learned to embrace both sides of the coin. She is the delicate spin between the two. She knows her calling to heal the nations, but she also knows that it only comes from the One who has already healed creation at the cross. She knows that she is made to furiously love the people around her, but she is well aware that this love can only flow through her as she abides in the One who first loved her. Consequently, she has come to a place of peace within both dynamics of rest and work. The work is fiery and passionate, but it flows from a place of divine ease.

Instruments, Singers, and Charms

With this newfound unity between her great identity and her world-changing calling, Jesus now proclaims the following words over His Bride: *"How beautiful and how delightful you are, my love, with all your charms!"*

Jesus sees the full picture of His Bride and is stunned by everything that has come together in her life. Of course, He has always seen and understood this. He was singing about it even when she couldn't believe it herself (Sgs. 1:5). But now that these aspects of the church are outwardly blossoming, there's a new depth of joy in His Song. God is rejoicing over His Bride because a great desire of His heart is beginning to be answered through

The Song of the Ages: Part III

her—the prayer that it would be *on earth* as it already is in heaven. He is celebrating heaven's growing manifestation on earth.

Here, the Lord refers to her with the personal and possessive phrase "*My love.*" In saying this, Jesus is obviously referring to the Shulammite; yet there is another way of looking at this. He could also be speaking of His own love within her. "How beautiful and delightful is *My* love." Remember, the wine of His love has been poured out within her. She is one with Love Himself. So in saying *My love*, He could be referring to her *or to Himself.* Either way, this brings us back to the central thread of union running through the entire Song.

After this, the Lord declares that all of this delight comes from the Shulammite's "charms." As we come to the climax of the Song, we will find that the Hebrew word for charms is astoundingly fitting. Besides one other prophet in the Old Testament, King Solomon is the main biblical writer to use this word. He specifically utilized it in the book of Ecclesiastes. Reading this will give us more insight into the associations in Solomon's mind when he thought of this particular word:

> *I also gathered for myself silver and gold and the special treasures of kings and of the provinces. I acquired male and female singers, the **delights** of the sons of men, and musical instruments of all kinds.*
> *(Ecc. 2:8 NKJV)*

Solomon put the word "delights"—the same word translated as "charms" in the Song of Songs—right in the middle of a discussion about singers and instruments. In Ecclesiastes, he is recapping the glories of his pursuits as the richest man in the world; how he acquired all kinds of musical instruments and singers, referring to these things as the "delights of the sons of men." This comes right after he mentions his acquisition of

Arrival

silver and gold and the "special treasures" of kings. We can infer here that Solomon used his riches of silver and gold to purchase musicians, instruments, and vocalists. It is then that he uses the word delights, or charms, to speak of the music he brought into his life. Hence, this is a word that was connected, at least in his mind, to the treasures of music.

And so, when Solomon writes that the Shulammite was beautiful and delightful because of *all her charms*, it's not too difficult to make the prophetic connection to the ballad of heaven that the story points to. Here, the Lord is referring to the full musical ensemble of her life. In other words, Jesus (through Solomon) is beholding the complete orchestra of the church and the coming manifestation of the Music within her. He is taking delight in it as a king would delight in His most prized possession. Jesus, the King of all nations, has acquired the true silver and gold of those nations—the people that make them up. The people of the world are the true treasures of God. And, as we awaken to love, our lives become the instruments that play forth His Song.

Wind and Breath

Many of the instruments treasured by the Hebrew people were of the wind family, such as the flute or trumpet. At Solomon's coronation, the earth shook at the noise erupting from the people as they played these specific types of instruments (1 Kgs. 1:39-40). An interesting thing about these devices is how a musician must, in a way, kiss them and release breath into them in order for music to come forth. Such instruments release beautiful sounds when wind or breath passes through their inner chambers. This is because within them lies hollow cavities of different shapes and sizes that allow for the wind to come through and exit out of piped openings, creating an assortment of musical notes along the way.

The Song of the Ages: Part III

The connection to humanity is exhilarating. We are hollow clay vessels, empty and incomplete without the breath of God flowing through us. But when God kisses our being with His love—when He releases the glory of His Spirit through us—we become instruments of praise. And our praise is a dynamic life of supernatural power, gratitude, and kindness. Unless we receive that kiss for ourselves, we remain hollow, continually searching for the meaning behind our seemingly empty design. It is important to note, however, that even when an instrument isn't being played, there is still air inside of it. The same goes with every human being. The Spirit of God, who fills all things, is not separate from any person. Yet wind is meant to move and flow. Breath is meant to come in and out. So, when a person allows the fresh and vibrant breath of God to kiss their being, the air already within them moves and is released out of the pipes of their soul. The Spirit was there all the time, but now they are allowing Him to create beautiful music through their lives. In a way, that is what salvation is—the hollow instrument of a person's life coming alive to the Song of heaven!

In biblical times, much like today, musical instruments were made of wood or brass. As we've noted in previous studies of the Song, these materials are symbols for humanity (while precious metals such as gold are symbolic of the divine; hence, the Ark of the Covenant perfectly represents Christ since it was solid wood covered with gold—a picture of humanity and divinity). Brass and wooden instruments were specifically hand-crafted for breath and wind to pass through them in order to create different notes that could come together to form music. And of course, such instruments complement and enhance each other when they are played alongside each other.

All of this is an amazing picture of the Song of the Ages being released through the human church. As our seemingly hollow

Arrival

frames are filled with the kisses of grace—as we receive and drink of the Spirit of truth—we become instruments that play together. Out of this, a symphony of praise arises and fills the earth with the melodies of grace. In the church, the King of glory has found the perfect ensemble of "male and female singers…and musical instruments of all kinds." Through His own breath, God sings and plays through us to His absolute delight and pleasure.

Focus and Preparation

With all this in mind, let's remember that God Himself is the content of the music. He is the true Song we were meant to play through the instruments of our being:

> *Behold, God is my salvation;*
> *I will trust, and will not be afraid;*
> *for the Lord God is my strength and **my song**,*
> *and he has become my salvation.*
> *(Isa. 12:2 ESV)*

He is the focus of our music—and yet our union with Him gives us a fresh perspective on this. Because we are one with Christ, we are in fact the focus and content of *His* music. We are His Song! And so, once more we find two kisses colliding into one. He is the music and so are we. This is the splash of two wines and the kiss of two seas, as we discovered in the last volume. Thus, the words laid out before us remain true and eternal. How stunningly beautiful, how marvelously delightful we are, with all of our "charms," coming together in unity, wind, and Song! Prepare yourself to embark into the untold wonders hidden in this grand orchestra as it reaches its most beautiful lyrics and sounds…

2
Maturing the Nations

Your stature is like a palm tree,
And your breasts are like its clusters.
(7:7)

The Song goes on as the King continues to look at the full musical ensemble of His church. He then appropriately gives a description of her entire "stature," a word that means "full length" or the "whole size of a person's body." Earlier in the Song, the King and the on-looking world gave praiseful descriptions about the Bride from the head down to the feet (and back up to the head again). At this point, we are taking a step back and looking at her all at once, with each piece coming together in wonderful harmony. This is the poetic and musical summarizing of God's people. Jesus is looking at the Shulammite in the fullness of her stature and all the musical "charms" of her being. He is seeing both the identity and the destiny of the Bride merging in a glorious collision. Because of this, He proclaims these words: *"Your stature is like a palm tree, and your breasts are like its clusters."*

Now that we are looking at the full stature of the church, we find another description about the breasts, a symbol of nourishment to the spiritually young. This part of her identity

The Song of the Ages: Part III

is being highlighted because the next part of the Song is about fruitfulness and multiplication. That's where we're ultimately headed. First, however, we need to slow down and get a better look at the word "stature."

The Puzzle of the Word

Each word in the Song of Songs is a treasury of revelation and insight. Every single term is like a musical note, where if any of them were taken away, it would dampen the entire composition. Therefore, we must continue to tune our ears even to the smallest of notes within the Song by unpacking the significance of particular words. We've already done this with the word "charms," and we did it numerous times in our last study. To re-explain the importance of this, we need to remember something about the Bible. Though it is a book written by men over the course of thousands of years, there is a higher Author behind its frail make-up—a Composer who has hidden certain notes within it for us to discover and enjoy. Everything connects in the Bible, including specific words.

To use another analogy, the Scriptures are like a puzzle with many different pieces, all of which can be put together to unveil a hidden picture. However, reading Genesis to Revelation straight through like a textbook is not the way to put together the puzzle. The Bible from front to end is actually a jumbled mess of pieces, as though you are just opening up a puzzle box for the first time. The pieces can only be put together through a revelation of Christ and the New Covenant. This is also why the Bible is a living book with a living message. It's a not dead reference book to be read from front to back to get a lesson on morality and or to gain understanding on religious history. That is one layer of the book that can be useful in some regards, but there's a much more important message in the midst of it.

And so, in this puzzle even individual words can make up its individual pieces. You can take words out of books like Genesis,

Maturing the Nations

Exodus, or the Song of Songs and place them alongside each other to find the greater picture jumbled up in the Scriptures. As you do this, you find that the picture formed by this puzzle is the most beautiful image in all of creation—both in the heavens and in the earth.

Ark, Ark, and Temple

The Hebrew word for "stature" is *qowmah*. The first time it shows up in the Bible is during the construction of Noah's ark. As you probably know, the ark was a large wooden boat that would not only hold animals but also the family of the one righteous man left on earth. The *qowmah*, or stature, of this ark was specifically "thirty cubits" in height (Gen. 6:15). Keep all of that in mind. This is one puzzle piece that we'll put aside for a moment until we find another one that can connect right into it.

The next time *qowmah* shows up is in Exodus 25 during the construction of another significant item—the Ark of the Covenant. We mentioned this other Ark in the last chapter; how it was a wooden chest covered in gold, representing both the divinity and humanity of Christ. This chest was filled with the righteous law of God and other holy items. Already you can see a congruence between the Ark of the Covenant and the ark of Noah, which was a wooden structure containing a righteous man inside of it. But we'll put those two puzzle pieces aside and continue to look for more.

If you keep searching through the box of the Bible, one of the later times the *qowmah* piece shows up is in the building of yet another significant structure—the temple of Solomon. The temple was of course a physical building that hosted the presence of God in its innermost room; a room that lay beyond two other places called the outer court and inner room. Interestingly, Solomon's temple was specifically designed to be "thirty cubits in stature," just like Noah's ark (1 Kgs. 6:2). So already there's a pattern and picture

The Song of the Ages: Part III

beginning to emerge as we put all these individual Scriptures next to each other.

Now first and foremost, these images connect back to the person and stature of Christ. However, they also point *to us*. Humanity is the wooden ark of Noah, tossed in the floods of own destruction but preserved through the righteousness of Christ within. We're also like the wooden Ark of the Covenant, made to hold the true law of the Spirit within the tablet of our hearts (Rom. 8:2). Furthermore, we are the true temple of God (1 Cor. 3:17). Like the temple and its three main areas (the outer, inner, and innermost rooms), we too are made up of three main regions (body, soul, and spirit). Moreover, in the deepest place within us is the righteous presence of God. Thus, these are all images of our identity as God's greatest creation.

But the key point in all of this is that the height of our *qowmah* is "thirty cubits." In other words, the true stature of humanity is the very stature of God, which is what the number thirty represents. Three is a divine number—the number of the Trinity. Thirty just puts an added emphasis to the number three. Thirty is also the age when Joseph, David, and Jesus were all released into their full calling. Thus, it is also a number of maturation and fullness. At thirty years old, God declared His love over His Son, saying, "This is My beloved Son, in whom I am well-pleased" (Matt. 3:17). This is similar to the words of the Song, where Jesus speaks over His mature Bride and declares His pleasure over all her "charms" and "stature." He is saying to her, *"This is My beloved church, in whom I am well-pleased!"*

When we stand up into our full stature we look just like our precious Lord. Or—since the number thirty also points to the entire Godhead—we could also say that we look like the entire Trinity who lives together in grace and harmony. This means that our full mature posture is one of unity, love, and honor; all of which rises together into a great dance of faithfulness and intimacy.

Maturing the Nations

Even in the wooden frailness of our humanity, we can engage in this eternal dance because of the gift of righteousness inside of us.

True Apostolic Ministry

One of the main analogies we've used to describe the difference between the world and the Bride is that the world is asleep while the Bride is awake—and more than just awake, the Bride is one who has gotten out of bed and is now standing tall. We've seen this analogy over and over again; however, there is another metaphor the Bible offers on the same subject that's also very important. It has to do with infancy versus maturity. In this case, the difference between the world and the Bride has to do with growth. In other words, the world is stuck in a type of spiritual infancy while the true Bride is comprised of those who have "grown up" into the maturity of Christ.

This analogy comes up subtly when the apostle Paul explains his life mission to the Colossian church. He first says that his passion is to make known the mystery of "Christ in you" among the nations. This is then followed by an incredibly fitting statement that alludes to this analogy of infancy and maturity:

> *We proclaim Him, admonishing every man and teaching every man with all wisdom, so that we may present every man complete in Christ.*
> *(Col. 1:28)*

Now the analogy is unclear unless you understand the meaning of the Greek word for "complete." This is actually the same word used for "mature" or "full-grown." Hence some translations will render it, "so that we may present everyone *fully mature* in Christ" (Col. 1:28 NIV). The idea behind Paul's words is that the people of the world are immature. They are not full-grown. In the other analogy, you could say that they are not getting out of bed and standing up in the full stature of Christ. They are stuck in a bed

The Song of the Ages: Part III

of infancy. The world needs to come into maturity, and thus he wanted to present *every man* in such a way.

Paul addresses the issue of immaturity more clearly in a different letter of his. In 1 Corinthians he comes against sinful and divisive Christians (people who should be standing up in the stature of Christ) and compares their foolish ways to the people of the world.

> *And I, brethren, could not speak to you as to spiritual men, but as to men of flesh, as to infants in Christ.*
> *(1 Cor. 3:1)*

Most people think of the phrase "infants in Christ" and think of immature believers who need to grow up. But let's look at this verse more carefully. Paul is comparing the church—a people of the Spirit—to "men of flesh." He is comparing Corinthian believers to the people of the world who have not embraced the gift of the Spirit and the eternal life of Christ. He then gives another title to this kind of person at the end of the verse. He calls them "infants in Christ," or "babes," as the King James puts it. Paul is not directly calling the Corinthian believers "men of flesh." He's only saying that they are acting in such a way—*as* to men of flesh—*as* to infants in Christ.

Here's the point. Paul is saying that the people of the world are infants in Christ. They are immature infants in the revelation of who they really are as God's children. Like babies, the world has become egocentric, unable to share, and unable to stand up and walk. All humanity has fallen to the ground and crawled through the dust instead of standing up in the light of grace. As Paul says elsewhere, the whole world has sinned and *fallen* short of the glory of God (Rom. 3:23). It doesn't say they don't have the glory of God. It just states they have fallen short of it. They have stopped standing in the fullness of the glory they were designed to experience. But that glory is still there, and it squeaks out all the time. Whenever someone who doesn't know Christ acts in a Christ-like way, that is still the glory of God coming

Maturing the Nations

out of their life. Don't think it's the devil getting unbelievers to forgive and love another, or to sacrifice their lives or to respond with patience to difficult situations. That is the image and glory of God still resident within mankind, for they are actually *infants in Christ*. For this reason, Paul wanted to present every person *mature* in Him.

The problem with the world is that the glory only comes out here and there. It is only a crawl and not a constant walk in the righteousness of God. But the standing up—the awakening and arising—happens through the power of the Holy Spirit when a person receives the love of Christ and the knowledge of who they are in Him. That's when people begin to walk as mature children of God. That's where they receive authority and power to *become* who they already are.

> *But whoever did want him,*
> *who believed he was who he claimed*
> *and would do what he said,*
> *He made to be **their true selves**,*
> *their child-of-God selves.*
> *(Jn. 1:12 MSG)*

Everyone, no matter who they are, is a child of God; however, not everyone is living in mature sonship. That is what the Bride represents in this part of the Song—the *mature* sons and daughters of God standing in the full stature of Christ. "Men of flesh," on the other hand, are divine infants. Or in other terms, they are instruments sitting in the dust, broken and unplayed. And this is where Paul's great mission comes into view. The apostle's passion was to wake up the instruments—to make them men of wind and breath instead of flesh and futility. He wanted to present every man in full maturity by showing them who they already are. Think about it. A person sleeping in their bed has just as much potential to walk around as the person who is awake and standing. The problem is that their eyes are closed, which reminds us of something else Paul reflected on:

> *So this I say, and affirm together with the Lord, that you walk no longer just as the Gentiles also walk, in the futility of their mind,* **being darkened in their understanding***, excluded from the life of God because of the ignorance that is in them, because of the hardness of their heart.*
> *(Eph. 4:17-18)*

The entire purpose of apostolic ministry is to wake people up—or to bring them into maturity in Christ. And this is the work of all true ministry, including the fivefold leadership gifts mentioned in the same chapter quoted above. This is a subject we'll return to at the end of the book; for now, we'll just note that after Paul describes these five different gifts, he ends by saying that their work will continue until...

> *...we all attain to the unity of the faith, and of the knowledge of the Son of God, to a* **mature man***, to the measure of* **the stature** *which belongs to the fullness of Christ.*
> *(Eph. 4:13)*

This will come through proclaiming, admonishing, and teaching the revelation of *Christ in you*, the hope of glory—the hope of standing in the full stature of God.

Blossoming Righteousness

And so the King is marveling at His awakened Bride. He sees her standing in the full stature of His Son. He's always seen this and has always declared it, but now He's overjoyed because she's truly taking hold of it. But He's not just marveling at her ability to stand. He's also rejoicing over her ability to nourish the spiritually young. And that is

Maturing the Nations

the point of bringing up this analogy of infancy and maturity. This is where we connect it with the symbolic imagery of the Shulammite's breasts. For the breast of the mother feeds, nourishes, and helps to develop infants—*babes*. Here we come to a tremendous link between the apostolic mission of the church and the Song of Solomon. As the Bride rises into her full stature, this also includes the calling to bring every other man and woman into their full stature as well.

The Bride's stature is then compared to a fruitful palm tree. Once again, the word choice is not an accident. This is not the poetic whim of the writer. This is the inspired word given by the great Composer and Puzzle-Maker behind the entire Song. It's one more musical note and puzzle piece within this verse that we must listen to and put together before moving on.

As with many other puzzle pieces, it's usually best to start with the first time the term shows up in Scripture. In the case of the "palm tree," this word initially emerges after the Hebrews are delivered from their slavery in Egypt (Ex. 15:21-27). The Israelites' exodus leads to a scene where they find themselves in a place filled with palm trees, and it is there we uncover the full meaning of this piece. Interestingly enough, this scene begins after a *song* of deliverance is sung out by Moses's sister. The song is sung and the people celebrate, but the story continues and the people enter into the wilderness. There, they go three days without water.

After three days of thirst, the people come to a place they decide to call *Marah*, a word that means "bitter." This lovely title came about after the people drank from the water in that region. No matter where they cupped their hands and slurped, the streams of Marah were undrinkable. This becomes a spiritual picture of death and bondage, especially when you consider how the human body can't spend much longer than three days without water (particularly young children and the elderly, who comprised a

The Song of the Ages: Part III

good portion of the Hebrew camp). Thus, three days of thirst was leading to the bitter end of death.

But it is here that the Gospel's notes break through like a sweet chorus coming after a slow and twisted verse. Moses steps in for the people and God instructs him to take a tree and cast it into the bitter waters. Moses obeys the command and throws an entire tree into the water. Instantly, all the water in the region becomes sweet! Yet again, a beautiful picture of Calvary comes together here. Through the tree of the cross, Christ threw Himself into the bitter waters of death. And He didn't just dip His foot into these waters. He dove in completely. There, He remained for three days to show the utter finality of His death. But then, oh happy day, the bitterness of death turned into the sweetest of water! On the third day, our thirst for forgiveness and new life was quenched in the rising of Jesus.

Immediately after this great picture of salvation, the Hebrew people arrive at place they call Elim, which is a much happier word than Marah. This word literally means "Palm Trees." The reason for this is that this new region had twelve wells of water and seventy palm trees. Finally, they are in a place of refreshment and fruitfulness—a stark contrast to where they found themselves during the three days leading up to Marah.

The palm tree is known for its burgeoning fruit, and the imagery speaks of the fruitfulness that comes to our lives as we drink of the sweet waters of Christ's death. In Psalm 92, the writer declared, "The righteous man will flourish like the palm tree" (Ps. 92:12). The progression from Marah to the land of Palm Trees is a picture of salvation and its resulting fruit. When we drink of the righteousness that has been given to us in Christ, we begin to flourish like the palm tree. Through Jesus's death, we are instantly righteous by grace; however, we start to "flourish" as the righteousness already insides of us outwardly blossoms into the ripe fruits of salvation.

Maturing the Nations

Now the fact that the Israelites stumbled upon *seventy* palm trees is also significant. It's another connecting edge of the puzzle piece. We've well established the fact that the number seven is all about completion. This has come up several times throughout the Song of Solomon and it comes up hundreds of more times throughout the rest of the Bible. Seven speaks of completion, but *seventy* is a symbolic way of adding emphasis to it. In a way, it communicates mature completion—or, in other words, manifested completion. It's similar to the number thirty in this regard. And so again, the image of seventy palm trees speaks of our righteousness in Christ *blossoming and manifesting* as mature fruit.

The Israelites' move from Marah to Elim is like a micropicture of the larger move from Egypt to the Promised Land. All the wilderness wanderings contain messages of truth for us today (1 Cor. 10:6). For us, Marah to Elim is a picture of what comes about when we encounter the cross and drink of its truth. As we continue to drink from the sweetness of the simple Gospel, our righteousness manifests. We begin to rise into our full stature as the redeemed sons and daughters of God!

The City of Palm Trees

The Israelites' wilderness wanderings contain yet another puzzle piece of the palm tree. In fact, it appears at the very end of the people's journey as they prepared to enter the land of Canaan through the city of Jericho. In several different Scriptures, Jericho is referred to as the City of Palm Trees because it was renowned for being populated by these kinds of trees (Deut. 34:3). Jericho is an image we covered extensively in our last study of the Song, but now we come to a fresh perspective on it with this alternative name.

When the Israelites finally came to the Promised Land, they faced a giant wall blocking them from entering the famous City of Palm Trees. As we saw in the last volume, the walls of Jericho represent anything and everything that blocks us from entering the rest and righteousness of the Gospel. Ultimately, the walls speak of unbelief, religion, and fear. And now, as we look at the prophetic meaning of the palm tree, we see that the walls are specifically keeping people from entering into *mature fruitfulness*. In other words, they keep us from moving out of spiritual infancy and into the full righteousness of Christ!

Therefore, the walls of deception need to come down in order to unveil the "palm trees" of our true stature as God's kids. In a way then, this whole world is like a City of Palm Trees blocked by the walls of darkness and fear. These are the same walls the Shulammite encountered throughout her entire journey, which blocked the life of God within her from bursting forth. She was no different from anyone else in the world, because each one of us is called to be a palm tree of righteousness. As the Beloved said to the Shulammite earlier on, we are all "a garden locked, a spring sealed up" (Sgs. 4:12). The image of a locked garden also reminds us of Eden, which is where the first *wall* in front of the human race was ever erected. There, on the east side of the Garden, the entrance into Eden was locked and guarded by mighty cherubim (Gen. 3:24).

Carvings in the Temple

On that note, did you know that cherubim actually show up in the midst of palm trees later on in the Bible? The puzzle continues! This is an image that appears inside of Solomon's temple where there were carvings of "cherubim, palm trees, and open flowers" (1 Kgs. 6:29). These things were carved into the doors on the *east side* of the temple that guarded the path to the innermost rooms. All of this connects in an incredible way. As we've explained before, Solomon's design plans for the temple were just as prophetically inspired as the writing of his great love Song. Like each verse of the

Maturing the Nations

Song, every part of Solomon's temple carries immense revelation in and of itself.

The temple carvings of palm trees and open flowers speaks of mature and blossoming righteousness. But sadly, the temple design also reminds us of the doors and veils blocking the way into this reality. That is what the cherubim allude to. Like the sword-wielding cherubim at the east entrance of Eden, they represent the legal blockages keeping us from discovering the *innermost room*—the springs of glory locked inside of our innermost being. The doors of the temple and the walls of Jericho all communicate these same messages.

But that is again why we find the Song of the Gospel to be so sweet and so powerful. It destroys the bitterness of these walls and guides us into the way of true life. And of course, Jesus is that Way. In His own body He took on the dividing walls and *became sin* on our behalf. Therefore, when Jesus's body was torn, the "veil" of separation was torn as well (Heb. 10:20). This is how the way into fruitfulness and fullness was restored.

Later on in the Scriptures, palm trees show up in yet a different temple, but this time they are described with a more encouraging tone. Ezekiel has a vision of a future temple and describes another kind of palm tree carving inside of it. Look carefully at the following:

> *All the walls were decorated with carvings of cherubim, each with two faces, and there was a carving of a palm tree between each of the cherubim. One face—that of a man—looked toward the palm tree on one side. The other face—that of a young lion—looked toward the palm tree on the other side. The figures were carved all along the inside of the Temple.*
> (Ez. 41:18-19 NLT)

The palm trees here are surrounded by cherubim, but these are quite different from the ones described in Solomon's temple. They

The Song of the Ages: Part III

each have a single body, but their heads are composed of two different faces. One face is that of a man, while the other is that of a lion.

For some, the symbolism here might be glaringly obvious. These images really aren't pointing to angels. The carvings in Ezekiel's temple are now speaking to Someone else. This Someone is the Lion of the tribe of Judah, the human descendent of Judah who is also God in the flesh. This mysterious Someone, hidden in ages past and now revealed through the Gospel, is Jesus Christ—the One who has passed through the flaming sword of Eden on our behalf. He has taken that fiery death upon Himself, and in the same act has forever opened the way for us to enter back into Eden. Ezekiel's cherubim are shown to be heavenly symbols of the person and work of Christ. He's the One who is greater than the angels; who has overcome every hindrance to a mature and fruitful life!

Using the imagery of palm trees and cherubim, Ezekiel paints a hope-filled vision for God's future temple—the *church*. Ezekiel's vision is not about a future physical structure. It's actually a symbolic vision of redeemed humanity—mankind united with the Lion of Judah! It's a picture of humanity rising into their full stature as a "palm tree" of righteousness.

The Central Truth

Now at this point you might be lost in a forest of palm trees and symbolism. So let's just take a deep breath for a moment and come away from all this poetic imagery. Let's step back and look at the simple yet beautiful picture emerging from all these different puzzle pieces of the Word. As we do this, let's also remember that this is indeed the point of studying out these symbols and searching the Scriptures. The point is always about discovering and beholding the central truth of God's Word—the key note and the main chorus within His heavenly Song.

Maturing the Nations

This central truth is the reality of people being restored to their union with God. In and through Christ's work, the way has been opened for us to experience an Edenic life. A fruitful life. A life filled with a luscious harvest of tranquility and happiness, sacrificial love, and bottomless kindness. A life of relational health and intimate connection with the Trinity. A life of wholeness in every part of our lives. This is the life of the *full stature* of God's kids. And this is what the Beloved has been declaring over His Bride all along!

Kingdom Leadership

Of course, with this mature stature comes the call to lift others into their true stature as well. This brings us back to one last symbol from the story of Elim and its many palm trees. The story also says that there were *twelve wells* of water in that region. These wells, in the midst of seventy palm trees, are another key element that uncovers more of the true picture here.

Once again, the number of objects involved gives us some insight into its meaning. Thankfully, the number twelve is something we've covered before. In fact, seven and twelve are perhaps the most common numbers in the entire Bible. While seven speaks of completion, the number twelve speaks of the apostolic foundation of the church. It correlates to the number of patriarchs that founded the twelve tribes of Israel, as well as the number of apostles Jesus raised up to found the church. It's a number that speaks of leadership and foundation.

But how does this connect to the Shulammite?

As we drink from the sweetness of the cross and come into the place of maturity, we naturally become leaders in God's Kingdom—leaders who have become wells for the world to drink from. Just as the twelve tribes of Israel were like priests to the nations, the church is a royal priesthood who dispenses the drink of the Gospel to the world. We are an apostolic people. Through

The Song of the Ages: Part III

the fivefold leadership gifts—through proclaiming, admonishing, and teaching (and every other form of spiritual gifting)—we bring the knowledge of identity and redemption to the people of the world so that they can drink of this sweet water as well. Through this, they discover the hidden palm trees of glory that have been blocked behind the walls of guilt and shame.

This is what the twelve wells amongst the seventy palm trees is all about. The wells are the Bride's apostolic ministry to bring the water of life to the nations. This truth has been emerging all throughout the seventh chapter of the Song, but now it's being spoken in an overarching and summarizing way. As the Bride rises and flourishes like a tree, she will naturally give away the water of life—for it is already within her. She is now revealed as the unwalled City of Palm Trees. She *is* the land of Elim. Therefore, the twelve wells represent the same thing as the Shulammite's breasts. She brings both the *water of life* and *the milk of the Word* to the infant nations of the world!

Now, as more puzzle pieces come together to form this great portrait of the Bride, the picture will expand even further and include the fruits of her labor, leading to the end-time harvest of the nations…

3
The Song and the Apocalypse Pt. 1

———•◆•———

*I said, "I will climb the palm tree,
I will take hold of its fruit stalks."
Oh, may your breasts be like clusters of the vine…
(7:8a)*

The Beloved is overcome by the full stature of His church and in an outburst of rapturous delight He exclaims that He will take hold of her fruit.

Now let's be honest. Imagery like this can be quite difficult to study from a spiritual perspective. We mentioned in the beginning of the Shulammite's journey that Jewish boys were told to keep away from this book until a certain age. Today, much of the evangelical world teaches this book from a marital or sexual perspective, and they completely miss the forest for the palm trees. So, besides a relatively small number of people over the centuries, the treasures in this book have gone untouched by those who've handled it. It's funny actually, how the Lord chose to hide such powerful truths behind intimate language like this. He probably knew how awkward this book would be in certain hands. Like a jewel thief missing the diamond hidden underneath the unsuspecting pillow of the homeowner, many who have gone through this book have completely missed the jewel within. But perhaps in some way this has helped preserve the purity of its unsuspecting message. And what better place to hide the revelation of Jesus's Bride than in a romantic poem?

It's almost like God purposefully put some of the deepest revelations of Scripture here because He was waiting for a mature church to take hold of them. He was waiting for the church to be more deeply established in grace in order to open up the true contents of this book. Recall Solomon's wisdom when he wrote, *"It is the glory of God to conceal a matter, but the glory of kings to search out a matter"* (Prov. 25:2). God has concealed His glorious messages very well.

Thank God, we are well beyond the point of awkwardness. We've lifted the lid of an earthly romance and are now peering into the treasures of divine glory. That said, let's unpack more of this imagery and behold the mysteries within. Mysteries that speak to the great harvest of the ages, the time of the end, and the eternal mercies of God poured out at the cross...

Promise of the Harvest

Let's first focus on the Lord's statement about *taking hold* of the fruit stalks. This imagery is a message about Jesus harvesting fruit from the Shulammite's life. He says He will climb the palm tree and take hold of its fruit, which is what farmers would do in ancient times (and many still do today) when harvesting clusters of dates from tall and mature palm trees. In the land of Judea, the date fruit was a staple food that required the hard work of climbing high into trees in order to gather and export it throughout the region.

The Song and the Apocalypse Pt. 1

Indeed, the full "stature" of the Bride includes the abounding fruit of a great harvest. Her fruitfulness is more than just the fruit of the Spirit. It's also the fruit that comes from the nurturing love she gives to others. The Song has built up toward this, expounding on the promise of entire nations being drawn to the light of Christ within the church. Now we find the Lord making a declaration that He will harvest all of this promised fruit. "I *will* climb the palm tree," He says. "I *will* take hold of its fruit stalks!" Jesus intends on reaping a bountiful harvest of revival and transformation through a mature Bride. This is the promise continuing to grow throughout the Song's seventh chapter.

Rebirth of the Ancient Palm

Did you know that the oldest germination of a mature seed came from a Judean palm tree just like the one described in the Song of Songs? In 1965, the palace of Herod the Great in Masada was excavated, leading to the discovery of an ancient jar holding the seeds of date palms. These seeds were held in storage in Israel for forty years until 2005 when three of them were taken and planted in different locations. Miraculously, one of those seeds sprang to life. The seed was determined to be from the first century B.C., making it almost exactly 2000 years old. It's the oldest known tree seed ever geminated, and ever since 2005 it has continued to grow into a healthy date palm, even flowering and producing pollen so that it can eventually reproduce itself. What's incredible is that this specific type of palm tree had been extinct for over 800 years prior to this discovery! *This was quite literally an act of resurrection as the same tree mentioned in Solomon's timeless Song was reborn in our own modern day!*

There are incredible implications to this breakthrough discovery. Herod the Great, in whose palace this seed lay hidden, is the one who tried to kill Christ as a young baby. Think of the enormity of this fact. Herod is the one who failed to kill the young seed of salvation—the Messiah of Israel. 2000 years later, a literal tree seed from his own palace was recovered and proven to still hold life inside of it. The irony! This life was preserved for over 2000 years and has now emerged as a flourishing plant that is already bearing pollen that can multiply its life into other palm trees. Moreover, this is the same tree the Scriptures explicitly use to represent the righteousness of God and the flourishing Bride of Christ!

Jesus truly is the seed that died in the earth in order to bear much fruit (Jn. 12:24). Likewise, His life has been preserved within the seed of our own beings and 2000 years later there is a church who will believe this truth and flourish into the same *stature* as Christ.

It's also significant that this ancient date palm seed discovered in Herod's palace was hidden away for forty more years before it was planted and brought to life. Forty is the biblical number for trials and testing. It speaks to the forty years of wilderness wandering before Israel broke through the walls and entered the City of Palm Trees. In the same way, the true church has been relatively hidden under the shell of broken, divided, and man-controlled systems and walls. We've undergone great trials and testing. Nevertheless, all our hiddenness and pain will lead to the ultimate fulfillment of God's precious and magnificent promises. Once again, even 2000 years later, the life of Christ will spring forth from the dust of our beings and the church will come into full maturity! Jesus will certainly reproduce His life in a mature church throughout the world. This is a maturity that will lead to an abundance of fruit that will be harvested by the Lord Himself—and by His holy angels. The next part of the poem will help us understand this all the more.

Jacob's Prophecy

Right after He speaks of climbing the palm tree, the Beloved mentions the Bride's breasts and compares them to "clusters of

The Song and the Apocalypse Pt. 1

the vine." Even more harvesting language emerges here and a deeper revelation comes forth. But before we look at this, there's a powerful truth hidden right in the Hebrew word for "breasts" that we need to see. Once again, looking at the first time this word shows up in Scripture will give us a key in understanding its spiritual meaning. It's another unifying puzzle piece and it first surfaces in the prophetic promise spoken over Joseph by his father Jacob. The prophecy begins like this:

> *Joseph is a fruitful vine,*
> *a fruitful vine near a spring,*
> *whose branches climb over a wall.*
> (Gen. 49:22 NIV)

Like the Shulammite, Joseph is described as a fruitful vine. He's a vine with branches that are so expansive they reach out and extend over the walls that surround it. It's intriguing to find out that the word for "vine" in this prophecy is actually translated from the Hebrew word for *son*. Then the word for "branches" used here is taken from the Hebrew word for *daughters*. Thus, a literal translation of this passage would read, "Joseph is a fruitful *son* near a spring whose *daughters* climb over a wall." This is obviously a word about the many children who would come from Joseph's line. He is a fruitful vine who would reproduce many sons and daughters. Already we can see even more of a connection to the Bride in Solomon's Song. But the prophecy goes on and becomes even clearer. Jacob gives us the reason as to *why* Joseph will be so fruitful:

> *Because of your father's God, who helps you,*
> *because of the Almighty, who blesses you*
> *with blessings of the skies above,*
> *blessings of the deep springs below,*

The Song of the Ages: Part III

blessings of the breast and womb.
(Gen. 49:25 NIV)

Joseph's fruitfulness is due to the "blessings" of God—the sheer grace and goodness of the Lord, which are upon the breast and womb. The prophecy paints a picture of those who will be birthed and nurtured through Joseph's family line. This brings us back to the underlying theme emerging in the seventh chapter of the Song. Underneath the lid of physical intimacy, eternal mysteries are being revealed. When the Beloved says to the Shulammite, *"Oh may your breasts be like clusters of the vine,"* He is continuing to speak of the church's call to birth and nurture a great harvest of spiritual sons and daughters.

The Great Winepress

Yet this comparison to "clusters of the vine" carries much more insight than this. Like our last study, this involves a deep parallel between the Song of Solomon and the book of Revelation. As we've said from the very first volume, the Song of the Lamb in Revelation and Solomon's Song of Songs are spiritually united. The book of Revelation and the Song of Solomon are sister books that weave together two totally different colors and textures of thread; yet create the same tapestry of Christ and His Bride.

In John's Revelation, the phrase "clusters of the vine" is described in connection to a harvest. Ironically, it's mentioned only a few verses before "the Song of the Lamb" in Revelation 15. So already we can see a connection between this portion of Revelation and the Song of Solomon. But that connection will deepen as we look at it closer...

> *Then another angel came out of the temple which is in heaven, he also having a sharp sickle. And another angel came out from the altar, who had power over fire, and he cried with a*

The Song and the Apocalypse Pt. 1

*loud cry to him who had the sharp sickle, saying, "Thrust in your sharp sickle and gather the **clusters of the vine** of the earth, for her grapes are fully ripe."*
So the angel thrust his sickle into the earth and gathered the vine of the earth, and threw it into the great winepress of the wrath of God. And the winepress was trampled outside the city, and blood came out of the winepress, up to the horses' bridles, for one thousand six hundred furlongs.
(Rev. 14:17-20)

In this vision, the apostle John sees an angel holding a sharp sickle. While many readers might assume this was a large staff with a curved blade at the end, it was actually just a hooked knife. This was a common instrument used to cut off clusters of grapes from their branches. The clusters would be cut and then gathered together and brought into a winepress. There, the grapes would be trampled upon, typically by the feet of vineyard workers, which would allow its juices to be released into a container where it would ferment and later be turned into wine.

In much of the modern church, this passage is typically taught from the perspective of a literal bloodbath coming upon the disobedient. The "ripe" grapes are the matured sins of mankind being gathered together so that God's wrath can trample them down. Many believe this is speaking of Jesus and His angels coming to wage an apocalyptic war against the disobedient; the results being literal pools of blood reaching up to a horse's neck and going on for 1600 furlongs—*about 200 miles*. The idea is that Jesus will come galloping on a literal equine animal, cutting off the heads of military leaders like a first century Roman general, and then allow His horse to take its hooves and violently trample upon their skulls, ribcages, arms, and legs. As the bones crack and the skin breaks, a river of blood will be released into an entire region of the Middle East (a distance close to the entire nation of Israel

The Song of the Ages: Part III

from north to south). In all of this, the mercy revealed at Calvary will cease and Jesus will go into a righteous rampage of brutal execution.

Now before we look at another possibility for understanding this verse, let's first acknowledge that there are indeed many strange and varied teachings out there about the book of Revelation. These teachings often involve intricate charts and interpretative opinions, and they usually stem from those who take the visions of Revelation very literally (often interjected with their own personal visions they claim to have received from God). So, in all of this, let's remember that the Scriptures warn us to guard the message of grace by staying away from "strange and varied teachings" (Heb. 13:9). There's a simplicity to God's Word, even in a book as intense and outlandish as Revelation. This simplicity is rooted in the blood of the Lamb—the central character of Revelation. Indeed, the book is called the "Revelation of Jesus Christ," which can also be translated as the *Unveiling* of Jesus Christ. That is the true meaning of the Greek word behind *Revelation*—or *Apocalypse*, as it's sometimes rendered. This book is primarily about an unveiling of Christ and His victorious church.

So, let's look again at this violent passage in Revelation 14. One of the main problems with taking this literally is that there are not enough humans in the world to account for the amount of blood described here. People have actually done the calculations for the amount of human blood required to reach a horse's neck and then extend for 200 miles. They've found it would require the blood of more humans than have ever lived upon the earth!

On top of this, there's a serious issue of conflict with the heart of Jesus that was revealed at Calvary. The Lord told His own disciples they were to forgive their enemies "seventy times seven" times (Matt. 18:22). Most would agree this doesn't mean you have permission to stop forgiving after the 490th offense. Jesus was

The Song and the Apocalypse Pt. 1

talking about entering into the mercy of God, which never ceases. In fact, it *endures forever* (see Ps. 136). But some people assume Jesus doesn't follow His own commands and can choose to stop forgiving people at a certain point in history. Such an assumption is clearly disconnected from the character of Christ. Therefore, both physiologically and theologically, the violent interpretation of the passage has serious holes in it.

While the lampstands, stars, and dragons in Revelation are obviously all representative of something deeper, bloodthirsty Bible scholars have a hard time discovering the deeper meaning of this particular passage. As a result, they decide to choose where spiritual revelation ends and literal interpretation begins, picking out some images to be literal and some to be symbolic. But this is a dangerous road to walk down, and it is part of the reason the Bible is a double-edged sword. According to 2 Corinthians, one side of the Word kills (which is the *literal letter* of the law), while the other side brings life (the *spirit* of the law). We're called to stay on the side of *life*.

Thankfully, we don't have to whip out detailed charts and contrived explanations in order to discover the meaning of this passage. It actually becomes quite simple when the overarching focus of the "unveiled Christ" is put into view. To see this more clearly, we'll now need to look at the larger context of this portion of John's Apocalypse...

4
The Song and the Apocalypse Pt. 2

———•❖•———

I said, "I will climb the palm tree,
I will take hold of its fruit stalks."
Oh, may your breasts be like clusters of the vine,
And the fragrance of your breath like apples,
And your mouth like the best wine!
It goes down smoothly for my beloved,
Flowing gently through the lips of those who fall asleep.
(7:8-9)

We're looking at the incredible connection between the "clusters of the vine" in Solomon's Song and the "clusters of the vine" in the Bible's final book. In order to see its deeper meaning in Revelation, we need to look at something from earlier in the chapter where this phrase shows up. In Revelation 14, the apostle John sees a Lamb standing with a faithful group of people singing "a new song" (v. 3). Now take note here that this is not talking about a literal livestock mammal singing a song with a gathered crowd. Obviously, this is symbolic language, just like the winepress John sees a little later. The Lamb

The Song of the Ages: Part III

is none other than Jesus Christ and His song is the Song of the Gospel—the song of deliverance heralded throughout the entire Bible (see Ex. 15, Ps. 32:7, Isa. 25). It's a song of celebration and victory. In this passage, it's called a "new song," which makes sense when you read the following chapter.

In Revelation 15, a group of victorious ones begin singing the "song of Moses," which is actually an old song. However, the title of the track is then clarified when it is called the "Song of the Lamb" (Rev. 15:3). It's not the old song of the Mosaic law they're singing—it's a new Song of grace! This one is not about the blood of literal Passover livestock, but the blood of the true Lamb of God. This is the life-giving side of the sword of God's Word! Moses and legalistic literalism brings death, but the Spirit of the Lamb and the revelation of the Christ brings life. This is the true sword of the Spirit.

So, in between the "new song" in Revelation 14 and the "Song of the Lamb" in Revelation 15, you have this series of angelic visions, one of which is the bloody passage mentioning "clusters of the vine." Thankfully, these visions start off with something that explains the meaning and focus of everything else. Look at what it says:

> *And I saw another angel flying in midheaven, having an* **eternal gospel** *to preach to those who live on the earth, and to every nation and tribe and tongue and people; and he said with a loud voice, "Fear God and give Him glory, because the hour of His judgment has come; worship Him who made the heaven and the earth and sea and springs of waters."*
> *(Rev. 14:6)*

There it is. The eternal Gospel, which is synonymous with the Song of the Lamb and the "new song" of victory. This is the simple thread of truth strewn throughout each of these visions with one underlying message. John is seeing the proclamation of the Gospel over the nations. Remember now that the word *Gospel* is about celebratory good news. It actually involves glad tidings of great joy for *all people*—as another group of angels once declared (Lk. 2:10). Perhaps the angelic choir director who visited the shepherds keeping their flocks by night is the same one John saw flying in midheaven. Either way, their message is the same.

Now notice something else. Within this good and victorious news is the proclamation that *the hour of His judgment has come*. This note about judgment is part of the "eternal Gospel." Therefore, it's part of the exceedingly glad tidings. Fortunately, John gives us further insight into this statement in his personal account of Jesus's life. In fact, much like the Song of Songs, John's gospel intimately connects with the book of Revelation as well.

Judgment Has Come

In his gospel account, John records some powerful words Jesus spoke as the time of His crucifixion approached. The Lord declared *"the hour has come"* and *"for this purpose I came to this hour"* (Jn. 12:23 & 12:27). The "hour" Jesus was referring to was the hour of His glorification—the moment of His triumph on the cross. Jesus then says the following:

> ***Now*** *judgment is upon this world;* ***now*** *the ruler of this world will be cast out. And I, if I am lifted up from the earth, will draw all men to Myself."*
> *(Jn. 12:31-32)*

It turns out the real and ultimate judgment happened at the cross! It was there that Satan (the great dragon of Revelation) was cast out of heaven as Christ ascended to the right hand of God (see Rev. 12). In that act of judgment, Jesus took on the sin of the

The Song of the Ages: Part III

world and broke the accuser's power. He did this by drawing all men and all judgment to Himself. This is why the Gospel carries such happy tidings. Christ's sacrificial body has fully paid the penalty for the broken body of humanity's sins.

If you think this is a misunderstanding of Jesus's statement in John 12, then look carefully at the words of Paul who taught this even more explicitly:

> *For the love of Christ controls us, having concluded this, that one died for all, therefore* ***all died.***
> *(2 Cor. 5:14)*

When Jesus died, all died. How? Because at the cross, Jesus *drew all to Himself* and took on the full judgment that was due to sin.

In other words, there was a bloodbath at the cross.

There was a massacre of all humanity's sins. Judgment and wrath poured out on humanity like never before.

But this was the purest kind of wrath. It was the *wrath of the Lamb*. It turns out God's wrath is not divorced from His mercy, for the Lord God is one. He is not a two-faced deity with schizophrenic conflicts within Himself. He is perfect Love and within His Love is the wrath that deals with sin in the most praiseworthy way. This is why the eternal Good News and the hour of judgment are one in the same!

The word for "wrath" in the Greek is a word that means "strong passion." At the cross, God's furious passion for His children was released like never before. The Lamb laid down His life for us as He released the roar of a merciful Lion. This is a wrath unlike the wrath of man, for God's ways are not our ways, nor are His thoughts our thoughts. This is a wrath that leads to healing and resurrection. It's a sword that releases life—not death.

The Song and the Apocalypse Pt. 2

The Real Grapes of Wrath

This brings us back to the bloody text about the "clusters of the vine" and the winepress of God's wrath. After the angel declares the hour of judgment has come, we see more symbolic passages about the destruction of evil, all culminating in the bloody vision of the winepress. When everything is put together, we discover that the cross of Christ is actually the winepress. And this makes sense when we remember that Jesus's own body was *crushed for our transgressions* (Isa. 53:5).

In His body, Jesus took on the sins of the whole world (Jn. 1:29). The ripeness of man's sins—the grapes of wrath—were gathered into His substitutional body on our behalf. The *ripeness* of the grapes in Revelation is an issue of timing. Christ's coming and crucifixion was the "ripe" time for man's sins to be dealt with. It happened at the "fullness of time." This is what Paul wrote about in the book of Galatians when speaking of the *first coming* of Jesus and His work on the cross (see Gal. 4:4-5). Jesus came to the earth at just the right moment, where He would die on a Roman cross and gather all sin upon Himself. In that instance, Jesus Christ was crushed at the winepress of Calvary. His body was laid in the ground and then a transformational fermenting process began. In the resurrection that followed, the wine of new life was released! This was the wine of a new covenant—the wine of unshakable peace and eternal love (Isa. 54:10). This is indeed the eternal Gospel hidden right in the book of Revelation!

Are you starting to catch the upbeat melody of this new song? Are you beginning to sense the good vibes behind the angelic messages of glad tidings? This is incredibly *good news*. The wrath of God is for us, not against us! God is not a bipolar deity who has a wrath side and a love side. That two-faced god has been propped up by countless theologians, but his days are numbered.

God is One.

The Song of the Ages: Part III

God is only Love, and His *wrath* is the hot and fiery overflow of that Love. It is His all-consuming passion to redeem His children, even it means laying down His own life for us. God's wrath eases our hearts because it reminds us that He will not relent until the utter wickedness and deception of sin is fully dealt with. It was out of this wrath that He sent His Son. This is the same as saying that God so loved the world that He gave His only begotten Son. This one and only Son would bear the weight of the whole world at the winepress of the cross and there His blood would become the sweetest of wine.

Outside the Gates

It's interesting that the bloodbath of Revelation 14 specifically happens "outside the city" (look again at verse 20). This is not an accident. Do you remember our warning about staying away from "strange and varied teachings"? That's a quote from Hebrews 13, where we are also reminded that Jesus Christ sanctified people through His own blood *outside the city* (Heb. 13:12-13). Indeed, Jesus was crucified on the hill of Golgotha outside the gates of the main city of Jerusalem. It was there that all humanity died on the cross and rivers of blood poured out for 1600 furlongs. And so, the number 1600 carries symbolic meaning as well.

We've well-established that throughout the Bible, and especially in the book Revelation, numbers carry great significance. For instance, in Revelation 13, the spiritual meaning of the number six is clearly explained. A chapter later, the number 1600 comes up and it too is filled with underlying purpose. Oftentimes in the Bible an important number gets multiplied or squared to emphasize or complete its meaning. For example, the number 144 shows up a good amount in Revelation. This is the number twelve squared. The number twelve has to do with the government and leadership

The Song and the Apocalypse Pt. 2

of God, and so 144 (or 144,000) speaks of the complete Kingdom and government of God being established on earth.

In the study notes of the Passion Translation, Dr. Brian Simmons highlights how 1600 is the number forty squared. We mentioned the meaning of forty earlier. It is the biblical number of testing and trial. Therefore, the squaring of forty intensifies and completes its meaning. Here, it represents the ultimate and *perfect* trial and tribulation. It speaks of Jesus's tribulation on behalf of the entire world! This too is the eternal Gospel of the Lamb.

Wrath, Sweet and Complete

It's about time we return to the journey of the Shulammite. This all started with a simple analogy from the Lord—*may your breasts be like clusters of the vine*. We heard these words and then walked into the strange terrain of Revelation in order to look at a similar phrase. If there's anything our trek through that apocalyptic landscape showed us, it's that things aren't always what they seem. When we tie together the threads of these two different passages, we discover it all points to the astonishing "judgment" of the cross—a judgment of mercy and restoration. Therefore, when the Beloved sings over the Shulammite and compares her body to clusters of the vine, we see that *the Bride is bearing the fruit of Jesus's suffering!*

On top of that, the Shulammite Bride is also nurturing the world with a pure revelation of God's wrath. A true understanding of this furious passion within God is key to bringing freedom to those who feel orphaned and alone. This freedom comes because people recognize they have a true Father who will stop at nothing to destroy the kidnapper and slave-master of sin, even when it means laying down His own life. The Bride does not "cheapen" the message of grace. Instead, she communicates the inestimable cost of forgiveness and the true motive behind the cross. When embraced, this revelation leads to a pure fear

The Song of the Ages: Part III

of the Lord, one that involves a deep reverence and awe as well as a sure and joyful repentance.

Now if there are any doubts as to this interpretation of the Song and its connection to Revelation, perhaps the following will help settle the matter. In the next line, the Beloved continues with another comparison:

> *Oh, may your breasts be like clusters of the vine,*
> *And the fragrance of your breath like apples.*

Here is where everything begins to come together in divine symmetry. The Hebrew word for "breath" here is *'aph*, which is a homonym. This is a word that can have two totally different meanings depending on the context. In our last study of the Song, we used the example of the English word *wave*, which could mean a movement of the hand or a movement of water. The word *'aph* can mean "breath," as is typically translated in this part of the Song. But the same word can have another meaning to it as well. *'Aph* can also be translated as *wrath*. In fact, the Hebrew word *'aph* shows up in the Bible as "wrath" or "anger" more than it does any other meaning. Here's an example from Deuteronomy where the same exact word shows up:

> *For a fire is kindled in My **anger** ('aph), and burns to the*
> *lowest part of Sheol, and consumes the earth with its yield,*
> *and sets on fire the foundations of the mountains.*
> (Deut. 32:22)

So let's start putting the pieces together. The Beloved compares the Shulammite to clusters of the vine and then talks about the fragrance of her "wrath." He subsequently compares this fragrance to apples. This should remind you of something from much earlier in the Song when the Bride was sitting under the "apple tree" eating its fruit. It seems her breath is now filled

The Song and the Apocalypse Pt. 2

with the scent of those same apples because she's been feasting on them throughout the entire Song.

But do you remember the meaning of the apple tree?

It's the same note and melody bouncing throughout the entire Song of the Lamb.

The apple tree is the tree of the cross.

So, the Bride's breath is filled with the sweet revelation of the cross.

But it's not just the fragrance of her *breath*. The fragrance of the apples is also the sweet fragrance of *wrath!* The Hebrew could be translated both ways. And this is because her breath does indeed radiate with the pure message of the cross, which is sweet and tasty and *good*. While others carry a bitter and poisonous breath that comes from misunderstanding the wrath of God, the true Bride is filled with its purest essence. In other words, her communication of the Gospel is becoming whole and complete.

The Best Wine

After comparing the fragrance of her breath to apples, Jesus says the following. This will complete the apocalyptic message hidden within this part of the Song:

> *Oh, may your breasts be like clusters of the vine,*
> *And the fragrance of your breath like apples,*
> *And your mouth like the best wine!*

Think about all of this. We have "clusters of grapes," then "wrath like apples," and finally the "best wine." Do you see the progression here? This is a parallel image from the Song of the Lamb that is heralded in the book of Revelation. It's the same Song, but with different poetry. The same tapestry, but different types of thread.

The Song of the Ages: Part III

The grapes were gathered at the cross, which was the winepress where the furious love of God was poured out. This was a love that was for us, not against us. The result of this was the *best wine*—the wine that flows out of His side and includes the life of every human to have ever existed. It's the wine of joy that was set before Jesus as He embraced the perfect and complete suffering of the cross.

And the *best* wine is really the *good* wine. The word behind "best" here is the same term that shows up in Genesis 1 when God describes the goodness of His creation. This is speaking about the wine of redemption! God's wrath has been revealed from heaven to conquer everything that enslaved His original creation and the stole the blessing that was upon it. And so, from the Shulammite's mouth comes this sweet declaration of the eternal Gospel. It's the same message heralded by the angel flying in midheaven. It's the glad tidings of judgment at the cross—and it's good news for all people!

Lips of Sleepers

And here is where we arrive at the majestic culmination of this entire portion of the Song.

> *It goes down smoothly for my beloved,*
> *Flowing gently through the lips of those who fall asleep.*

We're reminded here that all this amazing truth is being revealed in the context of a passionate kiss. The intimate language being used makes that clear. The Beloved is embracing the full palm tree of His Bride and tasting the wine flowing from her mouth. It's a moment of matured love as the Bride fully embraces her union with Jesus. The wine the Shulammite initially longed for has been discovered within her and she is pouring it back out to her King. Jesus is delighted to taste the wine of His own love coming out

The Song and the Apocalypse Pt. 2

of her. In the midst of this, the Shulammite gives an interesting response to His delight over their kiss. She says the wine of her kiss goes down smoothly *for Him*. However, it flows gently through the lips of other people—*those who fall asleep*. What's that about?

Here's a key to help unlock this particular verse. Though the Shulammite is talking about kissing her Beloved, this is happening as she gives the kiss of love away to those who are still spiritually asleep.

The literal Hebrew translation of this passage says that the wine flows gently through *the lips of sleepers*. So, the Bride is kissing the Beloved, but she is doing it by kissing the sleeping world! And does this not fit in with what we know of the Gospel? Jesus said that when we minister to the hungry, the thirsty, the naked, and the prisoner, we are actually ministering to Him! And note that the Song says the wine goes down *smoothly* and passes *gently* over sleeping lips. This speaks of ministering in a spirit of gentleness and grace to those who are still asleep. As we kiss those whose eyes are still shut—those still blind and stuck in spiritual infancy—we help awaken them to a pure revelation of their Father.

Come!

Remember that from the very beginning of the Song, the Bride longed for God's "Spirit-kiss divine" (Sgs. 1:2 TPT). Now that the kiss has come and she's experiencing its effects, we're starting to see how it's destined to overflow into ministry to the hungry and thirsty. As the Bride's lips unite with the Spirit, together they speak out one word:

Come!

Indeed, this is what is revealed at the end of John's Apocalypse. The Spirit *and the Bride* come together with this word:

> *The Spirit and the bride say, "Come." And let the one who hears say, "Come." And let the one who is thirsty come; let*

The Song of the Ages: Part III

the one who wishes take the water of life without cost.
(Rev. 22:17)

 We'll come back to this passage much later. For now, let's acknowledge who the Spirit and the Bride are speaking to in their kiss of union. They're calling out to those who are thirsty. They're speaking to those who are outside the gates (Rev. 22:15). These are the "sleepers" of Solomon's Song; the people who are still living in the illusions of darkness.
 The call is for humanity to come and wash their robes—their identity—with the blood of the Lamb in order to be rid of all guilt and shame. The call is come to the table of grace and sit under the apple tree of the cross. It's to hear and *trust* the eternal Gospel—the good news of the furious wrath of God poured out at the winepress of Calvary once and for all.

5
The Heavenly Mission Base

———•❖•———

I am my beloved's,
And his desire is for me.
Come, my beloved, let us go out into the country...
(7:10-11a)

The whole world is being summoned to dine at the table of the Lamb. The call is to "come," spoken by the Spirit and Bride together as one. But this call does not issue from idle lips. The Bride doesn't just sit around and shout at people to come. No. She is moved into action with an intense focus. It's as though her feet are being swept away by a strange and ferocious undercurrent. Her heart is being pressed and compelled to move in one singular direction—the direction of love.

This intensity of her heart and this new movement of her feet is the result of a simple declaration the Bride makes in the twilight notes of the Song: *I am my Beloved's and His desire is for me!* These words sum up everything the Shulammite has learned thus far. They come together to form the currents that now propel and guide the streams of her life.

It's amazing to think that earlier in the Song she really had no clue about these things. Her life had grown stagnant even though

The Song of the Ages: Part III

she was busy working in the vineyards of ministry. In reality, she was tired and burnt out, and found herself working *for love* instead of *from love*. But all that has changed. At the Summit of Truth, the Shulammite discovered the reality of her unchanging union with Christ, and through a journey of perseverance in this word of union, she began to wake up to who she is and what she's called to do.

By now we've well established the fact that the Shulammite knows the truth of God's love for her. This is just another reminder of where she's at and where her journey has brought her. But there's something else here that we discover about the Shulammite's confidence. We can see she also understands that God *desires* her. This is a fundamentally important part of the text, for someone can "love" another person out of obligation or through a sense of responsibility; however, when they actually desire the object of their love, the recipient of that love can have a much deeper level of confidence. This word for "desire" is quite intense. To say it differently, the Shulammite now knows that God *craves* her. It's as though He is a wild chocoholic and she's the perfect candy bar. In the past, she may have looked at herself as a dry vegetable sitting on the plate of the almighty chocolate Lover. But now she sees that she is a delectable piece of the finest quality chocolate and God's mouth is watering over her.

Over you.

When the realization dawns that God *desires* you in this manner, it changes how you pray and how you live. He's not put off by you. He's not looking at you and noticing pieces of mold or bitter rinds that surround the chocolate (the goodness) of your life. Because of the sweet work of Jesus, which we've amply covered, all He sees and smells is top quality cocoa. And so He longs for you. Right now.

The Heavenly Mission Base

The goal of this journey with the Shulammite is to be rooted and grounded in this love. This is what bears the fruits of a prosperous life. And of course, this rooting is not just head knowledge. The Shulammite has learned that feelings come and go, and circumstances change. She may not even *feel* the truth of this statement at the moment of her saying it. But still she speaks it because her heart has set sail on the ship of faith and has utterly abandoned a life ruled by feelings and circumstances. She is grounded and rooted, and because of this, she is being filled up with all the fullness of God—the One who was inside of her from the very beginning (Eph. 3:18-19).

Believe

Remember, beloved reader, this is about you. Never divorce the reality of the Shulammite's journey from your own life. Never allow a separation between you and the Shulammite to be built up in your mind, for God was thinking of you when He took hold of Solomon's pen thousands of years ago. He was not thinking of someone other than you. You were the one on His mind. The Shulammite is about you and your own destiny, just as much as she points to the church as a whole. Believe again that these words are yours—all of them. Receive a fresh revelation that all of this speaks to your own heart and journey. Take that in deeply as we follow the shifting currents of her life and embark on the new adventure that love is igniting.

Sailing by the Promise

Besides being rooted in her identity, the Shulammite has also grown confident in her calling. The reality of her great calling is what we saw unfold at the end of the Song's sixth chapter and the previous portions of the seventh. This young maiden from Shulam received amazing prophetic words and promises over her

The Song of the Ages: Part III

life, including her destiny to bring awakening to the entire world. But just like the words of her identity, she had to learn to take these world-changing promises by faith. This is not unlike the young apostle Timothy who had received great promises over his life and was urged by his spiritual father to stand firm in them:

> *This command I entrust to you, Timothy, my son, in accordance with the prophecies previously made concerning you, that by them you fight the good fight, keeping faith and a good conscience, which some have rejected and suffered shipwreck in regard to their faith.*
> (1 Tim. 1:18-19)

We're reminded here that many people set sail on the ship of faith into an adventurous life of love and ministry. But by losing hope in their prophetic future, they can suffer a shipwreck and crash into an island of isolation, bitterness, or perhaps just a quiet disconnect from their calling. (More devastating than this is when one loses hope in their righteous identity, which is where a bad "conscience" comes into play.) The choppy waters of contradiction and fear hit them, and they give up on what God has spoken over them. Disappointment and contradiction become more real in their eyes and they end up submitting to lesser voices. The sea calls them forward and the ship is easily repaired by remembering the truth (repenting), but unfortunately they stay stuck in hopelessness with a poor self-image (a bad conscience).

Again, the Shulammite has abandoned a life that submits to lies, including the ones that feel most real. This is a life ruled by the voice of opposing waves, forces that stand at the shoreline of our personal islands and yell at us to stay put. They tell us to build a fire and live a status quo life. In other words, they call us to just survive. They might allow you to yell *hello* to other boats as they pass by your island, and perhaps let you go so far as throwing some

The Heavenly Mission Base

money at the other vessels. But they do not want you to get back into your own ship.

Yet the Shulammite is different. She knows who she is and this knowledge has grown bigger than the rough currents in front of her. She knows she belongs to a God who craves her with an all-consuming addiction, and that she is destined to reform the entire earth. As the fulfillment of Eve, she is the mother of all the living, called to birth an incredible harvest of sons and daughters into the Kingdom of light. In light of these two things—her identity and her destiny—she knows that it's time to *go*. It's time to set sail and fulfill the Great Commission given to her by the Shepherd of her soul and the Bridegroom of her heart:

> *Go therefore and make disciples of all the nations,*
> *baptizing them in the name of the Father and the Son*
> *and the Holy Spirit.*
> *(Matt. 28:19)*

The heart-knowledge that says *"I am my Beloved's and His desire is for me"* has become the stronghold and fortress of her life. But more than a fortress, it has now become an outpost. Or perhaps a "mission base" might be a better word for where the Song is headed. The Shulammite has become a mission base that seeks to impact the entire world with the beautiful Gospel of Christ.

A Heavenly Mission Base

Now a "mission base" might conjure up a number of images in your mind. Please know that the kind of mission base we're talking about here is the most unique and beautiful one imaginable. It's not a dry and boring office space filled with lecture halls, archaic maps, and hard grueling tasks to prepare for war. Its hallways and courtyards do not carry the sounds of angry sergeants or army

The Song of the Ages: Part III

drills designed to whip up motivation from battle-weary attendees. This base is of a much different flavor.

The Shulammite Bride dwells in an outpost and mission base that has the most comfortable couches imaginable. It has majestic artwork adorning its walls; artwork that you can step into and explore. There are exotic scents and strange sights all around, and pervading the whole space is the sound of laughter and play. Slides and swings would be more fitting here than locker rooms and arsenals. This is because a true mission base reflects heaven more than earth. While the earth is filled with battlegrounds strewn with the weapons of war, heaven is filled with children playing and laughing. Likewise, the Bride's "ministries" and "missions" should parallel the childlike wonder of heaven, not the brutality of earth. And though we are speaking in such peaceful and non-conflictual terms, it doesn't mean that this kind of base is unengaged or ineffective. On the contrary, it is the most effective and efficient kind there is.

This fortress of confident love and awakened identity is a place of maximum impact. There the church abides and in her abiding she is moved by the currents of love, flowing like a river into the nations. This is not a stationary outpost that stays away from the world's troubles, but one that is right in the midst of it, like the tabernacle that moved through the wilderness. From a place of vibrant love, the Shulammite is called to go in and out of uncharted territory, bringing life and healing wherever she finds herself (see Ez. 47). She is truly a river of love that refreshes weary adults who have forgotten innocence and grace. She cheers the hearts of widows and causes orphans to sing, exposing the futility of wickedness by demonstrating the true and original nature of man.

In case you're getting lost in these analogies, we're essentially talking about the kind of atmosphere that should surround and undergird the church's work of missions and evangelism. At this

The Heavenly Mission Base

juncture of the Song, the Bride is shifting more purposefully into the work of ministry and it is so important we understand what this is meant to look and feel like. It might seem strange that we are only now embarking more decisively into the "ministry" part of the Shulammite's story. It seems to be coming so late in the Song. But that's the value Jesus attaches to having confidence in the cross and knowing the love of the Father before any "works" take place. The Lord spends the majority of the Song establishing the Bride in her identity and in His finished work before He really begins releasing notes and lyrics that have to do with action and ministry.

Of course, this isn't to say that ministry hasn't been happening up until this point. The Bride has been engaged in many different things even as she's been growing in the confidence of God's love. But in this part of the Song, we begin to see her true impact on the world. After having learned to abandon herself to the love of Calvary, the Bride is ready to step into her prophetic mandate. She's ready to walk on the water of God's Word over her life.

From "Have to" to "Want to"

Before we move forward, there's something absolutely vital we need to recognize here. The confidence that has so filled the Shulammite's heart includes the steady awareness that she is loved no matter what she does. The unconditional grace that pursued the Shulammite even when she resisted Christ's call has settled down into her soul and borne one particular revelation:

Even if she chooses *not* to go out into the world, she will *still be loved and accepted* by Jesus.

This conclusion is scandalous. It's not something the Shulammite would have learned from her "mother's sons," who we saw in the Song's first chapter. Spiritual leaders are not quick to acknowledge this, primarily due to the fear that such truth would lead to apathy. But obviously this is not the case with the

The Song of the Ages: Part III

Shulammite. On the contrary, this revelation has given her all the more passion and enthusiasm to go out and bless others. And what a different motivation this is than the guilt and pressure spewing out of countless pulpits and institutions who try to "mobilize" the church. In the Song, there isn't one ounce of guilt motivating the Shulammite anymore. She's been fully delivered from that spirit of bondage and is now free to choose from the heart. Either way, she knows her Beloved will be with her whether she stays or goes.

You see, in recognizing these things, the Shulammite has also discovered something else: *She is made to go.*

She must go.

This is an empowering realization that rises to the surface of your soul when you see that you don't *have to go*, and yet the desire still remains. Living from this place of the heart is the difference between a son and a slave (or one who works in the vineyard for a paycheck versus the Bride who lives in the house of the vineyard owner and shares his bedroom). Working and ministering from this place of freedom and sonship makes a huge difference in the value and substance of our work. The Shulammite's impact upon the world is part of who she is, not what she must become in order to please God or those in leadership. Such a realization allows for absolutely no boasting, for your actions now arise from a place of God-given identity, instead of a sense of performance or duty. Therefore, if we boast, we boast in the God who put this identity deep inside of us.

Re-creation of the Earth

In the very beginning of the Song, when its notes first broke free from the heartstrings of Christ, the Shulammite was searching for a love that wasn't based upon her personal work. Sunburnt and weary, she began her singing with two powerful words: "Let Him…"

The Heavenly Mission Base

Let Him kiss me with the kisses of His mouth!

And of course, that kiss came. It pressed upon her heart and rose like a geyser up to her lips in a growing confession of grace and truth. With this joyful eruption came a burst of new melodies, lyrics, and passions. Having been kissed by grace, she is now compelled to share this kiss with the weary world around her. As a result, she issues a new request using two words that are quite similar to what was sung at the beginning: "Let us…"

Let us go out into the country…

Now something amazing surfaces when you connect this part of the Shulammite's journey with Genesis and the creation account. The birth of this universe also began out of an eruption of love. From all eternity, the Trinity was simply enjoying one another and living in the place of total satisfaction. This is the larger story behind everything in existence. Really, our own existence is only a dot on the timeline of everlasting fellowship and joyful union amongst the Trinity. Events like the fall of man and the overcoming of evil are only passing moments in this greater story of Divine Love. Perhaps this is why only a slim portion of Solomon's Song is devoted to the actual work of ministry. This isn't said to devalue ministry, but rather to put it in proper perspective. The *main point of everything* is intimacy and love, which looks like righteousness, peace, and joy.

Out of the abundance of these things, the Father, Son, and Spirit gave birth to the cosmos. More specifically, the Divine Family gave birth to children—to us. And so the Shulammite's request in this latter part of the Song is similar to the Trinity's words in creating humankind—something that comes out of a joyful relationship. In Genesis 1, the Trinity speaks and says, "Let Us…"

Let Us make man in Our image and likeness.

The Song of the Ages: Part III

Out of deep love and passionate union, the Divine Family decided to get their hands dirty and begin the work of birthing and nurturing children. Realizing more and more that she is part of this same family, the Bride follows suit. She is finding total satisfaction in God alone and is thus all the more willing to say, *"Let us."*

Jesus once said, "Out of the overflow the heart, the mouth speaks" (Lk. 6:45). Here then is another way to look at what is coming out of the heart of the Shulammite…

> *Come, my beloved Jesus! I am overflowing with love and it needs to be shared with others! Let us go together into the country—the world—and multiply our love. Let us baptize the nations, immersing them into the Family name. Let us bring them into our fellowship! Let us share our joy and celebration with the entire world!*

This is the heart of the one that Jesus purchased by blood and washed in the waters of truth. This is the heart of the radiant Bride coming into full maturity. In the days ahead, this heart will be seen and heard more clearly throughout the church and it will redefine everything we know when it comes to concepts like missions and ministry. This is a redefinition that will lead to a true and lasting awakening in the nations. Such awakening will not come about because of our great business plans drawn up with milestones and objectives, as though unreached people are just a notch on the belt or a goal to reach (so we can secure more funding or boast in how many people we've "led to Jesus"). This is not about an agenda to collect a number of people who prayed a prayer so we can report it back to administrative overseers. Nor is it about proselytizing people to join a religious club and increase the membership base.

This is about individuals. Sons and daughters who don't know who they are or where they truly come from.

The Heavenly Mission Base

This is about finding precious gemstones buried in the dust; stones that intoxicate God with wonder as the dust comes off and their unique facets glimmer in the light of His face.

This is about reaching one person just as much as it's about impacting the multitudes. Because in reality, this is all about *family*.

It is God's great desire that it would be on earth as it is heaven—and heaven is not a business or a club or an organization with a mission statement. Heaven is a family table, decked out with mouthwatering breads and the finest of wine. It is a table filled with the sounds of laughter in an atmosphere of belonging. It is the dance of myriads of angels moving in joyful celebration like a spiral of light leading to a bright center of intimate communion. This is what Jesus's "Great Commission" is really all about—the expanse of this luminescent circle to every nation, until all have sat down at the table of fellowship.

This is what we're stepping into as we follow the Shulammite out into the country. But there is another part of her plea we need to look at more closely. The request *"let us go out into the country"* has erupted like lava from within her burning heart, and of particular interest to us now is the word "country." As we take our time with this word—and allow it to cool—we'll find that it forms a glorious rock of revelation…

6
A Mystery in the Field

Come, my beloved, let us go out into the country...
(7:11a)

The Hebrew word for *country* is more literally translated as "field." So the Shulammite is saying to her Beloved, "Let us go out into the *field*," which reminds us of Jesus's own words about the harvest fields. For instance, Jesus said this in the gospel of John:

> *...I tell you, open your eyes and look at the **fields**!*
> *They are ripe for harvest.*
> *(Jn. 4:35 NIV)*

The Bride's eyes are certainly open. She sees the fields of humanity and beholds the treasure hidden within, which brings up another statement the Lord made:

> *The kingdom of heaven is like a treasure hidden in the*
> ***field**, which a man found and hid again; and from joy*
> *over it he goes and sells all that he has and buys that **field**.*
> *(Matt. 13:44)*

The Song of the Ages: Part III

For the joy set before Him, Jesus gave everything He had to buy the treasure buried in the field of humanity. Now His Bride is pursuing this same joy. But there is more to the Shulammite's words than meets the eye. The Hebrew word for "field" is *sadeh* and there is treasure hidden even within the word itself. Once again, Solomon takes a tiny puzzle piece from the Scriptures—a single Hebrew word—and places it in his text to point us to an even bigger message. As before, this puzzle piece can be best understood when you go back to the first time it's used.

A Contradicting Scripture

Sadeh first shows up in Genesis 2 and it is there that we will find a connection between the Song and the creation account once more:

> Now no shrub of the **field** was yet in the earth, and no plant of the **field** had yet sprouted, for the Lord God had not sent rain upon the earth, and there was no man to cultivate the ground.
> (Gen. 2:5)

This passage can be quite confusing when you read the full creation story. Before this passage, in Genesis 1, we're told that the earth had *already* brought forth vegetation and plants before man came about:

> Then God said, "Let the earth sprout vegetation, plants yielding seed, and fruit trees on the earth bearing fruit after their kind with seed in them"; and **it was so**. The earth brought forth vegetation, plants yielding seed after their kind, and trees bearing fruit with seed in them, after their kind; and God saw that it was good. There was evening and there was morning, a third day.
> (Gen. 1:11-13)

Mystery in the Field

In Genesis 1:11, God spoke a word with utter confidence and finality: "Let the earth sprout..." The text then says, "And it was so." All kinds of plant life began to sprout and "God saw that it was good." The third day was complete. But then we learn something different in Genesis 2, which comes after the seven days of creation. It says, "No shrub of the field was yet in the earth, and no plant of the field had *yet sprouted*." It then follows up with the reason for this: "God had not sent rain upon the earth, and there was no man to cultivate the ground." But this is somewhat of a contradiction from the first chapter of Genesis.

Most scholars will say that the author of Genesis simply utilized two different accounts of creation. Whether that's true or not, the true Author of Genesis has planted a deeper message into the text—a message pointing us back to the redemption plan of Christ. Beyond scientific and apologetic explanations for the differences between Genesis 1 and 2, there is a spiritual revelation hidden in the *field*. And like every other mystery and puzzle piece of the Word, it all comes back to Christ and Him crucified.

The Finished Work in Genesis

In Genesis 1, God speaks a word that was only in seed form—spiritually and literally. A seed is a promise of a greater reality. In the seed, God sees the finished product before we do. He sees a whole forest hidden within one speck. Therefore, even if the earth looked barren, God could still say *it was good*, because He knew His word would not return void. He is the One who speaks "things that are not as though they were" (Rom. 4:17 NIV). He has complete confidence in the seed of His word, even if it's hidden away in the ground and new life seems impossibly far away. To Him, the word is not a vague hope, but a solid reality that is already settled.

God spoke the word of organic life and declared it as a finished work. He entered into rest, even before anything grew out of the

The Song of the Ages: Part III

ground, which is what we see in Genesis 2. There we find that the life hidden within the *fields* of the earth had not yet sprouted. This is because God had not yet sent precipitation upon the earth, and there was nobody to cultivate the soil. So even though the word was spoken and the work was finished in God's eyes, there was a special plan for it to unfold. This plan would involve a man and his wife—and the help of rain.

The story of the first creation ultimately points us to Christ and the new creation. At the cross, Jesus spoke the words *"it is finished"*—a much bigger statement than any of us can imagine. It was there humanity was fully redeemed and creation was renewed. The work of redeeming the universe had been completed in that very moment. All darkness and all corruption had been sucked into His servant body and perfectly destroyed. On the third day, the words "it is finished" were proven by the resurrection. Jesus's body *sprouted* from the earth, just like seed-bearing life came forth on the third day in Genesis. Jesus's resurrected body was the proof of a restored and "very good" world.

And yet, to the natural eye, this may not have seemed like a universe-transforming moment. The resurrection event only appeared to be one Man rising from the dead; one speck in the vast and barren field of a world still torn and broken. But the truth is that all creation rose anew from the garden tomb that day. In God's eyes, all the cosmos were blessed and renewed in the resurrection of Christ. God beheld His beloved Son and saw Him as the firstfruits of a redeemed planet, bearing seed that would multiply after its own kind. All things had been raised to new life through His resurrected body because He is the One who holds everything together in the first place (Col. 1:17-20). Therefore, God could once again look at His creation and declare, *"It is very good!"* And thus, God could enter into a true Sabbath rest.

Mystery in the Field

The Lord Jesus has truly *finished* the work of redemption. But yet it's obvious that this reality has not fully blossomed throughout creation. The message of the Gospel remains true, but the fruit of it has not broken through all of humanity's earthen fields. Dust, pain, and barrenness still fills much of the landscape of the world. But this where the prophetic story of Genesis 2 comes into play. God has chosen to use a Man (Christ) and His wife (the church) to cultivate the soil of humanity and bring the promises to fruition. In the aftermath of the cross, God has chosen to beautify the earth in and through us! So, we come back to a truth we visited in our earlier studies of the Song. In the story of Genesis, Adam and Eve are prefigures of Christ and the church (Eph. 5:32). Eve and the Shulammite both represent the same thing—the fruitful Bride of Christ.

In Genesis 2, Adam was given the task of cultivating the soil and tending the Garden that God had already planted. Afterward, he was put to sleep and Eve was formed through an opening near his heart. Eve became his helper in the work God had given him. In like fashion, Jesus was put to the death on the cross, and as blood and water poured from His wounded side, a Bride was brought forth. This Bride—the church—is a co-laborer with Christ who is called to go with Him into the fields of the earth in order to cultivate the soil of humanity. We are called to tend the Garden God has victoriously planted!

"Works of Service" and Heavenly Rain

The word for "cultivate" in Genesis 2 is also powerful. It can actually be translated as "serve." It has to do with attending to another's needs and making oneself a servant. So, Adam and Eve were literally called to *serve* the soil. Now recall the fact that the human race was made from this same soil, for we all come from the dust of the earth. Therefore, when it says the man was called

The Song of the Ages: Part III

to *cultivate* the soil, it's a picture of Jesus coming to *serve* humanity. And naturally, His helper—the church—is called to join Him in this work of service. In fact, the fivefold ministry we mentioned earlier is all about equipping the Bride for *works of service* (Eph. 4:12). For it is as we serve those around us—as we go into the fields and wash the feet of others—that we awaken the seeds of destiny that have been spoken over every human being.

But there is another important element in the account from Genesis 2. No matter how hard Adam and Eve tried to cultivate the soil, nothing would come forth without the help of rain. This is a wonderful reminder of the church's need for the Holy Spirit in the work of the harvest. Throughout the Bible, rain is so often connected to the person and work of the Spirit. The Holy Spirit is the only One who can bring about true spiritual growth. Our calling is to serve others in love and truth, but it is the Spirit who awakens the seed of life within those we're serving.

This brings us back to the importance of Pentecost when the Spirit first fell upon the early church. Before that happened, Christ was crucified and resurrected. Again, the work was completed at that moment and God entered into His rest. However, the full fruits of His Word had not been revealed, for the rain of the Spirit had not yet come. The work was finished and the Word was spoken, like Genesis 1, but now it was time to manifest that work and cause it to bloom—like Genesis 2. Thus, on the day of Pentecost, the Holy Spirit fell upon the hearts of people, awakening them as the sons and daughters of God and giving them power to walk in their redeemed identity. This is where the Bride emerged as one who would work alongside the Spirit of Jesus in harvesting the rest of humanity (see Acts 2). What God spoke at the cross and revealed on the third day would now be multiplied throughout the earth. The Spirit and the Bride were joined together and now they would

Mystery in the Field

go out and speak the word *"Come!"* Together they would enter the fields and issue the invitation of the Gospel:

> *Come forth from the grave, from underneath soil and rock,*
> *and arise into new life!*
> *Turn from the dust and blossom with the life of God!*
> *Awake, O sleeping seeds, and rise from the dead!*

The First Great Commission

We're spending a lot of time on this one verse in the Song because it represents a major shift in the music. It is the overflow of the arrival and climax of everything revealed so far. The Song in the Bride's heart is continuing to spill out into the world around her. We'll move on shortly, but there's one more aspect of this word *sadeh* that needs to be dug up and examined.

Besides *country* or *field*, this word can also be translated as "the wild." The Beloved's Song is thus propelling the Shulammite to go into the *wild places* of the earth. In other terms, the Shulammite is saying she now desires to go into uncharted territory where there is still the uncultivated land of corruption, wickedness, and fear. She wants to go and cultivate this hardened soil and transform its twisted landscape through the plow of the Gospel and the tools of grace. This aspect of cultivation reminds us of the very first "commission" given by God to the original man and woman in Genesis 1:

> *God created man in His own image, in the image of God*
> *He created him; male and female He created them. God*
> *blessed them; and God said to them, "Be fruitful and*
> *multiply, and fill the earth, **and subdue it**; and rule over*
> *the fish of the sea and over the birds of the sky and over*
> *every living thing that moves on the earth."*
> *(Gen. 1:27-28)*

The Song of the Ages: Part III

Adam and Eve's call to "subdue" the earth had to do with treading down the wild places and beautifying the land. This points to the greater calling placed upon Christ and His church. In fact, this commission in the first book of the Old Testament is only a foreshadow of the Great Commission in the first book of the New Testament—Matthew 28. There, Jesus said all authority in heaven and on earth had been given to Him. He then called His Bride, the disciples, to go out and make other disciples ("be fruitful and multiply"), and to subdue the wild terrain of humanity. Jesus knew the world was never meant to exhibit a harsh topography of injustice with the imposing weeds of poverty and prejudice, as well as the overgrown thorn bushes of disease and death. Rather, it was meant to be a garden filled with righteousness, joy, and peace. Therefore, the Great Commission was not just about going and making converts so people could go to heaven when they die. It was to teach the nations the ways of the Kingdom, which included healing the sick, raising the dead, and ministering to the poor. As we said before, this is about bringing heaven to earth (Matt. 6:10).

Quite a large task. But that's why Jesus ended His commission by reminding the disciples He would be with them always, even to the end of the age. In other words, they could be assured that the "rain" of His presence would be with them no matter what. Whenever they set their hands to bless human soil, the atmosphere would always be ready to release drops of life-giving rain and power.

The Continued Vision of the Bride

At the end of our last volume, *The Kiss of Two Seas*, we looked at humanity from a heavenly vantage point and discovered these same truths. We saw what God showed the prophets Isaiah and Habakkuk when their vision was filled only with darkness and bloodshed. To them God revealed the reality of His glory, which

Mystery in the Field

already fills the entire earth and will one day manifest—or *sprout*—everywhere. This is the great viewpoint to which Christ brought His Bride as well. Now that she has awoken to this reality, her eyes are like the fish-pools of Heshbon—she sees the fish of humanity through the perspective of the Spirit (Sgs. 7:4). She knows all have been included in the death and resurrection of Jesus. *Therefore, she is no longer intimidated by the barren and ugly landscape of the earth, for she knows a true garden lies underneath.* Even in the valley of the driest of bones—the bones of genocide, slavery, and hate—there lies the seeds of life and the hope of glory.

The prophet Isaiah perhaps gives us one of the best pictures of where things are headed due to the finished and spoken Word of God:

> *For as the earth brings forth its sprouts, and as a garden causes the things sown in it to spring up, so the Lord God will cause righteousness and praise to spring up before all the nations.*
> *(Isa. 61:11)*

The same Hebrew word for "sprout" in the creation account shows up here in Isaiah's prophecy. God is promising that the earth will finally "sprout" with the Word of His finished work. This means the righteousness and justice God already sees in the one person of Christ will fully emerge upon the soil of the entire planet. In *all the nations*, it says. Indeed, the nations will be harvested and come into the "full stature" of Christ. This will happen through the loving service of the Bride and the precipitative power of the Holy Spirit. And all will finally see that there has been a garden of glory underneath the earth all along. The Kingdom was always here—it was just waiting to be cultivated.

Of course, this is what the Shulammite had to learn about her own life as well. She needed to trust in the reality of an inner garden

The Song of the Ages: Part III

over and above the weaknesses and struggles of her outward experiences. Now, after embracing the truth of her own identity, the Shulammite has begun to understand the identity of the entire world. She has found that people are inestimably precious—so precious that they are worth dying for. And that's where we're reminded once more of the words of the apostle who gave his life to go into the harvest fields and herald this same message. Paul said, "The love of Christ *compels us*, because we judge thus: that if One died for all, then all died" (2 Cor. 5:14 NKJV).

The Bride has come to this same conclusion. Not as a nice theology, but as a revelation of the heart that brings about passionate action and a reformation of ministry. You might call the results of this "missions" or "evangelism" or "discipleship," but in essence, it is simply awakened passion. It's a passion that springs from seeing the beauty of Jesus in yourself and others.

Now it's important to remember that this calling also comes with the pain of cultivating hard and rocky soil. Oftentimes, the soil rejects your hands and spits out thorns and rocks as you seek after that hidden garden. Sometimes it looks like you're just moving around piles of dirt with nothing to show for it. In many cases, you never actually see the garden manifest and you have to move on to new fields while you question the legitimacy of your previous work. Or perhaps your work leads to some fruitfulness, but then a time of spiritual drought comes or demonic winds blow through and all your hard work appears to shrivel up and die.

Even in the midst of these things, we can still hold to an unfailing hope and a confident love. For we know that God has planted a holy and victorious seed in the soil of humanity—a seed of glory that will prevail over the dust that so often covers it. While this "dust" of humanity has a choice to cooperate with it or not, the seed God has planted is of an indestructible quality (1 Pet. 1:23). It is filled with a mercy that will endure forever. Therefore, righteousness and justice

Mystery in the Field

are destined to sprout in *all the nations*, for mercy always triumphs and love never fails. In light of this, a seemingly barren world can never take away our joy. We can rest even as we vigorously work because we trust in the One "who sits in the heavens and laughs" (Ps. 2:4). God is not sitting on His throne wondering if all will be well in the end. He's resting in the reality of His Word, even as He bears patiently with the self-inflicted chaos of the nations. He waits patiently for the world to awaken to love.

And as He waits, He calls His Bride to join Him on this co-laboring adventure.

A New Kind of Dominion

That leads us to one final note before we actually go with the Shulammite into the fields and further off into the villages and vineyards. We must remember that taking dominion and "subduing" the earth does not come by force. This is an upside-down Kingdom with a different kind of King and a countercultural strategic plan. As we said before, this looks nothing like the battle plans of man's armies or the business strategies of our corporations. This is a subduing that comes only through the purest of love. This may seem like an obvious point by now, but it needs to be said again and again. It's part of the reason as to why God doesn't just wave His hands and instantly force everything to "sprout." True awakening can only happen through love, as we've seen in the Bride's own journey—the one who is a "first-fruit" of the nations.

"Do not awaken My love, until she pleases," the King has said.

So now we will continue on in the journey. The sheets of religion have long been cast aside, and the bed of fear which they covered is no longer present. The Shulammite is awake, standing tall in the full stature of Christ, ready to now give her life to awaken others. She dives headfirst into this great *labor of love*, setting her heart toward the wild places of the earth.

The Song of the Ages: Part III

"Come away, my lover. Come with me to the faraway fields. We will run away together to the forgotten places and show them redeeming love."
(Sgs. 7:11 TPT)

7
Dismantling Shadows

...Let us spend the night in the villages.
(7:11b)

These latter parts of the Song of Solomon carry a grand and sweeping overview of the purposes of God. Its lyrics continue to plumb the depths of our glorious identity in Christ while also exploring the heights of the prophetic destiny rising up from our divine DNA. Yet in the midst of such panoramic truths, we must never forget that all of this carries very small and practical implications.

For instance, whenever we step out and release the kiss of grace to someone who has been abandoned or rejected, we're participating in the work of re-creation. Whenever we show the lonely or guilty that their Heavenly Father has included them in the life of Christ, we're doing the same. When we take of our time and resources to pour into the orphaned and widowed, we're awakening seeds of new life. The Kingdom of heaven expands every time we bring life to the hopeless or declare the truth of God to the broken. Eden re-emerges even in the simplicity of giving a cup of cold water to the least likely candidates.

The Song of the Ages: Part III

The Shulammite can smell the scent of this new creation lying just on the horizon of people's hearts as they too wake up to the truth. And so, as the modern proverb puts it, this is where the rubber hits the road. We've spent a good amount of time talking about her calling to go out into the "fields," but now we will actually go there and see what this entails. First though, let's look at the full scope of her words and take note of something important:

> *Come, my beloved,* ***let us*** *go out into the country;*
> ***Let us*** *spend the night in the villages.*
> ***Let us*** *rise early and go to the vineyards;*
> ***Let us*** *see whether the vine has budded and its blossoms have opened,*
> *and whether the pomegranates have bloomed...*
> *(Sgs. 7:11-12)*

It's significant that she says *let us* four different times. Throughout the Bible, the number four is representative of the entire earth. It speaks to the "four winds" or "four corners" of the world (see Mk. 13:27 & Isa. 11:12). And so first and foremost we see that the Shulammite is heeding the call to go out into the *whole* world—every corner of it—in order to see Eden blossom once again. No person or place is excluded from the call of this beautiful Gospel. No spiritual territory or physical environment is off-limits. The church is called to go *everywhere* with the love and grace of Christ.

Lighting Up the World

With this in mind, we can begin to look at her heart for the "villages." Apparently, going out into the fields will involve spending *the night* in such places. From this one statement, we can conclude that the Shulammite is willing and ready to delve into the night season of this world—places that have not yet embraced the light of Christ. This continues to mark a deep shift in the Song

Dismantling Shadows

because earlier the night had intimidated the Bride and shook her faith. We saw this in the Song's second chapter when the Shulammite was called to trust in her righteous perfection and to rise up and minister in resurrection power upon the mountains of the world. It was there we saw her fear of the "foxes" that were ruining the vineyards, leading her tell her Beloved to turn away until "the *shadows* flee away" (2:17). At that point in her journey, the Shulammite was intimidated by any form of darkness that seemed to contradict the truths of His Song.

This issue was then amplified in the Song's fifth chapter when the Bride began to open the door of her heart to the Beloved's words. Upon opening this door, she was confronted by the shadows of contradiction once more and began to doubt His words again. Because of this, she went back to the watchmen of religion in order to find the Lord, and this only led to deeper frustration and greater persecution. This was a crisis moment that eventually brought her heart back to the indwelling Christ. It was the hinge of the entire poem and the moment of breakthrough for the Shulammite. She finally accepted that a garden of eternal daylight was already present within her soul (6:1-3). The Lord was there, and He would never leave her nor forsake her. With this revelation, she awoke to an inner Eden that was stronger than the barrenness of this world.

In the sixth chapter, the Bride took her full stand upon these truths. Her feet landed on the most solid rock imaginable—which also functioned as a trampoline that would catapult her into greater and greater impact. The people around her began take notice and they declared, "You are as beautiful as the full moon, as pure as the sun" (6:10). Since then, everything changed. The Shulammite is now ready to walk through the shadows around her, for she has learned something absolutely astonishing…

She is the light of the world.

The Song of the Ages: Part III

Poetry in Motion

Physically speaking, when you look at darkness, you are only seeing the absence of light. In a way, it looks like you're seeing something tangible and black, when in reality it's only an empty area of space devoid of light. Moreover, when you go into the dark and experience the dropping temperatures that can result from it, you may also think you're feeling something tangible called the cold. But the principle is the same. The cold is only the absence of light's energy. Feeling the cold and seeing the dark is simply the experience of being in less and less light. It's all a chilling nothingness that has no power of its own, other than what the absence of light gives it. Thus, when light confronts darkness, it immediately displaces it.

This is why all the darkness of the universe cannot wipe out the burning of one sun. Its light illuminates an entire region of empty space, exposing all the beauty and color around it (and even allowing for new life to arise). Obviously, this all parallels spiritual truth. When you realize *you are light* in the Lord (Eph. 5:7) and you shine like the stars of the universe (Phi. 2:15), darkness loses the power of its intimidation. For you know your presence immediately displaces any and all darkness around you. Like the sun, you are an energy source that completely shifts and warms the atmosphere, no matter what things look or feel like. As a result, darkness is way more fearful of you than you are of it.

But of course, this isn't to deny that the look and feel of darkness can be quite overwhelming. Poetic descriptions about these things might seem nice on paper, but if we're honest, we're often left with the question: *how does this apply to the harsh realities of life?* What about when you look into the eyes of an abused child or a psychotic inmate or visit a Holocaust museum and survey the exhibits of genocide? For many people, this is where the rubber tire of the Gospel hits a broken road that is seemingly impossible

Dismantling Shadows

to tread. It's where the sweet metaphors and poetic truths of Solomon's Song seem to drop, like music hitting soundproof foam. It's where we come face-to-face with the questions the Shulammite herself had to wrestle with...

Was the cross of Christ victorious—or not?
Was the love displayed there true?
And if it was victorious and true, does it still hold power today?

Confronting such questions can mark our greatest crossing point in the faith. Such confrontation is where we decide whether this poetry connects to a solid reality, or if it's just empty words written by a lovesick king in the ancient Middle East. This is where we take the bushel off our lives and find out whether or not there's a real flame underneath.

The truth of the Gospel either has weight and power behind it or it's just a good idea. Unfortunately, good ideas that are devoid of power won't change the world. However, good ideas with rocket fuel attached to them will. An idea with rocket fuel is one that carries an intrinsic force that erupts when it's believed, spoken, taken hold of, and acted upon. But you can't discover this supernatural energy until you step out and place the key of faith into the ignition of your own heart, mouth, and actions. That's when its power is manifested and you explode into new spiritual heights.

Earlier in the Song, the Shulammite was not willing to test the solidity of her Beloved's words. As a result, she wanted to avoid the opposing spaces of darkness at all costs. Though her Beloved had told her the coldness of winter was over, she felt and saw otherwise. Fear and unbelief prevented her eyes from seeing a new world of light and hope. Though revolutionary fuel sloshed inside her soul, she was afraid of taking hold of its truth in each area of her life by turning the inward key of faith. There were certainly moments when she began to turn that key, but the lies of

The Song of the Ages: Part III

darkness would continually tempt her to turn it back the other way (or completely take it out of the ignition and give up). Thankfully, the Lord's grace would not let her go. He taught her to persevere in looking beyond her natural sight by gazing upon the beautiful cross of Calvary. All along, Jesus was building strength and resiliency in His Bride, exposing more of the shadowy nothingness behind her fears. This is what He taught her at the Table of the Lamb, under the apple tree of the cross, and at the House of Wine. Soon, these experiences moved beyond good ideas to sweet and precious (and non-negotiable) realities, filled with an otherworldly power.

Here's another way to describe this. The Shulammite learned to follow the voice of the Good Shepherd in the first chapter of the Song (1:8). Because of this, she learned to lay down in the green pastures of grace. From there, she experienced the desire to stand up in her full stature and walk through the valley of the *shadow of death*. For laying down in the grass of Jesus's finished work teaches us that death is only a shadow. As painful and enduring as it can appear and feel (including all its decrepit forms, from abuse, to deterioration of the mind, to mass murder), death is not a *real entity*.

This isn't to say that shadows don't exist, but rather that they are see-through, insubstantial, and not as big and scary as they appear. They aren't as lasting as they seem either. As the apostle John said, "The darkness is passing away and the true Light is already shining" (1 Jn. 2:8). On top of this, each and every space of cold darkness is redeemable. Darkness is turned into potting soil in the hands of the Father, who takes it and makes it a space for the flowers of new life to emerge. God is never the One sending the shadow, for how can perfect Light cast forth darkness (Jms. 1:17)? Rather, He is the One turning it all around for good, like a farmer turning over soil to prepare the ground for its greatest purpose. And so, anyone who goes out in His name to the fields of darkness

Dismantling Shadows

will only find a springtime of light following close behind them. For they serve the One who brings beauty even out of ashes.

The Conviction that Leads to Bravery

With such conviction in her heart, the Shulammite is ready to walk into places where humanity is in deep pain. She's become more confident in the joyful notes of her Beloved's wedding Song than in the sour and dark tones of the world's funeral dirges. For the funeral of the Lamb has become a wedding Song for all humanity. Darkness has been forever swallowed up in the all-encompassing death of Christ. Thus, the Bride is willing to look right into the eyes of the broken, the abused, and the trafficked, and not turn away from their pain. She's ready to step out and light the match of the Gospel in places that are desperate for an explosion of hope.

Song of Songs 7:11 is a beautiful turning point in this eternal ballad, painting the picture of a brave church willing to endure the momentary pains of love and rejection. For even if the Shulammite brings her light into the villages and it is utterly rejected, she knows that sowing the seeds of love will still prevail, whether she sees it with her own eyes or not. In fact, those out in the "villages" who have experienced the worst kind of loss, abuse, and rejection are surrounded by the most fertile soil for new life to emerge. Though it may look like a cold and ugly space, it's actually the spot where some of the most magnificent flowers and the hottest burning suns can bud and ignite.

We cannot overemphasize enough that all of this ties back to what the Shulammite had to learn for herself in the first six chapters of the Song. She had to face the shadows of her own life and realize their emptiness. She had look and see the greater truth of righteousness within. What she perceived as a dark and barren space was actually a fertile field ready to produce a life-giving garden—one that was already there, just somewhat hidden beyond the horizon of her limited perspective. Now her perspective has expanded, so much so that it now includes the villages around her!

And herein lies another gem buried within the poetry of King Solomon…

Covered

When the Shulammite says the word "villages," she is using a Hebrew term that has a parallel meaning to it. It is the word *kaphar*, which shows up as "village" only a few times in our English Bibles. Most of the time it shows up as "atonement" or "reconciliation." The word *kaphar* has to do with "covering," which is its root meaning. Moses used this word when describing the atoning animal sacrifices that would cover and wash away the guilt of the Hebrew people. *Kaphar* is sometimes translated as "village" because it can describe a community that was "covered" and protected by a surrounding wall.

This insight greatly affects the implications of this verse. As we've seen before, Solomon could have chosen many other words for his lyrics. In this case, there are other Hebrew words to use when talking about a town or village. Yet this is the one his pen settled on and it shows us something quite beautiful in the text. For in her native Hebrew tongue, the Bride of the Beloved is saying something like this:

Let us spend the night in communities that are covered—places that are atoned for!

The Beauty Already There

Anywhere you can find people, you can also find the glory and goodness of God. Unfortunately, this glory is often hidden behind a veil of blindness. It may sound too simplistic, but deception is the only thing that muffles the light of God's love and righteousness from exploding within humanity. Multitudes of people remain neck-deep in

Dismantling Shadows

the nothingness of sin because they lack the *knowledge of God*. As we've seen before, this doesn't just mean they don't know who God is in all of His goodness and majesty. That's part of it; but it also means they don't know what *God knows* to be true. God knows we have already been reconciled by the blood of His Son. He also knows we have been redeemed and raised to new life in His Son's resurrection.

And that brings us back to the topic of shadows. Shadows form when a certain structure stands in the way of light. Therefore, the dark and evil spaces of society that seem to negate the truth of a redeemed world are formed only because of things blocking the exposure of that truth. This is why the apostle who vehemently ran into the villages of the world said his mandate involved "casting down arguments and every high thing that exalts itself against the knowledge of God" (2 Cor. 10:5 NKJV). These "high" structures take the form of "arguments" or lies that stand *against* what God knows to be true. So, when a lie is taken down, light hits a person and reveals the original color and beauty that was there all along, even though it remained hidden in the shadows.

This is what happened with the Shulammite and it's what can happen with each and every human being on the planet. Having discovered these things for herself, the Shulammite now represents a triumphant church who is looking at the world with x-ray vision—*cross-centered vision*. She sees the original blessing of glory upon each person. She looks at beggars and sees kings hiding under a false shadow of rejection and shame. She looks at prostitutes and sees worshippers who will give themselves fully to the King when they discover the safety in His presence. She sees leaders of gangs and cartels as future apostles and prophets who are called to be fathers and mothers in the family of God.

Put simply, she sees humanity as God sees them.

The Shulammite can look at entire cities without overly focusing on the strongholds of demonic influence or the problems on the

The Song of the Ages: Part III

local news networks. Instead, she sees streets and playgrounds waiting to be beautified by healed families. She sees office space and abandoned buildings waiting to be turned into gathering points for creative work and community partnerships. In all of this, she understands such things will easily come about as people wake up to the truth—as fathers begin to reflect the image of their Heavenly Father; as mothers see their true worth in the mirror of the Holy Spirit; as children grow up in their identity in the Son of God, cherished and beloved and treating one another the same; as employees and bosses recognize Christ in one another, engaging in work from the place of love and honor.

With this revelation, it becomes very easy to realize there is a plenteous supply of resources and strength hidden within every community, ever waiting to be discovered and tapped into. The prophetic promises of "rivers in the wilderness" is an acknowledgement of an underground water source already hiding in the desert. In other words, every solution to humanity's problems is hidden right within the problems themselves. For God said, "Let light shine *out of* the darkness" (1 Cor. 4:6). The Kingdom of light and a restored Garden of Eden is waiting to emerge right in the dust of humanity as people simply wake up to who they are and where they come from.

And so, the Song continues its sweet and luminescent melody, originating from the halls of eternity and passing through the believing soul of the Shulammite church. It rises up through her lips and begins to pour out onto the villages of a redeemed and yet sleeping earth. Her Song is the Song of Atonement and it calls for an end to every funeral dirge, inviting everyone from all corners of the earth to the dance of grace.

Seventh Selah

After dividing up titanic forces like gravity and light whilst arranging countless particles into breathtaking works of art, God entered into a *selah*. On the seventh day of creation, God rested (Gen. 2:2). This rest was a deep satisfaction with His finished work, a moment of enjoyment and celebration. Today, we're invited into this same satisfaction. To enter it is to embrace the very atmosphere of heaven. That wonderful atmosphere is a calm triumph buzzing with the frequency of hope. As we've said from the beginning, this atmosphere is all around us. You can actually relax right now and breathe it in. Like Jesus at the Last Supper, you can sit back and recline at the table (Lk. 22:14). Even if betrayal lies at your doorstep, there's a rest that overshadows any momentary affliction trying to steal your awareness of this pristine atmosphere of grace.

Selah.

As we've done in the previous two volumes, we want to continue with this life-giving practice. *Selahs* are meditative pauses and breaks that allow for rest, contemplation, and enjoyment. They are times to just *be*. They are also opportunities to meditate more deeply upon things that have touched your heart the most. But remember, sometimes the things that impact our hearts are

The Song of the Ages: Part III

surprising and subtle. Your heart may have even missed their touch while your mind was preoccupied with something else. So, allow the Holy Spirit to remind you of what's most important. Ask Him for help. As you bask in the finished work of God's Son, this help will come. Light and revelation will flutter to the surface of your conscious mind. You do not need to exert your energy and swim down into the depths of a bottomless ocean of truth. You can float on the surface and allow yourself to be swallowed by its surrounding glory. Indeed, stillness within His ever-present grace will bring you deeper than you can ever imagine.

8
A Door of Hope

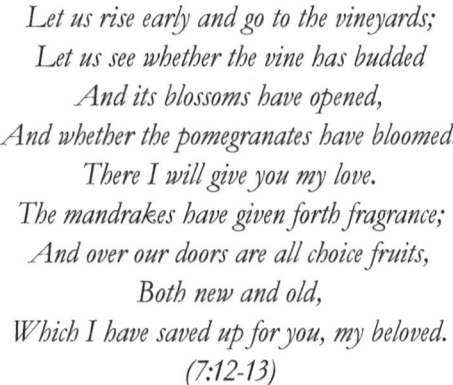

Let us rise early and go to the vineyards;
Let us see whether the vine has budded
And its blossoms have opened,
And whether the pomegranates have bloomed.
There I will give you my love.
The mandrakes have given forth fragrance;
And over our doors are all choice fruits,
Both new and old,
Which I have saved up for you, my beloved.
(7:12-13)

There are few people in the Old Testament who understood the Song of the Ages as much as the prophet Hosea. This man was called by God to marry a woman who would be unfaithful to him. Hosea did as the Lord said and, in the process, fell deeply in love with this woman. As a result, he began to embody the very heart of God toward the wayward people of Israel—and toward anyone who has struggled to stay true to the faith of the Gospel. His life became another instrument for the Song of the Lamb to play forth. Here's a portion of his writings directly coinciding with the present journey of the Shulammite:

The Song of the Ages: Part III

*I will return her vineyards to her
and transform the Valley of Trouble into a gateway of hope.
She will give herself to me there,
as she did long ago when she was young,
when I freed her from her captivity in Egypt.
(Hos. 2:15 NLT)*

 Toward the beginning of the Song, after a time of initial communion and intimacy, Jesus invited the Shulammite to come away and see "the vines in blossom" (Sgs. 2:13). It was an invitation into even deeper intimacy and greater fruitfulness. But the Bride declined this invitation, citing her worry about foxes in the vineyard. It was at this point that we saw the Shulammite's spiritual adultery with both fear and legalism. Fueling this affair was the false belief that Jesus was on "the mountains of Bether," a place signifying separation and distance. Gratefully, that affair has long been broken and the power of fear has been annihilated. Now, by the grace of God, Jesus's invitation to the vineyards remains and the Shulammite is taking hold of it. Like Israel in Hosea's prophecy, the Shulammite has been given back her vineyards. However, it's more like she has taken them back herself. For God was never the One keeping them from her. It was rather her own unbelief blocking her access to them.

 The beauty of the Song of the Ages is not only measured by the scope of its revelation, but also by the impact it has on the human heart. It opens up a willingness inside of us to explore places that may have seemed impassable before. When we tune in to the greatness of its melody, fearless love breaks forth from within, forging new paths forward in our attitudes and emotions. Limitations and fears are removed under the weight of its truth. Because of this shift in our hearts, situations and places where we've been stuck in the past and unable to move forward are transformed into doorways of hope.

A Door of Hope

The Vineyard in the Village

And so, the Bride walks through the door of this invitation knowing that on the other side is the hope of a transformed world. She enters the darkened villages of humanity and now speaks of *rising early* to go to the vineyards that reside there. It's important to see that when the Bride enters these villages, she immediately turns her attention somewhere else. She goes into the villages at night, but at the break of day—which is what "rising early" signifies—her desired destination changes to a vineyard.

Throughout Scripture, a vineyard is almost always associated with a community of faith. In the Passion Translation, the Shulammite says, "Let us arise and run to the vineyards of your people" (Sgs. 7:12 TPT). Whether it's referring to Israel or the church, a vineyard is intrinsically tied to a community or nation that God Himself has planted. In Isaiah, the prophet sings about his Beloved planting the "vineyard" of Israel (Isa. 5:1-2). In the New Testament, Jesus says that His Father is a "vinedresser" and His disciples are the branches connected to the Vine (Jn. 15:1-5). The vineyard represents a place where God's sons and daughters are growing together and bearing the fruit of the Holy Spirit.

The shift from villages to vineyards shows us that everywhere the Shulammite goes, there is a very specific mission and hope. When the church goes into the world (whether it's as one individual believer, two or three gathered together, or a whole community), the purpose is to bring the illumination of a new day. But more than that, it's to see darkened communities turned into places bearing the fruit of the Spirit. It's for cold villages to be transformed into playful, wine-infused vineyards of sunshine and grace. Look now at how another translation puts this part of the Song:

The Song of the Ages: Part III

Dawn shall find us in the vineyard…
(Sgs. 7:12 KNOX)

In reality, the vineyard was already there, but it was hidden in the dark. It was not until daylight emerged that the vineyard could be seen. Literally speaking, this is what would happen if two lovers during Solomon's day entered a village during the night. They would have to wait until dawn to explore the vineyards in that area. Yet, this would be different if those lovers *were the dawn themselves*. In the sixth chapter of the Song, this is exactly what we found regarding the Bride. Because of her union with Christ, she was described as one who "grows like the dawn" (Sgs. 6:10). Now, in the seventh chapter, we're continuing to see how this plays out. The Sun itself is lodging in the villages, revealing the fact that there's a whole lot more than just streets and homes in these places. There are also rows upon rows of vines and branches waiting to be touched by the waters of grace and soaked in the light of truth.

We've seen over and over how the "dawn" ultimately speaks of Christ's resurrection. But Christ's resurrection was bigger than one Man rising from the dead, or even a special group of people arising. Rather, it was the resurrection of all humanity, for all were united to Him at the tree. Like the recurring beat of a good song, these truths need to be repeated over and over again in order to keep in step with the overall rhythm of the music. As we embrace that rhythm, we can see more clearly what the Bride sees—a vineyard of new life hiding right within the villages of the world. Even though its fruit may be locked away behind the darkness of closed buds, the Shulammite knows what's hiding inside. And it is with this continued confidence that the Shulammite embraces her mission of transformation.

A Door of Hope

The World and the Church

When we strip away the poetry and symbolism, this part of the Song is simply a picture of the church's apostolic work amongst the nations. It reveals the church going out and planting more church communities right within the everyday world. It's the unfolding of the Great Commission, which we've seen building throughout the entirety of the Song's seventh chapter. But in all of this is that same thread and rhythm of grace. There's a simple and inclusive element to this work in the villages. Within this passage, we find how the global expansion of the church is simply the blossoming of the Holy Spirit's love, joy, and peace amongst humanity. It is sons and daughters awakening to love and reflecting the true image of Christ within.

This reminds us that there was never meant to be any division between the "world" and the "church." Both things—villages and vineyards—are meant to be contained within each other. Yes, the apostles tell us to come out of the world (2 Cor. 6:17), but this refers to the *world system* of deception that completely lacks the fruit of the Spirit. But the world itself (as in the one "God so loved") is filled with glory. Glory worth sending His only begotten Son to. Thus, this blood-bought world is meant to *become the church* as people draw their life from the Son.

The world of everyday things, from houses, to businesses, to theaters, and traffic, contains acreage marked out for the Kingdom of God. All of it has just the right soil for a vineyard to thrive. Too often, we think like the Pharisees; the ones whose name meant "Separatists." We imagine the church as this separate plot of land established outside the dirty and defiled streets of humanity. We often think in physical terms as though the church were a literal city with a heavenly zip-code that is only filled with Bible studies, church picnics, and worship concerts. Then, across the dividing highway of holiness, is another city, more putrid and defiled. It's

The Song of the Ages: Part III

the city of Babylon filled with casinos and brothels. But this is somewhat of a muddied understanding of the world and the church.

In reality, the city of the New Jerusalem, with its open gates and flowing river, is not found in a high mountain far away from the everyday world, fenced away through intense membership classes and religious rules and restrictions. On the contrary, it exists in every place where someone's heart has awakened to grace. This is why the fornicator, the murderer, and the idolater cannot enter this city, for their heart remains in a place of falsehood and fruitlessness (see Rev. 21:27 & 22:15). This is similar to saying that a pool of water cannot enter a block of solid steel. One object has to change its entire nature in order to enter the other. The sinner cannot enter the gates of the Kingdom, because if they did, they would no longer be *a sinner*. To embrace the Kingdom is let go of the false and sinful identity of Adam. It's to take on the name of Christ as His true Bride.

As this happens amongst the nations, there is certainly a need for spiritual organization and structure. God's awakened children will need to gather together, for what healthy family doesn't meet up regularly? There will also be different gifts and roles that form within these gatherings of God's kids, for even though our Father's creation is filled with wild spontaneity, there is also a great divine order. Yet even still, the Bible will not give us cookie-cutter models for church. Instead, it gives us the core DNA of the Gospel with some accompanying characteristics such as communion, worship, and generosity. But like a little seed, this can germinate and grow in an untold number of ways. For as the Gospel of light penetrates the soil of humanity, the expression of church can be as colorful and variant as the nations themselves.

The church is simply people. And thus, it is a potential reality wherever we go.

A Door of Hope

Love Manifested

So, with her heart set on this great mission of expanding God's family, the Shulammite goes on to say, *"There I will give you my love."* There, in the villages and vineyards, the Bride will pour out her love upon the Bridegroom. This verse almost seems to be describing a honeymoon between two newlyweds who are going away to a beautiful place to enjoy one another. That is certainly the feel of the verse, and it fits in very nicely with the spiritual message behind the book—for the true "Christian life" can be compared to an ongoing honeymoon that overflows into ministry to the lost, poor, and broken.

Don't let any well-intentioned but misguided teacher tell you there will come a time when the "honeymoon is over." As though the season of excitement and passion in the faith needs to eventually turn into raw commitment and will. There may be a scent of wisdom in that, but if you keep on sniffing you will eventually pick up the stink of garbage surrounding it. Obviously, commitment will undergird us in times of difficulty and stress. But if the honeymoon of intimacy and passion ends, Jesus will surely come with fire in His eyes to tell us to return to the place of our first love (Rev. 2:4). We're called to stay continually fixed and drunk on this love, knowing that any discipline or commitment will flow out of that intoxicated place.

This truth has already been well established, so it doesn't need further defense. What we need to do now is understand the type of "love" being given to the Lord in this ongoing honeymoon of grace. In light of what we've seen so far, giving our love to Jesus looks like something very specific. The Shulammite *gives* her love to Him by becoming a blessing to the world around her—by going into dark places and pouring out water and light. This is a more poetic way of explaining the famous verse from 1 John:

The Song of the Ages: Part III

If someone says, "I love God," and hates his brother, he is a liar; for the one who does not love his brother whom he has seen, cannot love God whom he has not seen.
(1 Jn. 4:20)

We give Jesus our love by loving people, by celebrating their lives, and by proclaiming and teaching the Gospel of grace. We saw this earlier in verse 8, when the Bride released her kiss to the Lord and described it as wine going over the "lips of sleepers." Her own kiss of grace is being poured out over those who are asleep; those buried under the pressures of life and covered by the darkness of deception. The Lord receives all of this as though it were a kiss to Himself. For that is how much He identifies with the people of the world, no matter how lost or broken they appear. Our outpoured love to others is like wine to God, intoxicating and enriching, and it is served in all kinds of differently shaped glasses. Some come in the form of compassion, some in friendship and service, some in speaking and teaching. The varieties are endless, but the wine is forever the same.

The Fruit of Passion

It makes sense then that the next statement is, *"The mandrakes have given forth their fragrance."* In the ancient world, mandrakes were known as aphrodisiacs. In the Hebrew, they are sometimes translated as "love-apples." This fruit was thought to awaken an intimate passion between lovers. For the Shulammite, passion manifests in *compassion*, which is being released in the villages and vineyards. That is what has been awakened in her heart, and it now comes from a place of deep desire instead of dry obedience. (And, to reiterate previous points, this isn't saying we need to always "feel" like loving people in order to love them. However, if we're only loving the world out of a depressed sense of duty, something

A Door of Hope

is missing and there is a definite need to feed afresh on the love-apples of the cross.)

Besides awakening passion, mandrakes were also believed to enhance fertility. This is probably why Rachel asked Leah for her son's mandrakes in Genesis 30. This is the only other place in Scripture where this fruit shows up. For years Rachel struggled to conceive and so she figured that mandrakes might help things along:

> *Now in the days of wheat harvest Reuben went and found mandrakes in the field, and brought them to his mother Leah. Then Rachel said to Leah, "Please give me some of your son's mandrakes."*
> *(Gen. 30:14)*

Notice this happened during the time of the "wheat harvest." This is a clear symbol of the harvest of God's sons and daughters throughout the world. Rachel wanted a harvest of literal children and sought after Reuben's mandrakes to make it happen. It was soon after this that she gave birth to her first child, Joseph, who would become the most influential and fruitful of all Jacob's children (Gen. 30:22-24).

Now Rachel was deeply loved by her husband, even before she could bear him children (Gen. 29:18). In like fashion, the Shulammite was always loved by Christ, even when she refused to go to the vineyards of fruitfulness. Nonetheless, by feeding on the mandrake-like fruits of His mercy, fertility came all by itself. The valley of a barren womb became the birthing canal for new life. And of course, this is another beat and melody rising and falling throughout the entire Song. It's the prevailing truth reminding us that when we feed on His love, empowerment comes to us and we are able to bear fruit in every other area of our lives. The mature union of love between Christ and His Bride always leads to a harvest, which is what we're seeing emerge in these final parts of the Song. This is the door of hope that stands wide open before the awakened church.

A Constant Expectancy of Victory

And as the Shulammite walks through this door, she speaks the following words over this rising melody of empowering grace:

"Over our doors are all choice fruits!"

The Shulammite understands that every situation, no matter how troublesome and difficult, is only an opportunity to bear "choice fruits" for Jesus. Whether it's the fruit of patience, love, or salvation, there's always power and victory when walking with Christ. Even when we go with Him to the most depressed and darkened villages, the gateway of hope is there as well. For every single person belongs to Him, and every square inch of this world is the inheritance of Christ (Ps. 2:8).

Therefore, in the mind of the awakened Bride, fruitfulness is not a matter of *if*, but *when*. And such a mindset is absolutely needed if the church is going to fully take hold of the Great Commission. All authority in heaven and earth has been given to Christ. Every knee will bow and every tongue will confess His Lordship. These are truths that permeate the heart of the Bride and it gives her an otherworldly confidence in her ministry and outreach. Again, we can see this attitude displayed through the life of the apostle Paul. He had an anticipation of fruitfulness and an expectancy of victory wherever he went. Here's one example that stands out:

> *I do not want you to be unaware, brethren, that often I have planned to come to you (and have been prevented so far)* **so that I may obtain some fruit among you also**, *even as among the rest of the Gentiles.*
> *(Rom. 1:13)*

A Door of Hope

Even though he'd been prevented from going to Rome, Paul was still bearing fruit in his current location. But he knew that if he could make his way to the capital city of the Roman Empire, fruit would be obtained there as well, just as it did "among the rest of the Gentiles." Paul had both experienced and understood that wherever he went, fruitfulness would follow. This was an assumption rooted in the promises of God as well as his own experiences of stepping out and taking risks based upon those promises. Like the Shulammite, he was established in the truth of Christ's finished work, through both revelation and follow-up encounters. He knew the truth of His own redeemed identity, as well as the redemption of the world around him. And so, he lived and ministered accordingly.

Possessing the Gates

Though the foxes of deception have eaten away at the vineyards of humanity, and the winter of sin has frozen its branches and stifled the growth of its grapes, Jesus has declared a word of hope over the nations. From the beginning, He has said to His awakening Bride that a new day has come. The winter of sin's power is over and gone. The floodwaters have subsided. The dove of the Holy Spirit is now released upon mankind and a new creation has begun to emerge. The vineyards are wide open for the taking and the gates of death will not prevail against them. (For as we learned before, those gates are only a passing shadow anyway.)

This is the promise God gave to Abraham for all of his descendants, including everyone reading this book. God promised Abraham his descendants would "possess the gate of their enemies" (Gen. 22:17). The gateway, or doorway, the enemy had once occupied would be reclaimed and restored. Hanging over those former gates of death are now the choice fruits of the harvest, and they hang there like grapes waiting to be picked by those who believe.

The Song of the Ages: Part III

The Israelites foreshadowed this when they lived in Egypt. For a period of time, the Egyptians would enter through the doors of Hebrew households and kill any newborn son within the home. Both slavery and death were possessing the "gate" of their household. For even if the family did not have a male child, they would still have to walk through the door every morning and go to work in a bitter and long day of slavery. But of course, all this changed when the blood of the Passover lamb was placed over those Hebrew doorways. This symbolic act reversed the curse of Egypt and set people free from both genocide and slavery. It was a picture of the "choice fruits" of Jesus's suffering hanging over their doors and breaking the power of death. After that event, the people walked out their front doors and, for the first time ever, headed toward a Promised Land of fruitfulness and freedom. On top of that, the Egyptians gave them gold and silver along the way! (Ex. 12:35-36)

The same reality has been offered to each one of us. Everywhere that death and slavery has persisted is now covered and overcome by the blood of Christ. As we take hold of the fruits of His suffering and walk forward in faith, we'll see that any and all slavery is long behind us. All that is ahead of us now are the promises of God! Joy, peace, and salvation will manifest left and right, and we will inherit the precious gold and silver of God's lost children as they too come back to the family of grace.

The Tying Thread

The Shulammite ends these declarations by saying all of this fruitfulness she's now experiencing has been *"saved up"* for Christ. This one statement holds a tremendous reminder of the redeeming work of God. It shows us that even when the Shulammite was fearfully neglecting her calling in earlier parts of the Song, nothing was actually lost. The fruitfulness she missed before was only being "saved up" for a future time. But that time has come. Love has led

A Door of Hope

her into a new season where she's tasting all the fruit she previously passed by. The seasons of missed opportunity and deep trouble have been turned around for the greater good!

God is able to do this…He is that good!

But perhaps the final two words of this verse are the most significant. The Shulammite concludes her thoughts by exclaiming, *"My Beloved!"* This brings us, yet again, to the thread of intimacy that ties up every loose end of revelation throughout the Song. It brings us back to the simple and eternal love of Christ. And this love is not a means to a certain end. We don't enjoy the love of Jesus just so we can experience greater power or have a bigger harvest. The love of Christ *is the end*. In fact, it's the beginning and middle too, and the harvest bursts forth along the way.

This is what everything is about, and it brings us right back to the words of Hosea. For after he spoke of the restoration of vineyards, the prophet immediately followed up with this:

> *"When that day comes," says the Lord,*
> *"You will call me 'my husband'*
> *instead of 'my master.'*
> *(Hos. 2:16 NLT)*

This is what everything has led to—a mature and confident love between Bride and Bridegroom. A love that is free from slavery, free from the fear of punishment, and free from the fear of letting Him down. And with all of this, it is a love that still compels us to go out into the villages and vineyards.

Peter's Valley

A final thought as we leave this chapter of the Song. There's a story from the life of Peter that connects with the Shulammite and it warrants a few more moments of reflection.

The Song of the Ages: Part III

Like the Shulammite, the apostle Peter had his own valley of trouble that God would transform into an opportunity for greater fruitfulness. This happened in the final hours before Jesus's crucifixion when Peter displayed a horrible act of unfaithfulness. Like Hosea's wife, he'd been unfaithful to his Beloved. First, Peter fell asleep in the Garden of Gethsemane after Jesus specifically asked him to stay awake and keep watch. This was much like the Shulammite in Song of Songs 2 when the Beloved asked her to rise out of bed and come away with Him. Like Peter, she fell back asleep. For the young apostle, this happened three different times (Mk. 14:41). Immediately afterwards, Jesus was arrested.

Soon after the arrest, Peter went on to publicly deny His relationship with the Lord. When someone questioned if he was a disciple of Christ, Peter began to curse and swear, assuring people that he did not know the Lord. This also happened three different times, and on the third occasion a rooster crowed—another symbol for awakening. At that moment, Peter was overcome by sorrow and fell into the worst valley of his life. Yet it was here that Jesus's faithfulness would overcome Peter's unfaithfulness. Jesus's awakened love would overcome the disciple's sleeping heart.

After He was resurrected, the Lord spoke to Peter on a shoreline off the Sea of Tiberius (Jn. 21). Over breakfast, He asked him the same question three different times. For each denial, and for each moment of falling asleep, Jesus asked Peter, "Do you love me?" Initially, it hurt Peter to be questioned this way, but a deeper revelation was coming to the surface. Jesus was not questioning Peter's love in a doubtful or condemning way, for He knew all things. He knew Peter did indeed love Him. Like the Shulammite, Jesus knew Peter's true identity. He knew that he was still "the rock." But He wanted Peter to see it. He wanted Peter to *wake up and get it.*

A Door of Hope

And that he did. After the third question, Peter said to Jesus, "My Lord, you know everything. You know that I burn with love for you!" (Jn. 21:17 TPT) It was at that moment that Peter's heart crowed and his true identity as a lover of God was confirmed. Instantly, his troubles were turned around and a doorway of hope was opened before him. For as Peter's love was affirmed, Jesus said to him, "Feed my lambs." The Lord immediately affirmed Peter's destiny and called him to be who he truly was—a lover of God, unafraid to take back the vineyards and eat their choice fruits.

This is the grace and power of God toward each and every one of us. Still, the Lord calls to us, inviting us to awake to His love and take hold of the harvest. This is the destiny of the entire church, embodied in the ancient story of the Shulammite. And as we read further, we'll find her taking this invitation to its furthest conclusion.

9

Full Circle: Back to Jerusalem

———•◆•———

Oh that you were like a brother to me
Who nursed at my mother's breasts.
If I found you outdoors, I would kiss you;
No one would despise me, either.
I would lead you and bring you
Into the house of my mother, who used to instruct me.
I would give you spiced wine to drink from the juice of
my pomegranates.
(8:1-2)

It is here in the church's climactic advance into the nations that we're reminded of the resistance that still stands against love. The Bride speaks here of people *despising* her and rejecting her love for Christ, which in essence is a rejection of her love for them. For when she speaks of kissing the Lord "outdoors," this still involves her love and service to the villages and vineyards of humanity. Of course, resistance doesn't come as a surprise. The triumphant church is a reflection of the One who faced intense persecution, even to the point of death. And so, in this portion of the Song, as the Bride reaches full speed and maximum capacity, she expresses a desire for greater boldness to stand in the face of such things.

Peter's Story Continued

We see these same realities playing out in the book of Acts when the early Shulammite church began to embrace the Great Commission. The disciples—fully awake to the resurrection of Christ—brought a great deal of light to the darkness around them. In partnership with their Beloved, they were healing the sick, raising the dead, declaring good news to the afflicted, and pouring out compassion upon the people around them. As a result, the atmosphere was transformed. People were coming to the Lord left and right and generosity was being multiplied. The poor and needy were being cared for while joy and celebration poured out of the wine being served at the communion tables in people's homes (Acts 2:41-47).

In other words, villages were being turned into vineyards!

One of the key leaders during these events was the apostle Peter. Having been recently restored to his identity and calling, Peter was at the helm of bringing the love of Christ into the "villages" around him—particularly the city of Jerusalem. Yet in this renewed work of ministry, resistance soon followed. Along with the disciple John, Peter was arrested and interrogated. We then find the following account of what happened:

> *When they saw the courage of Peter and John and realized that they were unschooled, ordinary men, they were astonished and they took note that* ***these men had been with Jesus***.
> *(Acts 4:13 NIV)*

Full Circle: Back to Jerusalem

Peter and John had certainly "been with Jesus." They had physically walked with the Lord and continued to be enveloped by His Spirit's presence. The intimate relationship these two "unschooled, ordinary men" shared with Christ was now erupting into the villages and vineyards around them—leaving people "astonished." Yet even though others were being impacted by their love, many still stood against it. At the forefront of this resistance was the same religious leadership that came against the Lord. These leaders began threatening Peter and John, insisting they stop displaying their affection for the Lord. Essentially, they were *despising* the Shulammite's love for Christ. And so, when Peter returned to the church community and reported what had happened, the entire church issued a prayer to God that parallels the words of the Shulammite:

> *"Now, Lord, consider their threats and enable your servants to speak your word with great boldness. Stretch out your hand to heal and perform signs and wonders through the name of your holy servant Jesus." After they prayed, the place where they were meeting was shaken. And they were all filled with the Holy Spirit and spoke the word of God boldly.*
> *(Acts 4:29-31 NIV)*

Like the Shulammite in Solomon's poetry, the early church was bringing transformation to the world around them, but opposition still came against their love and threatened to quench its flames. Because of this, they desired even greater boldness to release the Kingdom of God on earth. Another way to look at their request is that they wanted to experience a greater manifestation of Christ within. They wanted to walk in the same boldness as the One who fearlessly faced the cross.

The Song of the Ages: Part III

The Likeness of Christ

This is where we come back to the Shulammite's strange request to her Beloved: *"Oh that you were like a brother to me!"* At first glance, this seems like a contradictory statement to what has been revealed thus far. It was made clear a long time ago that the Shulammite is a "sister" to the Lord (Sgs. 4:9). So why would she now dismiss that truth and wish that He was "like a brother" to her?

On one hand, this could be simple, poetic language expressing her desire for the world to become more accepting of her passion for Jesus; and that the culture of heaven would be accepted and intertwined with the culture of earth. However, there's more to be uncovered in the Shulammite's words here. When the Bride says, "Oh that you were *like a brother* to me," she could also be speaking of her desire to manifest more of the *likeness* of Christ.

To be sure, the Shulammite understands she's been redeemed to the perfect image of Jesus. She knows she's filled with all the fullness of God, and that Jesus is both her Spouse and Brother. Nothing greater could possibly be attained than what she already has through her union with Jesus. However, this verse suggests that she still desires for the glory within her to burn more brightly on the outside. Like flames upon a lampstand filled with inner oil, the Shulammite wants to outwardly burn with more of the inner life of Christ. This relates to something the apostle John spoke about in his first letter:

> *Beloved,* **now** *we are children of God, and it has not appeared as yet what we will be. We know that when He appears, we will be* **like Him**, *because we will see Him just as He is.*
> *(1 Jn. 3:2)*

Likewise, the Shulammite understands that *now* she is a child of God. If this is so, then Jesus is her Brother through and through.

Full Circle: Back to Jerusalem

Nonetheless, the fullness of her identity has not yet manifested. In the "appearing" of Christ, the Bride's true identity will be fully known.

Now most people recognize John is speaking here of our final bodily resurrection (1 Cor. 15). However, this passage also teaches us that anytime we "see Him," we reflect more of His glory. We outwardly bear more of Christ's likeness. When John says "appears," he's using a word that simply means *"to be made visible."* It reminds us that even though Jesus is always with us, His manifest presence (or the revelation of His presence) brings noticeable change into the environment of our lives.

This word "appear" actually shows up in another portion of John's writings, during that famous breakfast scene with Peter. There, we find that Jesus "appeared" on the shore of the sea (Jn. 21:1). Of course, Jesus had already been on the shore for a while before the disciples finally realized it. But in that moment of realization, everything changed. Beholding the One who was already present led to a transforming encounter. First, the disciples became more-than-human fishermen, and then they experienced a deeper fellowship with the Lord (Jn. 21:6, 12). This is also where Peter had his powerful moment of restoration.

Later, when we read the book of Acts, it's apparent that this encounter with Christ led to a greater boldness in the lives of both Peter and John. Then you have the entire faith community joining them after asking Jesus for this same boldness to flow through them as well. After they prayed this prayer, the Scriptures tell us, "The place where they had gathered together was shaken, and they were all filled with the Holy Spirit and began to speak the word of God with boldness."

The Holy Spirit is the One brings the fullness of Christ out of us, like fruit on the branch of a vine or fire upon the branches of a lampstand. This story from Acts is not suggesting the church

The Song of the Ages: Part III

lacked the Holy Spirit before this prayer. Obviously, this same group of people had already been filled with the Spirit during Pentecost. The immediate disciples of Jesus had received the Spirit even earlier (John 20:22). Like the Shulammite, we should be established in the truth that we already have the fullness of God (Col. 2:10). The Holy Spirit is the sap and oil continually running through our veins. Furthermore, this life-giving sap is a person who never leaves us nor forsakes us. So, in a very real way, we cannot have "more" of God—for He has already given Himself to us completely.

Nevertheless, the fullness of God within us can increasingly manifest on the outside. That's what a fresh "filling" of the Spirit entails. This is meant to be an ongoing reality as we enjoy our union with Christ. We are to be "continually filled with the Holy Spirit," just like the awakened disciples of the early church (see Acts 13:52). It's an overflow of the life already inside of us, which is where we look more and more like Him. That's what the church encountered in Acts 4 during a time of increased persecution. And such is the reason for the Shulammite releasing her own prayer to the Beloved as she encounters the same kind of resistance.

Now, as we continue to read, we see this is more than just a desire for greater boldness and power. Ultimately, the Shulammite wants to give her Beloved *"spiced wine to drink from the juice of my pomegranates."* Pomegranates, we discovered in an earlier volume, represent the fruitful seeds of the Gospel stored up in the Bride. She says she wants to turn this into "spiced wine." This is another way of describing "mixed wine." If you remember, the Bride's naval was filled with such a substance (Sgs. 7:2). Her naval was also surrounded by a belly of "wheat," representing the harvest. These poetic dots are important to connect. She's speaking of the lifegiving joy of the Spirit within her, as well as the promise of birthing a harvest of revival and transformation. Her words at the beginning of the eighth chapter reveal this is now what she wants to pour out upon her Bridegroom. This portion of the Song is then a prayer for the bold power of the Spirit to birth every one of God's promises over her life!

The pomegranate fruit being turned into spiced wine speaks of the global impact of her love. But it is when we look at the Shulammite's words right before the mention of pomegranate wine that we understand more clearly what this global impact is all about. There is an underlying motive and goal attached to her entire prayer. It's here that we discover there's been something much bigger going on in the Shulammite's travels through the villages and vineyards. The Shulammite says that if she did indeed have more boldness to pour out her love for Christ, she would eventually lead Him back *"into the house of my mother, who used to instruct me."* This simple statement opens up a massive revelation that ties together everything we've been seeing through the last few chapters of the Song...

Returning to Mother Israel

The Shulammite's "mother" has shown up quite a few times throughout her journey. In the very beginning of the Song, we saw the Shulammite laboring in the vineyards of her "mother's sons" as she toiled under the weight of religion. We noted how her mother can represent Mother Church, including the religious systems of Christianity where many young Shulammites get their start. Nevertheless, there is a wider lens to use when interpreting the image of the Shulammite's mother. When we look at the entire biblical narrative, we can see the mother in the Song also represents the nation of Israel. In this perspective, the Shulammite's labor in her mother's sons' vineyards speaks to her labor under the law of Moses, which was instituted through the Hebrew nation. Israel is the mother "who used to instruct" God's people before the revelation of grace (Gal. 3:19). It speaks of the nation that

The Song of the Ages: Part III

was given the law, temple worship, and the covenantal promises of God—as well as everything else that pointed to the coming Messiah.

And so this is what we see emerging in the final chapter of the Song. As the church goes out into the villages of the nations, even in the midst of persecution and rejection, there is a deep longing to bring the Gospel full circle to the place where it was birthed. The Shulammite Bride wants to bring the Good News of Christ right back to Mother Israel. We see this same desire bursting out of the heart of the apostle Paul in his letter to the Romans:

> *For I could wish that I myself were cursed and cut off from Christ for the sake of my people, those of my own race, the people of Israel. Theirs is the adoption to sonship; theirs the divine glory, the covenants, the receiving of the law, the temple worship and the promises.*
> *(Rom. 9:3-4 NIV)*

In the same way, the Shulammite burns for her "mother" to know the indwelling Christ. This deep and passionate plea gives us a poetic glimmer of the completion of the Great Commission. In this final chapter of Solomon's Song, we see the great plan of heaven to bring the Gospel back to where it started—*Jerusalem*. Paul's words to the Romans continue to echo these truths:

> *My beloved brothers and sisters, I want to share with you a mystery concerning Israel's future. For understanding this mystery will keep you from thinking you already know everything. A partial and temporary hardening to the gospel has come over Israel, which will last until the full number of non-Jews has come into God's family. And then God will bring all of Israel to salvation!*
> *(Rom. 11:25-26a TPT)*

Full Circle: Back to Jerusalem

The Scriptures declare that as the fullness of the Gentile world embraces the Kingdom, the entire nation of Israel will eventually join them. In other words, the Gospel will go full circle around the globe, uniting Jew and Gentile as the redeemed Bride of God's Son!

This revelation brings us back to something we passed over in the last chapter. Earlier, when the Bride spoke of going through "doors" of opportunity and taking hold of "choice fruits," we didn't mention her description of that fruit. In the last verse of Song of Songs 7, the Shulammite said these fruits were "both new and old." This directly relates to what we're seeing in the eighth chapter. The "old" fruits speak to the beloved people of the Old Covenant—the house of Jerusalem and its children throughout the earth. Meanwhile, the "new" points us to the Gentile nations who are called into the presence of God through the New Covenant. The "mystery" Paul lays out in Romans simply gives us a more specific picture of how this will all come together. The Gospel of Christ is destined to go full circle around the world until it comes back to the "mother" who birthed the church.

What's stunning is to learn that church history follows this revelation. As the historical Shulammite travelled throughout the "villages" of Gentile nations, there's been a growing movement, especially in the last century, to bring the message back to the resurrected nation of Israel. Thus, what Solomon symbolically prophesied thousands of years in advance is coming together in our own day and age. But let's take a moment to look more closely at the history, because it will help us appreciate the historical unfolding of the Shulammite's symbolic journey.

Back to Jerusalem

The fires of the Gospel were initially lit on Pentecost in the city of Jerusalem where it then spread into the surrounding villages of

The Song of the Ages: Part III

Judea and up to Samaria. After this, the Song of the Gospel began its orchestral march to the ends of the earth (Acts 1:8). This began mostly in the Roman Empire with its sprawling terrain covering a good portion of modern-day Europe, North Africa, and parts of the Middle East. After many years, the message of Christ then crossed the Atlantic into North America (even as its original fires continued to burn in other parts of Europe, Asia, Africa, and beyond). Out of North America came a sweeping move of the Spirit that went down into South America before winding its way back East. All along the way, the villages of humanity were hit with the wine of grace and spiritual vineyards emerged in different varieties and settings. Obviously, this is a rough sketch that doesn't include many other areas touched by the fire; however, it does give a broad picture of how the church expanded. In all of this, a lot of confusion, religiosity, and pain spread as well; however, at the heart of everything was the indestructible seed of the Gospel being planted throughout humanity (see Matt. 13:31-35).

In modern history, the greatest movement of village-transformation is arguably the spiritual awakening that hit China in the last century. As the tiny and unconquerable seed of the Gospel winded its way back East, it was soon planted in the Chinese nation. What began as a very small outreach to certain parts of mainland China eventually led to millions upon millions of people falling in love with their heavenly Bridegroom, Jesus Christ. This movement marked a major acceleration in the Gospel's travels, even as it burned through other nations in the East such as South Korea and the Philippines. As this happened, the Song's loop around the globe began to near its completion.

In the early days of this eastern harvest there was a prophetic call from the Holy Spirit given to the young Chinese church. In the 1920s, several spiritual leaders within China felt compelled by the Holy Spirit to equip the church to bring the Gospel back to

Full Circle: Back to Jerusalem

Jerusalem. Of course, this did not just mean going straight to Judea, but also to minister in the many places lying between China and Israel. The Chinese church recognized that bringing the Gospel to Israel is just as important as bringing it to any other nation, for all are included in the finished work of Christ. In the end, this is about "one new man" arising on the earth, both Jew and Gentile together (Eph. 2:15).

Ironically, the area between China and Israel includes many of the places that have yet to hear the Gospel. They are *villages* that still lay under the darkness of a songless night. Thus, the church has been continually invited by the Holy Spirit to go into such places and play the chords of healing and forgiveness, singing out the lyrics of reconciliation which have the power to bring about a beautiful family reunion upon the earth. This includes the Middle Eastern regions where the children of Abraham have grown particularly estranged from one another. Consequently, the call upon the church in recent decades has involved going through places that have demonstrated some of the greatest resistance to the love of Christ throughout history. To use Solomon's language, some of these nations have adamantly *despised* the kisses of the Shulammite. This puts even more of an emphasis on the Bride's prayer in Song of Songs 8:1. As the Great Commission reaches its climax, the desire for greater boldness will continue to proceed from the lips of the rising church.

Remarkably, several significant things happened in the years following this vision given to the young Chinese church. First, their objective to complete the Great Commission and go by "night" into darkened regions was followed by them learning how to persevere through a flood of persecution in their own nation. In the midst of this, the Chinese church experienced an absolute miracle where, in the face of that unrestrained persecution, they grew to tens of millions of people. To this day it continues to grow, testifying to

The Song of the Ages: Part III

the promise of fruitfulness within the Shulammite church. Again, this is something Solomon wrote about in his ancient love poem thousands of years prior!

But this all interconnected with an even greater miracle. Not long after the vision in the 1920s to bring the Gospel back to Jerusalem, the entire nation of Israel was miraculously reborn two decades later! In 1948, the impossible happened as the Jewish nation was recreated, leading to the capital city of Jerusalem being reestablished as well. This was something that seemed totally unrealistic for nearly 2000 years, and it was no less so in the 1920s. But it all came together just in time for the Gospel to circle back to where its fires were initially kindled.

Coinciding with these events, Israel and China have experienced significant economic growth over the years. This has allowed for more trade and other interactions to spark between these two regions, paving the way for the Gospel to travel to-and-fro. On top of this, there's also been the explosion of computer technology, which actually began accelerating around the same time as Israel's restoration. Such technology has connected the world more than ever before, thus opening up even more doors for the Gospel to go through. As all of these moving parts have begun to align, the dream given to the Chinese church has become more doable than ever.

Awe and Worship

It's astonishing to see how history has brought us to this point, starting right in the original city of Jerusalem. Against all odds, a small sect of Jewish people who fell in love with a crucified Savior has exploded into almost every part of the globe. This group of people is now rising into the glorious Shulammite of Solomon's Song. The Lord is now answering her prayer to bring this love back to the place where it all started. When considering how all

Full Circle: Back to Jerusalem

of this has come together in the advance of the Gospel, it's truly overwhelming. The sovereignty of God is a beautiful wildfire that consumes everything around it.

And of course, this happens without forcing love to be ignited. This wildfire burns with a different kind of power. Like Christ on the cross, it comes with arms wide open, swallowing up hell's resistance with the heat of mercy. The loving providence of God has invaded human history, marching against the worst floods of rejection and unbelief. To this day, the Song advances, and it will continue to advance—for many waters cannot quench it (though that's getting a little ahead of ourselves). Perhaps this is why the apostle Paul ends his thoughts in Romans about Jews and Gentiles with the following words of awe and worship:

> *Oh, the depth of the riches both of the wisdom and knowledge of God! How unsearchable are His judgments and unfathomable His ways! For who has known the mind of the Lord, or who became His counselor? Or who has first given to Him that it might be paid back to Him? For from Him and through Him and to Him are all things. To Him be the glory forever.*
> *Amen.*
> *(Rom. 11:33-36)*

10
Still Asleep (Reprise)

*Let his left hand be under my head
And his right hand embrace me.
I want you to swear, O daughters of Jerusalem,
Do not arouse or awaken my love
Until she pleases.
(8:3-4)*

Through dark villages and budding vineyards, the Shulammite's quest to her mother's house marches on. We're looking at the climax of the Great Commission; a reality that will emerge as the church is unveiled as the co-steward of the earth standing confidently beside her heavenly King in the place of authority and peace. Her work is the overflow of participation in the life of the Trinity—a life of other-giving love culminating in the healing of the nations. Such is the true meaning of terms like evangelism, discipleship, or missions. These things are the eruptions of love—a fiery rocket blast off the platform of awakened identity. And the only true and stable launching pad for such explosive transformation are these words:

*"I am my Beloved's and His desire is for me."
(Sgs. 7:10)*

The Song of the Ages: Part III

Yet at the peak of this revelation, the Shulammite's language begins to shift. Old notes start to surface, coming from what feels like the distant past. As the Song nears its finale, familiar words return to her lips. *"Let his left hand be under my head,"* she says, *"and his right hand embrace me."*

This part of the Song is a *reprise*, a musical term for when an earlier passage of a composition returns to the forefront. If God's Word is a Song, then there are many such reprises throughout its stories, poems, and parables. Consider for example the rock that followed the Israelites throughout their time in the wilderness (Ex. 17:6). When the New Testament comes along, there is a reprise of that rock (1 Cor. 10:4). As with musical reprises, scriptural ones like this come with new understanding as well as an enhancement of the original melody. Oftentimes, they bring a purifying of the original melody, as though some unnecessary instruments were quieted down in order to highlight the essence of the music. In the instance of this wilderness rock, we discover that it was Christ Himself all along.

In the case of these reprised lyrics from the Shulammite, we will attempt to distill its underlying melody and uncover its deepest meaning. In order to do that, we will first go back through the Shulammite's journey and gain a clearer perspective of the entire Song. This will then position us to reach the end of her mission. Consider this chapter as a moment of hindsight that will unveil the bigger picture behind the Song of the Ages—a picture that will usher us into the true and final climax of its music…

A Melody in the Wilderness

Much earlier in her journey, when the idea of laboring in vineyards brought about feelings of anxiety and frustration rather than passion and confidence, the young Shulammite was led to a delicious apple tree (Sgs. 2:3). There she found rest under its shade

Still Asleep (Reprise)

as we discovered the tree represented the very cross of Calvary. The Shulammite learned to truly taste of salvation and of the love poured out at the cross. She found there was no shelter more fortified and comfortable than these truths:

That Jesus Christ would give His entire life for us to be whole and safe.
That He takes delightful pleasure in our health and joy.
That He is only Love. All of His judgments are unto our healing and restoration.

Taking this into the heart and mind changes everything, and that's what coming under the tree is all about. Sitting under the canopy of its protective branches, stretched out like the Messiah's arms on Roman wood, the Shulammite found herself transported into the place of spiritual intoxication. In Song of Songs 2:4, the King led her to the House of Wine. Like blood from pierced arms, the juice from the tree's fruit dripped down and became the sweetest of wine to her taste. This drink of redemption gave birth to bliss, and soon the tree transformed into a victorious image before her eyes. She beheld a bright *banner of love* waving over her life, providing deep meaning to her existence and a safe rallying point for the battles of life. In reality, this tree and banner had been there all along, following her around like the rock that followed the Hebrews in the desert. It was a home in the wilderness offering an end to all wandering and fear.

But as she began to taste of the pleasures of Christ's comfort, an ancient deception started to creep into the Shulammite's mind. She began to turn her attention back upon herself, feeling as though she needed to "sustain" these encounters, as though she had to personally do something in order to remain in the place of bliss. It was then that she expressed her longing for the Beloved's left hand to be under her head and His right hand to embrace her (2:5-6).

The Song of the Ages: Part III

On a natural level, these lyrics are obviously about physical intimacy. Yet through a spiritual lens, it's clear this is about the Bride's desire for union with God. In her mind, this is what would help her take hold of the heavenly realities set before her. In the first volume of *The Song of the Ages*, we discerned how all of this points to the church's age-old problem of pursuing something we already have—union.

This request for union is quite understandable. Certainly, the desire behind it is very good. Yet it exposes an ongoing issue the Song has been confronting since its beginning—a lie that sits at the base of all our despair. The lie of separation. This is at the root of humanity's brokenness and it is the very cornerstone of our false towers to heaven. In reality, this goes back to the lie the first humans embraced at another famous tree in the Bible—the Tree of Knowledge.

This is when Eve, a foreshadowing figure of the church, was told there was something she needed to do to become "like God" (Gen. 3:5). Eve bit into this lie and consequently bore the fruit of deception, living in a false separation from her Father (even though God remained with Eve and her children, following them into the wilderness and establishing His prophetic covenants with them over and over). And so, the apple tree in Solomon's Song is the true solution to the bitterness of human existence. With every bite of the Beloved's apples, the poisonous effects of the false tree are reversed, bringing about a new revelation of wholeness and oneness. This is the true cornerstone upon which humanity rises into the heavens, for it carries the truth that we have already risen there with Christ.

Yet still the Shulammite would follow Eve's pattern. Still she felt there was something she needed to *do* in order to take hold of these truths. The seeds of law began to surface within her heart and soon we discovered a sleepiness covering her eyes like a thick

Still Asleep (Reprise)

and itchy blindfold. This was the sleep of religion—man's efforts not only to become right with God, but to be united with Him as well. And yet with unyielding patience, Christ responded to her misled statements with words that would also be reprised in the finale of the Song:

"Do not awaken my love until she pleases."

Here it became evident that the Bride was still asleep and that much of the Song was about waking her up from the lie of separation. And yet, this was coupled with the Lord saying not to awaken His Bride until she *pleases*—a word that means to take delight in something. In other words, don't force her to wake up until she *wants* to. The awakening of the heart can only come through the purity of love. But even still, we can only love through first tasting His love for us. Therefore, much of the Song's composition went on to plumb the bottomless depths of God's love for us—*for you*—and helping the Bride rise out of her slumber in a natural way. A way that leads to the overflow of worldwide transformation and harvest.

We began to see these things more clearly in the latter half of the Song's second chapter. It was there that the Shulammite was standing behind a wall of perceived separation—the wall of the Old Covenant. Unfortunately, she was believing that the victory of Christ and the fullness of His presence was only found across a vast mountain range called *Bether*, a word in the Hebrew that can be translated as "separation" (2:17). It defines the essence of man's historical pursuit of union wherein oneness is believed to be found by crossing some vast valley between two mountains. On one mountain is our pitiful human existence while on the other is the glory of Jesus's resurrected life. In the valley between these mountains lies certain ideals such as suffering or discipline, and the way we're taught to cross this chasm is through personal sacrifice

The Song of the Ages: Part III

and death. Thus, death becomes an idol promising salvation instead of an enemy Jesus came to totally eradicate.

These lies seek to hide the truth that it is the myrrh of Jesus's death—not our own—that brings about union and victory (1:13). It is grace alone that brings about the eternal life of the Spirit (Gal. 3:2). There's a subtle spirit of unbelief that denies these realities. So, it was an exposure of this unbelief that took us into the third chapter of the Song where the Bride was still on her "bed," still seeking after Christ through the broad ways of man (3:1-3). In her false dream state, the Shulammite searched the highways and byways of religious institutions and methodologies looking for the One with whom she was already united by blood. The fourth chapter then continued this theme with further longings for her Beloved. At the end of that chapter we found the Shulammite crying out for the "wind" of the Spirit to come into the garden of her being, which was met by a stunning reply from Christ:

"I have already come into My garden" (5:1).

Like minor and major chords, the lie of separation intertwines with the truth of union throughout the Song; although it is always building toward a chorus where the sounds of union triumph. This chord progression was amplified in the fifth chapter where the Shulammite increased her rigorous pursuit of the Lord, returning to the watchmen of the walls. These were the guardians of religious ideology who only brought about more pain and struggle in her life (5:7).

Yet before the sweet sounds of grace could be drowned out completely, the great chorus of union broke through the crashing silence. In the transition between the Song's fifth and sixth chapters, we saw the birth pangs of religion dissipate as the long-coming truth was birthed in her heart—the revelation of the ages. The minor notes of law gave way to the majors of grace as the

Still Asleep (Reprise)

full Song plucked her heart and she surrendered to the truth of a perfect union with God. The Bride declared with finality and assurance that *the Beloved dwells within the garden of her being* (6:2-3). Come what may—feelings, circumstances, loss, or gain—the truth of the cross would be the Rock, Banner, and Tree of her entire life. No matter what, she determined to walk by faith in this truth and not by sight. This was the alignment of her heart with the Song of heaven—the "new song" of the Scriptures (Ps. 98:1). It was her transition from the Song of Moses to the Song of the Lamb.

Suddenly, the embrace of this truth helped the Shulammite step into who she was all along—the mother of all the living; the great co-steward of the earth. We learned that resting under the cross leads not only to personal refreshment and spiritual peace, but toward a transformative impact upon the world. The "queens, concubines, and maidens" of humanity are drawn to the light that shines from one who has embraced the apple tree and found rest under its shade (6:8-10). This is what brought about the Shulammite's advancement through villages and vineyards (7:10-13). And this is also what brought her full circle as she prepared to bring the beauty of this Song right back into her mother's house. Her hope is that all humanity—the fullness of Gentiles and all of Israel—would awaken to its glorious sound (8:1-2).

But now, something strange occurs. Having been fully awakened herself, the Shulammite returns to her old request for union. What seemed like nonstop progress in a victorious march of love across the earth seems to come to a standstill. In the final melodies of the Song, it appears that once more the Shulammite is looking for something she has already attained.

Has she fallen asleep again?
Has she forgotten the Word of grace?

The Song of the Ages: Part III

It seems that this might be the case. However, this assumption will lead us into great encouragement, if we'll heed the word of caution that comes with it.

Living Hope Deferred

Earlier, when the Bride was overwhelmed by her experience in the House of Wine, she requested that the Beloved's hands embrace her. We found that she was looking for something to sustain the life of the Spirit *within*. Now it seems that she is overwhelmed by sustaining the life of the Spirit *without*. And so, she says the same words again.

Think about it. The Shulammite has been circling the earth, joyfully bringing the Gospel of grace to everyone around her. The Lord has brought her from prophetic promise to literal fulfillment as she embarked upon the actual work of fulfilling her calling. But work like this can lead to weariness, which in turn brings about sleepiness. Or, in other words, a return to the dream-state of self-effort.

Intense persecution combined with the magnitude of our calling (birthing *and* nurturing an awakening in every tribe, tongue, and nation) is quite the challenge. If the focus remains too much on the work and not on the original place of rest under the tree, this can subtly re-open the door to that deceptive spell of separation. Much like Eve pursued something good through the serpent's temptation (becoming *like* her Father), the place of rest can be forgotten in the pursuit of good things. This is behind Paul's warning to the Corinthians, something we've discussed many times before:

> *For I am jealous for you with godly jealousy. For I have betrothed you to one husband, that I may present you as a chaste virgin to Christ. But I fear, lest somehow, as the*

Still Asleep (Reprise)

serpent deceived Eve by his craftiness, so your minds may be corrupted from the simplicity that is in Christ.
(2 Cor. 11:2-3 NKJV)

It is possible that the seeds of forgetfulness were sown when the Shulammite requested that the Lord "were like a brother" to her (8:1). We looked at this from a positive perspective before, but there is a potential blind spot in this request as well.

Remember that the Shulammite wanted to bring the kiss of the Gospel back into the house of Mother Israel. This would require a lot of grace and power, and so she prayed for more of Jesus's *likeness* to manifest in her life. This included the boldness to press through persecution. That prayer opened up a fresh discussion on the difference between truth and manifestation. In reality, the Bride is completely united with Christ and already *like Him*. But of course, this union has not been outwardly revealed—and it can't be fully revealed until Christ's revealing (1 Jn. 3:2). So, this entire commentary on the Song of Solomon is not denying our future hope nor is it minimizing the legitimate longing for more of heaven to manifest on earth. In the face of many challenges, the Bride expresses a longing for more manifestation. This is a good request that comes from a pure motive; however, there is still a caution here. If we're not careful, our longings and desires can be subtly twisted by the enemy of our souls.

Solomon wrote elsewhere in the Bible that "hope deferred makes the heart sick" (Prov. 13:12). Consequently, putting our hope solely upon future (deferred) realities can bring about heartsickness, which in turn can produce spiritual slumber and religiosity. Hope deferred, and the discouragement that results from it, has often led the church right back into the arms of religious watchmen. These are people of influence who build ministries and teachings on the foundation of separation and deferment. Such a foundation has little room for the expectancy of power and joy to break through

The Song of the Ages: Part III

in the present moment. It is always about looking for the next big thing, whether good or bad, instead of tapping into the fullness that is already ours.

Hope deferred makes the heart sick, but when our hope is the *hope of glory*—Christ in us *right now*—the heart remains healthy and alive. Religion wants to twist our hope into something that does not yet exist (and has all these conditions and valleys between it). But when our hope springs from what was already accomplished, there is a constant and renewable release of strength and power. With this renewed position of the heart, even our outlook toward future realities get brightened.

The apostle Peter affirmed that hope is something *living*. Hope is not a concept nor is it something *only* about the future—though we don't see all of its blessings with our physical eyes just yet. Hope is something that is alive. And of course, that something is a Someone. It is the hope of the living Christ within.

> *Blessed be the God and Father of our Lord Jesus Christ, who according to His great mercy has caused us to be born again to a **living hope** through the resurrection of Jesus Christ from the dead.*
> *(1 Pet. 1:3)*

Now it's imperative we point out something else here. This revelation of hope probably took Peter a long while to grasp himself. There were lots of ups and downs throughout his journey and his letter was written much later on in his life. Earlier, we looked at Peter's beginnings as an apostle, particularly from when he denied the Lord and was restored to his identity and calling. From there, we looked at the power and confidence that followed this restoration and how it paralleled the Shulammite's journey in the Song of Songs. We then looked at the entire early church community and the prayers for greater manifestation and boldness

Still Asleep (Reprise)

following Peter's arrest. This too was right in tune with the Bride's desire for boldness in her request to publicly pour out love upon her Beloved. We saw all these elements from the early church as good and pure pictures of walking with Christ, both as individuals and as whole communities. However, when go further into the New Testament, we can see the subtly of that age-old deception of separation creeping back in—even to bold and radiant individuals. And even to entire communities.

Peter's Story Continued, Again

In his letter to the Galatian church, Paul shares a very unflattering story about Peter. He tells of a time when Peter came to the newly birthed church in Antioch, the capital city of ancient Syria (Gal. 2:11-13). We'll look at this briefly, and as we do, keep in mind that this story happened a long time after Peter's restoration, his arrest and release, and several years of further experience and maturity in the Lord.

According to Paul, Peter had gone up to Antioch to spend time with the growing church of that region. Initially, he hung out with the non-Jewish believers who resided there, which was a beautiful expression of the heart of Christ from someone who had personally walked with Jesus in the flesh. As a Jewish leader spending time with Gentiles, this was a radical bridging of two cultures in a time when such bridges were never constructed. In fact, at this point in human civilization, the building materials for such a bridge hadn't even been dreamed of yet. Nevertheless, Peter displayed the inclusive heart of Christ—that is, until another group of people arrived on the scene.

Soon after Peter's arrival, several other leaders from Jerusalem also came up to join the festivities (or rather, to ruin them). When they arrived, this group refused to eat with the non-Jewish crowd. The reason for this was due to their continued honor of the law,

The Song of the Ages: Part III

which, as we've explained many times before, is the same law that the New Testament calls a "dividing wall." Unfortunately, Peter embraced this attitude and began to disassociate from the Gentile believers as well. His influence was so strong that even Barnabas, one of the other leaders of the Antioch church (and a man "full of the Holy Spirit"), joined in Peter's hypocrisy as well.

Paul understood that this resistance to eating with Gentiles would have a radical impact upon the community. Just as it took one simple act of eating for Eve to destroy the joy of divine fellowship, the same would be true with Peter's eating. This is because the table is the place of fellowship. It is the place of communion and thus the greatest reminder of our inclusion and union with the life and presence of God. Such an atmosphere would leave the non-Jewish believers with a sense of lack and distance. They would begin to feel that they were in some way unholy or less-than. All of a sudden, there would be a huge mountain range called *Bether* placed between them and the Lord. *Bether* would bring new questions to their innocent minds, strangling and corrupting their simple joy in Christ's finished work. These questions essentially would come down to how they could bridge the gap and share fellowship once more with Jesus's original disciples. The answers would then involve circumcision, dietary restrictions, and a whole host of other religious works.

Now what's possibly the most concerning element of this story is that this group of people were sent from the apostle James (Gal. 2:12). James was the recognized leader of the church of Jerusalem—the same community who had prayed for boldness and power years before this event took place. Like Barnabas, the Jerusalem church was full of the Holy Spirit and had brought much light and love to the villages around them. But this encounter in Antioch leaves us with a lot of evidence that the ancient slumber of separation and religion crept back in to the Jerusalem Bride. It

Still Asleep (Reprise)

seems that an affinity for the law is hard to break, and as a result, large portions of the early church fell back into that problematic dream-state (Gal. 3:1).

Thankfully, Paul took his stand against this. He called out Peter and the gang and then shared this story with future churches as a warning. Now some people could have read his letter and accused him of gossip or negativity (or perhaps trying to make himself look like a better apostle than Jesus's former righthand man). But Paul could care less about such accusations. He knew his heart. He was more concerned about the Gospel of grace losing its clarity than what people thought of him as a leader. Indeed, this kind of conflict with Jewish believers seemed to follow him throughout his entire ministry and some believe that these people were actually his "thorn in the flesh" (2 Cor. 12:7).

Now it's important to remember this incident was not limited to a problem amongst the early Jewish followers of Christ. The whole purpose of the book of Galatians was to rebuke an entire Gentile church of doing the same thing! Paul was warning the people about being bewitched, which is another way of describing spiritual slumber. Like the Shulammite, the Galatian church was pursuing good things—miracles and the emboldening power of the Spirit—but they were doing so without a central revelation of the cross.

What has happened to you Galatians to be acting so foolishly? You must have been under some evil spell! Didn't God open your eyes to see the meaning of Jesus' crucifixion? Wasn't he revealed to you as the crucified one?
(Gal. 3:1 TPT)

It seems that losing sight of the apple tree is a common thread throughout church history, even in its earliest days.

The Song of the Ages: Part III

Falling from the Beginning

Many commentators might disagree with this interpretation of the Song's eighth chapter. Some may think that the Bride's request for the right hand of the Lord to embrace her is simply her desire to experience more intimacy with Christ, even as she continues the journey back to her mother's house. This is entirely possible. The process of scriptural interpretation often resembles a multitude of ears listening to the same song. There are many layers of instrumentation and even varying messages within the lyrics that can strike the heart of different listeners in different ways. But that being said, there is still a deep and consistent undercurrent to Solomon's music. There is a heartbeat to it, and we want to keep as close to that beat as possible.

Hopefully, as we've surveyed the Bride's journey, the blood-flow of union and awakened love has become very clear. In view of everything we've seen, it appears that a moment of forgetfulness is once again sneaking up on the Bride at the end of the Song, especially as she looks to accomplish the great task set before her. Though it doesn't last for long, a subtle closing of the eyelids creeps in. This may come as a surprise this late in the game, but it can also bring encouragement for any of us who still struggle with the tug-of-war between faith and sight. For if victorious leaders like Peter (who had personally tasted of Jesus's grace in his life) can fall under the influence of a religious slumber, then we can certainly give ourselves grace for the times we forget about our union with God.

As we've realized, this issue goes way beyond Peter to the entirety of church history. There was a falling away from grace right from the start, leading to a variety of stumbles and trips as things developed. It would take us too far from Solomon's Song to give a detailed survey of church history and the ensuing examples of this fall, but the situation in Antioch hopefully offers enough evidence on its own. Well before its Roman politicization, the

Still Asleep (Reprise)

church of the first three centuries had succumbed to a religious spirit even in the midst of incredible harvest and shining leaders who were full of the Holy Ghost. This is quite different from the outright heresy that tried to wedge itself into the church in its earliest days. Spiritual leaders held their ground against obvious attacks on the person and work of Christ, but they weren't always as savvy against the subtly of religion. And this makes sense if you think of Eve, who was someone who had walked in the clear light of God before falling to deception. Eve probably wouldn't have bit the fruit if the serpent had claimed God was not God or that He was not worthy to be obeyed. It was the combined *twisting and acknowledging* of God's Word that was the real problem. And the same is true with the Shulammite church throughout history.

In the centuries after she was birthed, the soothing voice of separation continued its efforts to establish itself as the only song being sung by the Shulammite. Even in moments of historical awakening and revival, where the chorus of grace broke out afresh on the earth, we find this same pattern occurring. After a period of experiencing tangible power in the Holy Spirit, spiritual communities and entire regions were influenced by other voices that perverted the Gospel's sounds. These perversions caused the atmosphere to deaden and crust over, usually in the name of things like righteousness or order. As a result, most places that were once considered "hot spots" of revivalism are now the furthest away from the power of the Gospel. While many would blame the world and the devil for that, it seems the prophetic story of the Shulammite uncovers the real root of the problem—religious bewitchment.

You can track the Shulammite's wayward travels in every branch of the church, from mainline denominations to underground charismatic communities. Entire denominations birthed in the fires of grace have often grown cold and systemic as Shulammite believers made their way back to the broad ways of religion with its overseeing watchmen. Even in the early 1900s, when the church saw an acceleration of harvest and fresh encounters with the Holy Spirit, it did not take long before religiosity crept back in there as well. As vibrant and "village-transforming" as it has been, the Pentecostalism of the last century has often succumbed to the same lies that Peter and the Galatians embraced almost 2000 years prior. This is no less true amongst eastern believers as well as modern Jewish (Messianic) followers of Christ. Whether it's in places of evangelistic passion or in the embers of long-burnt out revival, the temptation to fall back asleep and forget the finished work of Christ is everywhere. Hearts are often in a good place, and the work of missions usually continues, but still the Bride finds herself looking to accomplish what has already been done once and for all.

Two Reprisals

But this does not have to be the end of the story. In fact, according to the eternal Word of God, *it will not be*. For there is always a reprise in the story of redemption. Just as religion itself has been reprised in different varieties and forms, so too will the triumphant chorus of grace return to the forefront. Thankfully, the Scriptures give us a wonderful precedent and hope for this. It's found in the lives of Adam and Eve.

When Adam fell, it was like a crash in the symphony of creation as the music of his life appeared to go forever silent. Yet thousands of years later, the music started up again in the coming of Jesus. Initially, there were similarities to the original composition. In likeness to Adam's nakedness and shame, Jesus was born into the world naked and left the same way as He hung shamefully on a cross. Yet this time, the crashing silence at the end of His life gave way to a new sound of triumph. The song of the first Adam was reprised and redeemed by the resurrection of the last Adam!

Still Asleep (Reprise)

But there is a great mystery hidden within Scripture regarding Eve's part in all of this. As we've seen many times now, the Shulammite church is the fulfillment of what Eve always pointed to. She is indeed the *reprisal* of Eve. And so, early on in the composition, Eve's song fell into notes of despair and toil as she found pain and labor under the tree of separation (Gen. 3:16). In that moment, the song of her life appeared to be totally finished until thousands of years later when it played once more through the church. Unfortunately, there have been similar notes of anguish and toil in this renewed ballad. However, like Adam, all of it is making way for a new and final sound of triumph.

Today, this victorious reprisal of Eve is already emerging. There's a different sound being trumpeted in our day, which will coincide with the narrative of the Shulammite in the Song of Songs. This sound is not tied to one movement or region; rather, it is penetrating every sector of the church little by little. From the East to the West, the drumbeat of His blood is rising. We live in an incredibly exciting time. The church is looking at tangibly completing the Great Commission and bringing the kiss of Christ's Word into every "village" across the world, even back into the house of Mother Israel. As all of this happens, Eve will be reprised and redeemed as she finally chooses the apple tree of her Beloved—the Tree of Life. There she will discover peace in place of toil, and rest in place of painful labor.

But even still, this particular passage of the Song gives us pause. It reminds us that the temptation to go back to sleep is still present, even in the midst of divine joy and fellowship. And so each one of us, no matter who we are, needs to continually guard our heart against this old spell of deception. *We need to cling to the Song of grace more than ever.* For its melody is the only true backdrop for the final verses of world transformation...

11
Waking the Harlot

I want you to swear, O daughters of Jerusalem,
Do not arouse or awaken my love
Until she pleases.
(8:4)

In response to the Bride's sleepiness, the Lord speaks once again to the daughters of Jerusalem, a group of people who have come up a few times already. In the past, we've compared this group to immature believers or to those still growing in their faith. But we've also seen how they can represent the entire world since the city of Jerusalem does not always represent the household of God (see Gal. 4:25 & Rev. 11:8). Thus, being a "daughter" of this city can expand beyond the scope of Israel and the church. In either case, these daughters include the "queens, concubines, and maidens" that we looked at in the last volume. A brief recap of this would be helpful.

From a natural perspective, these ladies were literal women in Jerusalem who had different degrees of relationship to King Solomon. Some, such as queens and concubines, had a relationship that entered into the bedroom. Maidens, on the other hand, were the virgins of the land who had not been with the king. To use

The Song of the Ages: Part III

biblical vernacular, they had not "known" Solomon. As a result, we found these characters representing a wide spectrum of people's relationship to God. The Lord takes Solomon's polygamy and turns it into a metaphor for people's varying "knowledge" of Him. This is a powerful facet of the Song that requires maturity to see. God is not endorsing polygamy nor is He sanctioning the conscription of concubines. Like everything else in this broken world, God turns around man's evil and fashions it into something good. In this case, He incarnationally writes Himself into Solomon's corrupt version of love and transforms it into an illuminating lesson on divine intimacy.

And so, the "maidens" represent those who have never *known* the true King. They speak to people of the world who have not embraced any form of relationship with God. Maidens are those who have not yet left their father's house, similar to people who have not embraced being born anew into the Kingdom of Christ. "Concubines" are those who may know Him, but in a superficial and shallow way. At best, their relationship is based on what they can produce, which corresponds to the work of a concubine in securing additional heirs for the kingdom. A "queen" can then sum up all humanity in one way or another. Being a queen was more about title than intimacy. The queens of Solomon, as with all ancient kings, were usually not married for relationship. Often it was just for political purposes. Nonetheless, a marriage was enacted and there was still some measure of authority given to these women via their title. In like fashion, all humanity has been given a royal title through their creation in the image of God, yet not all have embraced true intimacy with their Maker.

This leads us back to the key difference between the world and the Shulammite. The main issue here is about the intimate knowledge of God, and that is indeed what salvation is all about (see Jn. 17:3). Such knowledge is what the Shulammite sought after in the very beginning of the Song. After discovering God's love

Waking the Harlot

for her (and His choice of her), she willingly embraced the bridal calling upon her life. Though this calling is reaching out to every single person in the world—every daughter of Jerusalem—not all have embraced it. In other words, not all have *awakened to love*.

The End of the Bible

This phrase *"do not awaken My love until she pleases"* is a repeating theme that gets at this key message of the book. It can also be translated as "do not awaken My love until she *chooses*—or *wills*." The request reminds us that love cannot be strong-armed. The Bride is the one thing in this universe that will not be forced into creation. God will certainly go to intense lengths to awaken her heart. He may even knock her off her high horse at times (Acts 9:3-4). But there is still a response of the heart that's necessary on our end, especially since we're made in the image of a God who is totally unfettered and free.

The significance of this dynamic between the Bride and the world becomes extremely clear when you turn your attention to the last part of the Bible. The final six chapters of Scripture paint a contrasting image between two symbolic women. Now pay close attention here, for this is going to begin unlocking something quite significant as Solomon's Song reaches its finale.

At the end of Scripture, we find two women—a harlot and a bride (Rev. 17-22). The parallel between these two cannot be more striking. A prostitute's "love" is something that can be bought or forced. Accordingly, a harlot engages in a form of love—a form of *knowing* another person—that is defiled and artificial. This becomes a sobering portrait of the religious systems of this world as well as the spiritual idolatry in which mankind has participated. Meanwhile, a bride is totally different. A bride's love is actually *love*. It's pure and it comes from the heart.

The Song of the Ages: Part III

Of course, in some cultures marriage itself can be forced or bought; nonetheless, the intimacy that truly makes one a bride instead of just a legal spouse can never be bought. Now this may require a word of clarification when talking about Jesus and our own bridal identity, because the Scriptures declare that Jesus has "purchased" us as a Bride for Himself (Acts 20:28 & 1 Cor. 6:20). But there is a huge difference between how Jesus went about this and how people in the world go about this. His way of payment was unlike any of the typical dowries found in this world. A dowry is a payment a man would offer the family of a sought-after bride in order to secure her hand in marriage. The family would then have a choice to accept the payment or not. Christ Himself gave a dowry for us, but it was one devoid of any manipulation or control. He offered a dowry by laying down His life for us, using His own blood as payment. Instead of the word "buy," you might say that He *earned* our love. This is why He is the One who is *worthy* to be praised, adored, and followed. The Scriptures put it like this: *"Worthy are You...because You were slain"* (Rev. 5:9).

It's amazing to think that the crescendo of the whole Bible—as well as all of human history—comes down to these opposing images of love. But more amazing is the revelation that true love will ultimately win out (Rev. 18:8 & Rev. 21:2-4). This helps us to understand the whole purpose of life and to see what God has really been up to throughout human history. All along, He's been wooing the nations towards their true identity and calling. This calling involves leaving our harlotry and awakening the flames of bridal love.

Since we're nearing the end of the Song, we're now able to go back with fresh eyes and see some things in previous chapters that would not have been as impactful as they are now. By doing that, we'll see how much this message has been hidden in its music, even from the beginning. And this is the beauty of the eighth chapter. It

Waking the Harlot

unveils things that were not as clear in previous verses. As we move forward now, we're going to discover that this final chapter is much like a surprise ending in a movie. When surprise endings are done well, they make you want to go back and watch the whole thing over again. You're then able to spot details that were previously unseen because a major part of the plot had not yet been revealed. Such endings are powerful, not only because they reveal things that were there all along, but because they infuse the entire story with new meaning and perspective.

Let's go back then and see some things we may have missed. We'll start right at the beginning in the very first chapter...

The Veiled One

In Song of Songs 1:7, the young Shulammite expressed that she did not want to be *"like one who veils herself."* Although we passed over it in the first study of the Song, this statement was quite significant. Most scholars and translators recognize this phrase is speaking very bluntly about prostitution. Several Bible translations go as far as including a statement about this in the footnotes. The reason is that in ancient times, prostitutes were known to cover their faces with a veil.

Now most commentators would argue that the Shulammite is just using a metaphoric comparison here and that she was not engaged in actual prostitution; however, the comparison is strong and leaves room for the possibility that she was. This wouldn't be a foreign concept to the rest of the Scriptures either, especially when you think of how the true King of Israel, Jesus, transformed the lives of women who were caught in immorality (Jn. 4:17-18, 8:7, & Lk. 7:37-39). Hosea's wife is another definitive example of this.

From a more practical perspective, it stands to reason that prostitution might have at least been an option for the young maiden of Shulam. In the beginning, we saw her living under the

The Song of the Ages: Part III

influence of poverty as she sung about working outdoors under the harsh treatment of her brothers (1:6). In those days, women of wealth and influence (including the queens and concubines of Solomon) would never be given such a task. Therefore, we know she was a woman of less desirable economic means. Now while this provides little proof that she was engaged in actual prostitution, there's definitely the possibility of it since poverty and harlotry often go together. Wherever poverty flourishes, prostitution and trafficking are one of its premier fruits. Thus, it's not entirely unrealistic that in her poor state the Shulammite had engaged in the unwanted prostituting of herself.

Whatever her circumstances were, we know the Shulammite was tired of the way things were when she cried out in desperation, *"Why should I be like one who veils herself?"* She was ready to leave the religious systems around her with their heavy labor and spiritual abuse, and find a love that was pure and true. She wanted the kisses of One who was without manipulation, coercion, and cruelty. And so, whether it was literal, metaphoric, or both, the Shulammite was ready to leave the prostitution of this world and discover who she truly was.

There's an interesting story in the Bible that intersects with this. It centers around a woman who was not truly a prostitute and yet acted like one. It's the story of Tamar, the daughter-in-law of Judah (Gen. 38). Judah was one of the twelve patriarchs of Israel whose linage would inherit and establish the city of Jerusalem. With that in mind, Tamar is symbolically a "daughter of Jerusalem"— although it might be more accurate to say that she was a daughter-*in-law* of Jerusalem. In the story, Tamar is a widower who ends up facing the death penalty after engaging in harlotry. Thankfully, Tamar is spared this fate when people discover who the father of her child is. The story of how this all goes down is fascinating.

Waking the Harlot

The Righteous Harlot

Tamar was married to Judah's firstborn son Er who, because of his wickedness, ended up dying before having any children. Judah then told his next son Onan to marry Tamar in order to perform his duty in raising up offspring for his deceased brother. Centuries later, this command is something that would become part of the official law of Moses (Deut. 25:5). The brother of a man who died before having children was required to help their sibling's widow secure heirs by marrying her and having children with her. Nonetheless, Onan resists this command from his father and also ends up dying. Afterwards, Judah tells his daughter-in-law to wait until his youngest son Shelah is old enough to marry her. Yet for whatever reason (probably for fear that he'll lose another son), Judah goes back on this promise and Tamar is left as a childless widow. Up to this point, her life is a long trail of law, barrenness, and death.

Years later, this daughter-in-law of Judah comes up with a plan to solve her predicament. She puts on a veil and poses as a temple prostitute in a city where she knows Judah is about to visit. She must know that Judah has a thing for prostitutes because she meets him at the city gate and immediately secures his attention:

> *When Judah saw her, he thought she was a harlot, for she had covered her face. So he turned aside to her by the road, and said, "Here now, let me come in to you"; for he did not know that she was his daughter-in-law. And she said, "What will you give me, that you may come in to me?"*
> *(Gen. 38:15-16)*

Judah gives her some of his personal items as collateral for a later payment. These items included his seal and cord, very important objects during that time. They essentially identified who a person was and were used to sign off and make approvals for

The Song of the Ages: Part III

certain purchases and deals. After giving her these items, Judah sleeps with the supposed prostitute, who then mysteriously leaves the city without collecting the final payment and revealing who she was. Instead, she holds on to his collateral and now carries something else of his—a child within her womb.

Three months later, when Tamar starts showing a little bit of belly, the rest of the family finds out and accuses her of harlotry since they know she didn't remarry after Onan. Unaware of whose child she bears, Judah demands that Tamar immediately be put to death. Yet right before this can happen, Tamar reveals that he is the father by unveiling those personal items that were still in her possession. Upon hearing this, Judah declares her to be "righteous" and she is saved from her death sentence. Six months later, it turns out she is pregnant with twin boys, one of whom becomes a direct descendent of Jesus Himself! (Matt. 1:3)

This is an incredibly strange and painful story. It takes a lot of care and delicacy to sift through its contents and find something redeemable inside. Like most other people in the world at this time, the individuals in this story are significantly broken and influenced by a primitive culture with a twisted sense of justice. But despite all of this, God can still be found within the story if you look hard enough. No amount of brokenness can hold back the invasion of His presence. If you tune your ears and listen beyond its obvious discord, you can hear the Song of the Ages playing through the human instruments in this story. Fortunately, God's singing breath is able travel through the very ugly and rough-hewn holes of human lives.

So first of all, this image of a woman putting a veil over her face in order to engage in harlotry is profound. The face is the most distinguishing feature of a person. Beyond any other part of the body, the face visually sets individual people apart from one another. The face therefore speaks to a person's identity. In

Waking the Harlot

Scripture, a prostitute veiling her face is *a portrait of humanity's true identity being veiled*. Because of this, Tamar putting on a veil provides us with an interesting parable of humanity's harlotry and the ways we have hidden our true selves.

Tamar, of course, was not a prostitute even though she engaged in its deeds. In similar fashion, humanity is not truly a wicked harlot, even though our widowhood (our turning from the Lord with a resulting barrenness) has driven us into a destructive lifestyle of law, sin, and death. Yet even in our acts of prostitution, the true Lion of Judah—the One who would come from that patriarch's immoral loins—would unite Himself with us. Just as Judah united himself with Tamar in her false prostitution, Jesus united Himself with us in our false identity of sin (2 Cor. 5:21). Moreover, Jesus freely gave us His own seal and cord. The Lion of Judah has given us His own riches and identity, thus saving us from the inevitable destruction of our own harlotry!

Before this act of union, Tamar was only Judah's daughter-*in-law*. But after this encounter—as well as its resulting pregnancy—Tamar became Judah's bride, according to the culture of the day. Putting aside the extreme family dysfunction going on here, we can see even more of the diamond hidden in the rough of this story. Through the work of Christ, our harlot's veil has become a bridal veil! The old veil of Moses described in the book of Exodus—the veil he put over his face which pointed to law, sin, and death—has been permanently put been aside (2 Cor. 3:16). Now we are invited to switch from law to grace—from the identity of a barren daughter-in-law to that of fruitful and multiplying Bride! Because Jesus united Himself with our sinfulness, this means our spiritual barrenness is broken, and we now carry Christ within. Any inability to produce the life of God in our everyday existence has been removed.

The Song of the Ages: Part III

There's also a sparkling side-note to the diamond in this story. During the delivery of Tamar's twin children, one child stuck his hand out of the womb first, leading the midwife to tie a scarlet thread around his finger in order to show he was the firstborn son. This child was then named Zerah, which literally means "the dawning." But even though he was declared to be the firstborn, his brother broke past him in the womb and entered the world first. This resulted with him being given the name Perez, meaning "to breach." Therefore, in this story, the promised firstborn came *after* his brother.

> *Moreover, it took place while she was giving birth, one put out a hand, and the midwife took and tied a scarlet thread on his hand, saying, "This one came out first." But it came about as he drew back his hand, that behold, his brother came out. Then she said, "What a breach you have made for yourself!" So he was named Perez. Afterward his brother came out who had the scarlet thread on his hand; and he was named Zerah.*
> *(Gen. 38:28-30)*

The scarlet thread around Zerah's finger is another signpost signifying the person and work of Christ. The other biblical instance of a scarlet thread is from the story of Rahab in the book of Joshua. Rahab hung a scarlet thread from her window in Jericho's wall. This marked her with mercy and saved her from the destruction of the city. Interestingly enough, Rabah was a prostitute, which gives us yet another biblical connection between harlotry and God's grace.

With a scarlet thread around his finger, Zerah is literally *pointing* to the merciful One, Jesus Christ. But more than that, he is pointing out the fact that Jesus is the true and promised Firstborn who existed *before Adam* (Col. 1:15). Even though Adam, the natural

Waking the Harlot

man, came first (1 Cor. 15:46), the promise of Christ was present from before the foundation of the world. When He was finally born into the world, Jesus's appearing was the "dawning" (Zerah) of a new day for humanity—even after we had "breached" (Perez) the original plan of God!

Where the Unveiling Happens

Let's return now to the Song of Songs. Look again at what the Lord uttered in response to the Shulammite when she compared herself to a veiled prostitute at the beginning of her story:

> *If you yourself do not know,*
> *Most beautiful among women...*
> *(Sgs. 1:8)*

Do you see that glorious thread of mercy weaving itself through the Scriptures? Hopefully, its scarlet color is growing ever more vibrant in your eyes.

Even in the beginning, the veil covering the Shulammite's face did not stop Jesus from calling her the *most beautiful among women.* He saw right through her veil and into the heart of who she truly was. This is the way He sees *all of us.* It is when a person finally gets tired of their deceptive veil that Jesus shows them the way out. Like the Shulammite, He calls them to follow a different trail than the one of law and fear. He calls them to follow in "the footsteps of the flock" (1:8). We are not led to some obscure or complicated road, but to the pathway of faith that has been passed down once and for all to God's flock (Jude 1:3). It is this path that leads to a table; a table where wine has already been poured out. This wine is the wine of union, where the uncovering of true love and true identity takes place.

With all that said, there's a reason we're looking more closely at this previously unexamined element of prostitution. All along,

The Song of the Ages: Part III

the Song has been opening up a huge doorway of revelation regarding harlotry and love—a revelation that stretches across the entire Bible. Now that we are in the eighth and final chapter of the Song, this element will reach a climax as this mysterious line from throughout the Shulammite's journey is repeated once again:

Do not awaken my love until she pleases!

We've seen how these words are speaking about the nature of true love—but now we must focus in a little bit closer and consider the context of this statement. As we pointed out in the beginning of this chapter, this command about not waking up the Shulammite is always spoken in the presence of the daughters of Jerusalem. It's the same with every previous instance where the Bridegroom uttered these words (see Sgs. 2:7 & 3:5). There's a reason Jesus is speaking these things to this particular group of people—a reason we haven't totally uncovered yet. In order to see it, we must first understand something else we passed over in previous studies of the Song. This is another things we can now appreciate with greater hindsight. It has to do with the word *daughters*.

The Watching World

Like so many words in the Hebrew language, this word is a loaded homonym with several possible meanings. Translators do their best in figuring out which meaning to use, obviously using context and other elements to make the final translation. Typically, this word is rightfully translated as the physical "daughters" born of an individual. Yet in many instances, the word can mean something totally different. It can also be translated as "villages." This whole time then, the Lord has been speaking to *the villages* of the people!

This is important because in the seventh chapter of the Song we saw the Bride's passion and determination to go into the "villages" of humanity. The villages did not represent the church, but the unchurched. Having studied that part out, we can further establish

Waking the Harlot

the fact that Jesus is speaking to *all* the people of the world. However, there's something else that confirms this interpretation even further. This has to do with a third possible meaning for the Hebrew word for "daughters." Though it's rarely used in this way, the term can also be translated as "pupil" or "apple."

As in *the apple of God's eye*.

This word for daughters is the same word God uses when He calls Israel the *apple* of His eye (Lam. 2:18). Tying together all the underlying textures of this one Hebrew word—whether "daughters," "villages," or "apple"—the revelation of how God sees people becomes even clearer. Each and every person is just as loved and treasured as His Bride. God sees through the veil hanging over the villages of humanity and still He calls them the object of His affection. It's no wonder we have John 3:16 in our Bible, for God sent His one and only Son out of this kind of love. Though many have not yet said *yes* to the priceless gift of Jesus, the people of the world are still as dear to Him as the precious pupil of His own eye. They are indeed the focus of His vision and, like the Shulammite, the "most beautiful among women." Thus, the daughters of Jerusalem truly include the Tamars of the world—people who may be living like harlots even though it's not who they truly are. When God looks at them, He sees potential carriers of Christ.

So again, it is before the entire world that Jesus opens His mouth throughout the Song and says, *"Do not awaken my love until she pleases!"* That much is clear, but why is He saying this particular phrase?

For Better or Worse

The reason is quite simple. The world has been watching the journey of the Shulammite unfold from the very beginning and along the way they have been learning something of eternal

The Song of the Ages: Part III

significance. God is teaching the world through the life of the Shulammite. This is indeed the way He has always operated. God's plan has been to teach the nations through chosen vessels called to display His radical love. Throughout Scripture, the Lord is constantly developing covenantal partnerships with people in order to advance His purposes on the earth. This is the reason He came to Abraham and his little tribe which grew to become a great nation and taught the world many eternal truths. But that was only the foreshadowing of the ultimate covenantal partner—the church of Jesus Christ. The church would become God's true "witness," called to manifest His love from Jerusalem, to Judea, to the ends of the planet. To put it in Solomonic poetry, the church is His witness to the daughters of *Jerusalem*, and unto the queens, concubines, and maidens of the earth! In essence, this is why this line keeps coming up and why it's being directed at the watching world. *Through the Shulammite's many ups and downs, God has been teaching the world the way out of harlotry into the Kingdom of true love!*

This is not only a Song for the Bride, but a Song that is sung *through* the Bride.

Now of course, the church has not always been the best witness. Oftentimes, we have shown more of what bridal love is not instead of what it is. Like the woman from Shulam, we have gone back to sleep many times over, seemingly putting the veil of harlotry right back over our eyes. This happened again and again throughout the Song and it has happened over and over throughout church history. Now that we're at the final chapter of Solomon's music, we're still seeing the Bride's temptation to fall back asleep. But in the midst of our religious failings, there is hope. The Lord is still making us an instrument of truth to the world, even in our adulterous sleep. When He speaks to the villages of the world about not waking His sleepy Bride *until she wants to,* God is teaching the nations about the true nature of His grace. He is showing them

Waking the Harlot

that He is in the business of redeeming prostitutes, not creating them. Furthermore, the patience and mercy He displays toward us is an expression of the same mercy available to everyone else (see 1 Tim. 1:15-16).

What an incredible calling we have as the Bride of Christ! We are the teachers and proclaimers of love. We are prophets of a New Covenant, admonishing all people to walk down the trail of true life. According to the book of Ephesians, we are even teaching heavenly powers and principalities (Eph. 3:10). We may stumble badly in this calling, but God is turning it all around for good and using everything for His greater purposes. For better or worse, for richer or poorer, we remain witnesses of grace both to earth and heaven!

Now, in the next verse, we'll see where this witness ultimately leads.

12
Rising from the Wilderness

———•❖•———

Who is this coming up from the wilderness
Leaning on her beloved?
(8:5a)

A response comes from the world as they observe all that remains of wavering love break off the Shulammite like a giant cracked egg, its final pieces falling away to unveil an otherworldly creature inside. This is a new kind of creature who emerges with the movements of free and unashamed love. It's a magnificent and strange sight to the eyes of the world, leaving them stunned and only able to ask a single question in response.

"Who is this coming up from the wilderness..."

But we've seen this before, haven't we? We've seen the world stunned and we've watched them gape and mumble out this particular question in the past. And yet, as we've been pointing out, so much more revelation has poured out since then. New understanding and new surprises are upon us. Earlier, the threads that formed the Song's tapestry were still weaving themselves together. Now, the entire embroidery is being formed before our eyes. The question at hand is thus incredibly significant. It has come up on two other occasions and has become a core part of the Song's design. At this precious juncture of music, we are coming to the Song's final and complete answer to the daughters' question. But in order to learn the answer, it is necessary to look back once again. We need to see some more things that may have been missed before. As you, dear reader, look more closely at what has been weaving itself together, may you be left as stunned and overwhelmed as the daughters of Jerusalem.

Gazing into the Wilderness

The first time this question was asked was way back in the Song's third chapter:

> *What is this coming up from the wilderness*
> *Like columns of smoke,*
> *Perfumed with myrrh and frankincense…*
> *(Sgs. 3:6)*

As the daughters of Jerusalem stared out into the wilderness beyond the city, something began to fill their vision. At first, all they saw was smoke, which communicated an obvious element of haze and a lack of clarity. And so it was that things were very unclear back then. The daughters knew they were seeing something of breathtaking holiness, but it was still ambiguous. Nonetheless, they continued to fix their gaze, and through the rising columns of smoke they began to see something more distinct approach them. Now let's re-examine what led up to this encounter, for this will tie together many threads of truth forming at the end of the Song. It started with the words of the Shulammite:

> *On my bed night after night I sought him…*
> *Scarcely had I left them*
> *When I found him whom my soul loves;*
> *I held on to him and would not let him go;*

Rising from the Wilderness

Until I had brought him to my mother's house,
And into the room of her who conceived me.
I adjure you, O daughters of Jerusalem,
By the gazelles or by the hinds of the field,
That you will not arouse or awaken my love
Until she pleases.
What is this coming up from the wilderness
Like columns of smoke...
(Sgs. 3:1, 4-6)

This portion of the Song was foreshadowing what we're now seeing in the eighth and final chapter. It was here that the Bridegroom spoke for the first time to the onlooking world, the daughters of Jerusalem, and asked them not to awaken His love until she pleases. We examined many of these elements in the first volume of the Song. We took note of how the Bride was sleeping on her bed even as she pursued union with God. This was the search of self-effort that led the Shulammite through the broad streets of the city in order to take hold of something she already possessed. When she finally re-encountered the Lord, the Song says that she grabbed "on to Him and would not let Him go." Here we saw her slumbering under the weight of religion as she tried to hold on to the One who was already holding her.

In the next verse we came across something we did not fully unpack at our first passthrough of the Song regarding the Bride's "mother." With more revelation and experience under our belts, we can now take in a greater measure of what was happening back then. In the first volume, we looked at how the mother could represent the larger and more religious "Mother Church" from which the Shulammite came. We've now seen how the mother goes further back to Israel, and even back to Eve herself. It turns out this was an early picture of the church's passion to evangelize both Jew and Gentile—the calling to bring the Gospel full circle

The Song of the Ages: Part III

to where it all started in Jerusalem. The Shulammite was already embracing her role as a witness to the nations. Unfortunately, she was expressing this passion while still in that dream-state of separation and fear.

So, the world was not witnessing a fully awakened Bride at this point. In fact, they didn't really know what they were witnessing. You can see this by the way their question is translated the first time it's asked. They ask *"what is this"* as opposed to *"who is this."* It was still unclear. What they were seeing was shrouded in smoke. But as we've discussed, the church has lacked a lot of clarity in her witness of truth. By living from that dream-state, religiosity has crept into our mission to bring Jesus into the house of our mother. Many man-made plans have been birthed in the process. As the veiled church played the harlot with political structures and other systems, these man-made efforts were dreamt up like nightmares in our sleep, often bringing about tragic consequences. The worst examples of this are things like inquisitions and crusades; however, it goes much deeper and even subtler than these extremes.

Religious manipulation, in partnership with legalism and the fear of punishment, has permeated every area of what we perceive as the church's domain, from ideas about membership, to leadership structures, to preaching, and everything else under the ecclesiastical sun. It has even attached itself as barbed strings to our acts of mercy and compassion. Therefore, at this part of her journey, the Shulammite was more of a witness of religion than love. And so perhaps the Lord's words—*do not awaken my love until she pleases*—has been as much a message to her as it has been to the onlooking world. The Lord has been saying all along, "Do not bring awakening in any other way!" The world's embrace of the bridal invitation must be pure. As some of our great stories proclaim, awakening must come by love's true kiss. The forced kiss of religion simply won't do it. Its fruits will be religious slaves at best and angry dissenters at worst (though perhaps it's debatable which of those two is better).

Of course, under the rugged soil of her religious pursuits has always been a seed of purity within the church. Jesus has been proclaiming this pure identity from the very start. Because of this, the Song has never become a church-bashing ballad. Crashing notes of condemnation are nowhere to be found when we listen to the lyrics proceeding from the Bridegroom's mouth. Jesus has seen through our control and manipulation, looking deeply into the very roots of sleep and blindness that cause such problems in the first place. Like a kind doctor with untold skill in his hands, Jesus can easily separate the disease from the patient. He loves His sleeping beauty even while despising the dirty bed she has been chained to in her own mind. Through it all, He looks with delight at the church's passion to bring His love into the house of her mother. It is a passion that has risen and grown like a flickering light within the cocoon of her religion.

That said, none of this is meant to deny how ugly and harmful the cocoon has been. The religious efforts of the Bride have often been so detrimental that it has caused the purity of the Good News to become distorted in the eyes of the onlooking world. It is no surprise then, that when the world looks at the emerging Bride, they are peering out into a wilderness. For the dirty bed goes hand in hand with this barren landscape. It is this very thing that the Bride has been slowing rising from, like a butterfly in the midst of metamorphosis.

The Crowning

Against the backdrop of this barren wilderness, Jerusalem's daughters continued their gaze and soon saw something of a unique and growing splendor. They didn't really see the Bride at this point, for she was still hidden and asleep. However, they did see something else. They noticed a "sedan chair," the royal

The Song of the Ages: Part III

seat of a king's carriage, carried by posts that were shouldered by royal servants (Sgs. 3:9-10). As the scene progressed, the people realized more specifically what they were seeing. It was the King of Jerusalem, the One who was just outside the city gates, approaching from the wilderness beyond. The people were then invited to gaze upon this King who had been "crowned...on the day of his wedding."

> *Go forth, O daughters of Zion,*
> *And gaze on King Solomon with the crown*
> *With which his mother has crowned him*
> *On the day of his wedding,*
> *And on the day of his gladness of heart.*
> *(Sgs. 3:11)*

Even though this verse was talking about the mother of the King as opposed to the mother of the Bride, Israel still fits the bill here. Jesus was born of Jewish stock. His mother Mary was a Hebrew descended from Abraham himself (and further back to Eve). Since we now understand more of who the mother is in the Song, we can see something else here that is quite monumental—something we previously passed over. That is, Jesus's mother—Israel—is the one who crowned Him as King.

Now you might be confused by this, thinking this would then be talking about a future time when all of Israel will embrace her Messiah. But this is not talking about the future, for this scene was from early on in the journey. Besides, Jesus is never called a soon-to-be King. He is King right now. Rather, this whole passage is speaking about the same thing the rest of the Song has been celebrating. It's about the One who went outside the city gates of Jerusalem. There, the people of Israel (in partnership with Eve's Gentile descendants) crowned their own King...*with thorns*. Hidden

Rising from the Wilderness

in a poetic mystery, the vision of Song of Songs 3 was actually a veiled picture of Jesus's crucifixion.

The king being carried on his sedan chair while surrounded by armies is a reverse image of Jesus being marched to His death, surrounded both by Roman soldiers as well as a mighty angelic legion He could have called upon at any moment (Matt. 26:53). After the leadership of Israel provoked Pontius Pilate to crucify Christ, the air became fragrant with the myrrh of His suffering and the sweet frankincense of His intercession (Lk. 23:34). Roman soldiers took away His usual garments and replaced them with a purple robe, twisting together briery branches to adorn His head with a crown of thorns. After slapping Him and spitting in His face, this armed band of men marched Jesus toward a cruel and shameful death, enthroning Him high upon a bloody hill. There, atop His wooden throne, was a sign created by Pilate: "This is the King of the Jews!" (Lk. 23:38) The coronation of Israel's true King happened here, upon the strongest throne ever constructed—one of selfless and fiery love.

This unfolds many more layers of the things we started to tap into during our first walkthrough of the Song. As we continue to look back at this ongoing question about the wilderness, we'll need take a deep breath and gird ourselves—for there is still a ways to go in discovering the full tapestry emerging before our eyes. The complete answer to the daughters' question is scandalous and it upturns much of what traditional Christendom has taught us…

Inside the Box

We'll continue by honing in on Solomon's sedan chair. This is a key strand of thread that will lead us to the full picture in the Song's eighth chapter. Early on, we found that this royal object connects profoundly to the Ark of the Covenant, the sacred item God commanded Moses to design in the wilderness and then carry

The Song of the Ages: Part III

into the Promised Land. The Ark was like a royal carriage held on the shoulders of priestly servants. It was the real "sedan chair" of Israel's King, bearing many similarities to the one the daughters have been watching come up from the wilderness.

The Ark is essentially a box that points to Jesus—which is interesting considering that God is infinite and cannot be put into a *box*. The Almighty Creator cannot be grasped by human hands nor understood by human minds. And yet, before God created anything—and thus could be called an Almighty Creator—*He was simply a Father*. Within the fellowship of the Trinity, God is eternally a Dad. And as a Dad, He longs to be grasped, touched, and understood by His children. Because of this, He has expressed Himself through the "box" of a human being, Jesus Christ.

But the Ark itself speaks about something else. The imagery surrounding this momentous item points specifically to Jesus's suffering and death. As we saw earlier, Moses's Ark was an object of wood covered in gold. This points us to the Roman cross, a wooden structure that was overlaid with the body of Jesus—more precious than all the earth's gold combined. Then you have the golden rings placed on the four sides of the Ark, each like a little limb hanging from its boxed body. Special poles were placed through the holes in these rings; and once they were in, they were *never* to be removed (Ex. 25:15). In the same way, the ends of Jesus's four limbs were pierced all the way through. Today, Jesus still bears the marks of this event. There are literal holes in His body right now, reminding us this piercing was an eternal work that can never be removed!

But the many connections to Jesus culminate at the top of the Ark. At its head was the special covering of the box called the Mercy Seat. Ironically enough, this covering was encircled by a crown.

Rising from the Wilderness

*And thou shalt overlay it with pure gold, within and without shalt thou overlay it, and shalt make upon it **a crown** of gold round about.*
(Ex. 25:11 KJV)

The meaning of all this can't get much clearer. The Ark is a timeless representation of both the person and work of Christ. He was the One who was pierced in each limb and crowned with thorns as He cried out words of mercy. But the Song of Solomon adds more depth to this as it brings together the imagery of the sedan chair and the crowning of Solomon. A whole threadwork of truth comes together around this emerging scene from the wilderness, ultimately revealing Jesus's coronation through suffering.

The cross was Jesus's kingly carriage on the day of His crowning!

But the Song goes even further than that. It shows us that this was way more than just a coronation. For as the daughters continued to gaze upon the King in His chair, they were told this was also *"the day of His wedding."* Like a thread of one color entwining perfectly with threads of other dyes, this wedding element fits right in with the other truths of suffering and royalty. For this divine sedan chair was specifically called the Ark of the *Covenant*.

The Unveiling

When God established the first covenant with Israel, He marked down its agreements and conditions upon tablets of stone. These agreements, which were to be placed inside the Ark, were essentially solidifying a covenant of marriage between God and Israel. This is why one of the things He wrote down was that the people shouldn't take His name in vain. The people were literally *taking His name* as a bride would take her husband's. So the box holding these agreements could rightfully be called the Ark of the Marriage Covenant.

The Song of the Ages: Part III

Sadly, when Moses delivered this covenant to the people it exposed the deeper problem within humanity. His face (which we saw in the last chapter is the centerpiece of a person's identity) had shone with the pure light of God. Nonetheless, the people were not ready to embrace such light and truth. Moses was forced to put a veil over his face, which was very telling of the Old Covenant's true purpose (Ex. 34:33). This exposed the harlotry of humanity and our choice of law over relationship; independence over union. In other words, it revealed our path of religious sleep over awakened love. Then, with ever-increasing intensity, the law revealed the fruit of this choice—a false face riddled with guilt and fear.

Of course, everything in the Old Covenant was temporary, like a fake tattoo of an arrow pointing ahead to something else. It was helping us see the truth behind a different covenant to come, one that was eternal and true. Instead of being inscribed on inanimate stones, this one would be permanently marked down on the hands and feet of Jesus. And herein lies the key note to which we keep tuning our ears. The cross of Jesus was the place where the *covenant of marriage* between God and man was redeemed. Such was the "joy" set before Christ when He endured His suffering (Heb. 12:2). Though dark and bloody from an earthly perspective, His painful crowning was in fact the day of His wedding—*the day of His gladness of heart!*

Marriage is all about union, and union is the very purpose for humanity's creation. From the very beginning we were made one with God, created as His earthly Bride to reflect His image and walk in faithful friendship with Him. Tragically, we played the harlot and put a veil over our face. Even though we continued to live and move and have our being in God, we lost sight of our union and began to live in a dream-state. A false reality. In our sleep, we embraced a broken understanding of God and ourselves. Fear and guilt compounded this problem, working together to

Rising from the Wilderness

thicken the fabric of our veil until it completely blinded us from any penetrating light. It left us unable to see the face of our Father with His sparkling eyes and His wide and infectious smile. This was more than a blinding; it was actually a complete distortion of our vision. The sparkle in His eyes became a dark mist and His smile was turned upside down into a scowl. It was the same God but viewed through a warped lens. To put this problem in the words of the prophets, God's face was hidden from us (Jer. 33:5).

This brings us to one final element surrounding Solomon's sedan chair. When the daughters looked out at the king's royal seat, they saw it was surrounded by an army wielding swords (Sgs. 3:7-8). No one would be able to make it past such a mighty band of soldiers guarding the king. Death would be the fruit of any such an attempt. This is reminiscent of something from the beginning of Scripture—the flaming sword of Eden blocking the eastern entrance of the Garden. As we've discussed from the start, Eden was the place of unhindered union and intimacy. It speaks of our original marriage to God. Millennia later, when designing the Ark of the Covenant, Moses was told to construct a thick barrier on the eastern entrance into the Holy of Holies where the Ark would be laid. If anyone crossed this barrier, death would be result. This barrier was referred to as the "veil of the testimony" (Lev. 24:3). It points to the sword of Eden and now it also connects to the smoke and swords surrounding Solomon's sedan chair in the vision of the wilderness in Song of Songs 3.

This veil is another key that unlocks the inspired poetry that has been flowing from Solomon's pen. Essentially, the veil and the wilderness are one and the same. All along, the daughters of Jerusalem have been watching the slow removal of this veil as the Shulammite's testimony unfolds—*as she rises up from the wilderness.* And contrary to popular opinion, both the veil and the wilderness were never about God's separation from us. This is about our separation from Him. You can see this in the story of the Israelites and their own experience with the wilderness. God didn't put them in the desert for forty years—they put themselves there because of fear and unbelief. This is all speaking to the same problem within humanity, which is an unbelieving stoniness of heart. A veil over the face.

And that is exactly what Jesus came to deal with in the New Covenant. He came to tear the ancient veil and restore our original heart of flesh that has been made one with God. This work of redemption began before time itself, but it was consummated—*completed*—at the cross. Hence, right at the moment Jesus finished His work, the actual veil of the testimony was torn in two (Matt. 27:51). Eden's flaming sword had been quenched!

The Consummation of the Wedding

Throughout many cultures of the world, especially during the time of Solomon's songwriting, people have understood marriage to be consummated by physical union. In the first volume, we looked at how the union between a new bride and her husband points to the union between humanity and God at the cross. We'll now take a moment to look further into the ancient covenant of marriage, for as we do, we'll find an even greater treasury of insight concerning this reality of consummation.

We'll start by looking at ancient covenants in general. In biblical times, the primary way two parties would enter into a covenant would be through sacrifice. The bodies of sacrificial animals would be torn into two and placed across from each other, leaving a pathway between them. The two parties would then pass through the bloodied aisle, which would seal the agreements of the covenant. The gruesome idea behind this is that if one of the parties broke their agreement, they would be killed in the same

Rising from the Wilderness

manner as those mangled animals. It was an intense, all-out oath demonstrating that you would be faithful to your side of the deal.

Now forgive the graphic nature of this, but this correlates to a husband entering a virgin bride; the tearing in that moment sealing the covenant established in their vows to one another. This is part of the reason physical union was seen as the completion of a marriage. From this perspective, blood literally seals the covenant. But as usual, God is using the shadows of ancient culture and human understanding to help us see higher and greater realities. He wants us to know that the marriage between Him and humanity has been completed. It is not a coming reality. The only thing to come is the full *unveiling* of this beautiful truth. An unveiling where people from every tribe, tongue, and nation will awaken and join the wedding feast that has already begun.

At the cross, Jesus truly completed a marriage covenant between God and man. As a Man, He took on our side of this covenant, which first involved dealing with our harlotry and its overpowering guilt and shame. He took this upon Himself, and through death, He crushed the power of this false identity. This simultaneously released the truth of God's forgiveness toward us. This was then proven in His resurrection where we were fully revealed as God's beloved Bride, forgiven and embraced. In this way, Jesus was not only redeeming, but re-revealing our true identity. He was tearing the religious veils over our minds and letting us see ourselves as we really are.

Through Jesus's death and resurrection, we also got to see the true heart of our Creator. Jesus showed us we were loved and forgiven by a beautiful and merciful Father. This great Father is One who is not counting our sins against us (2 Cor. 5:19). Though we were enemies of Him in our minds (Col. 1:21), the cross revealed we were tenderly loved in God's mind (Jn. 3:16). Again, the veil was our problem, not God's. This is what the blood of Jesus deals with. The blood doesn't wash God's heart of some deep stain of rage separating Him from us. Jesus wouldn't have been able to eat, drink, and hang out with sinners before the cross if that were the case. Rather, the blood of Christ washes our own hearts from the guilt, fear, and lies that keep *us from Him* (see Heb. 10:22). It cuts the veil and awakens us from our deep sleep. It breaks the harlot's mask and lets the light of heaven into the earth.

And herein lies the great beauty of the Song of all Songs. So much of Christendom has been content to talk about the legalities behind the Gospel, focusing in on topics like covenants, substitution, and prophetic promises. But there was *something so much more* going on. This is about the love between Bridegroom and Bride as well as Father and children. If the Gospel were put into a literal song, this would be the highest note and the crowning chorus. In heaven's eyes, the day of gladness has already begun. The marriage between humanity and divinity has been consummated. Thousands of years of foreshadowing with the Ark of the Covenant came to a head at the cross of Calvary, where we saw the greatest display of covenantal love imaginable.

So again, when Jesus cried out *"it is finished,"* He meant it. This marriage was totally and utterly *complete*. And that brings up another mystery; one we didn't look at before. The completion of this wedding ceremony is actually hidden within the very words Jesus cried out.

The Mystery of Kalah

In the Passion Translation of the gospel of John, Dr. Brian Simmons brings out a wonderful insight about this phrase. The words *"it is finished"* are recorded by the apostle John, the only gospel writer to mark down this particular statement from Jesus (Jn. 19:30). This phrase comes from one word in the Aramaic language. It is important to look at the Aramaic because that

Rising from the Wilderness

is the language Jesus would have been speaking when He hung upon the cross. Jesus wouldn't have been speaking Greek at the cross, but rather His own mother tongue. This is why the Greek New Testament gives us direct quotes in Aramaic throughout the gospels, including the account of the crucifixion (Matt. 27:46). It was also the language of the people gathered around Jesus on that fateful day. So, as Jesus drew His final breath and completed His work, the last thing He uttered was the Aramaic word *kalah*.

Much like the Hebrew word behind "daughters," this term has several possible meanings to it. Its chief meaning is "finished," but as with other words, its meaning depends on the context. For instance, if you were in the midst of a crowd and suddenly heard a man uttering something about a "band," it would be hard to determine what kind of band he was referring to without context. To most people, if all they heard was that one word, they would probably guess the guy was referring to a musical band. But to someone else with a different set of ears, they might hear it and think of a ring, as in a wedding band. One meaning is about music while the other is about marriage, yet the word could point to both things depending on the ears of those listening. And that's because, like *kalah*, the word "band" is another homonym.

The main meaning of the word *kalah* is the one most people would associate it with—completion. That's why our Bibles typically translate this as Jesus saying, "It is finished!" This is a true and accurate translation. However, for someone with a different set of ears they might hear something quite different, and yet still accurate. You see, the word *kalah* can also be translated...as *bride*.

This is unfathomably significant. The same Aramaic word behind "it is finished" is the same word behind "bride." As Jesus hung on the cross, His last word was wrapped up in these two interlocking strands of truth. The work of redeeming humanity as His Bride was finished! The celebration of heaven had penetrated

The Song of the Ages: Part III

the earth! When you think about it, it's amazing the apostle John was the one to record this phrase. After all, he's the beloved disciple who leaned on Jesus's heart and was then given a Revelation much later in his life. This Revelation would *finish* the entire Bible with a vision of the *Bride* (Rev. 21-22). *Kalah!*

Now let's bring this back to the Song of Songs. Remember that at the cross Jesus was surrounded by the onlooking world. These were the literal daughters of Jerusalem gathered around Him that day. More specifically, it was the queens, concubines and maidens of the land who were present. Some people at the crucifixion knew Jesus very well, such as His own mother and John. But there were others who didn't truly know Him, even though they had some form of a relationship to God, such as the Jewish leaders of the day. And then there were Roman Gentiles who were present as well—spiritual maidens who had little to no knowledge of the one true King.

In reality, this crowd represented the entire world gathered together to gaze upon the King on His holy Mercy Seat! At that moment, they were looking upon the One "greater than Solomon" (Matt. 12:42). And to the surprise of the entire cosmos, it turns out they were beholding Him on *the day of His wedding, the day of His gladness of heart!* Though mourning filled the air, shouts of victory were piercing the heavens. A new song filled the sky as the King of heaven and earth revealed His love for His lost Bride.

At the cross, this Song of all songs blasted like a trumpet, arriving only as a whisper in the hearts of those willing to listen. On earth, this blast traveled through ugly and broken instruments, forged in the emptiness of mockery, spit, and hate. But these things became the ugly holes which the breath of God filled with the sweetest of music. Music that carried the lyrics of His heart— the truth hidden within Him from eternity past. The truth that no matter what, He loves us—even at our worst. And He longs

Rising from the Wilderness

for us to return to Him. He longs for us to know before anything else that He is Father. And Bridegroom. And that we are sons and daughters. And brides.

Down through the centuries, the world has continued to look upon this Man hanging from the cross. Multitudes even wear the emblem of this event around their necks. But still, many do not understand the fullness of what they're looking at. Even when the people of Israel continue to look at images of Moses's Ark, many do not see what is really being communicated. The glorious truth still seems shrouded in a veil of smoke and swords.

> *What is this coming up from the wilderness*
> *Like columns of smoke,*
> *Perfumed with myrrh and frankincense...*
> *Behold, it is the traveling couch of Solomon;*
> *Sixty mighty men around it,*
> *Of the mighty men of Israel.*
> *All of them are wielders of the sword...*

Not all have woken up to the true image yet—for not all have applied the blood to their own guilty hearts in order cleanse their skewed and distorted vision. Instead, they continue to run around in the dark, holding on to the blindness that comes from the god of this age (2 Cor. 4:3-4). And that's not to say that the truth is easy to see. It takes revelation from heaven to behold the truth of the cross. On all accounts, the day of Jesus Christ's suffering appeared to be the worst day in human history. But what appeared to be a revolting and dreadful Friday afternoon turned out to be Good Friday, the greatest Thank-God-it's-Friday ever. Though it sounded like a funeral song was blasting from that dark Judean hill, heaven's ears were picking up an entirely different melody. A melody as sweet as honey and smooth as wine.

The Song of the Ages: Part III

This is what the daughters of Jerusalem were being invited to gaze upon back in Song of Songs 3, *and it's been unfolding in front of their eyes throughout the entire journey.* They are being invited to behold the slain King of Jerusalem, to eat of the honey within His sacrifice, and receive the sweetest news imaginable. The news that the original covenant of marriage between God and man has been redeemed and re-established. The funeral song of Christ has now become the wedding song between God and humanity. What the world saw as the sad day of His thorny crowning was in fact the revealing of mankind's true King!

And since the King has come, so has His Kingdom. Jesus is and always was King, but now He has been crowned by His mother—by humanity herself…

The Sour and the Sweet

On this note, there's one last thing here to take in. On the night before His suffering, Jesus shared a final meal with His disciples and took a drink of wine. This was during the Passover meal, a special celebration involving four cups of ceremonial wine. Many scholars believe Jesus would have been on the third cup of wine when He talked about His blood and the great covenant God was bringing to humanity. That was the moment Jesus instituted communion. There was still one more cup to go, but Jesus stopped at this point. He said, "I will not drink of the fruit of the vine from now on until the Kingdom of God comes" (Lk. 22:18).

Now fast forward to the next day when Jesus had endured His suffering and was about give up His Spirit. Do you know what Jesus did right before He announced *"it is finished"* and unveiled the true identity of both God and man?

He drank wine.

Look at this:

Rising from the Wilderness

After this, Jesus, **knowing that all things had already been accomplished***, to fulfill the Scripture, said, "I am thirsty." A jar full of sour wine was standing there; so they put a sponge full of the sour wine upon a branch of hyssop and brought it up to His mouth. Therefore* **when Jesus had received the sour wine***, He said, "It is finished!" And He bowed His head and gave up His spirit.*
(Jn. 19:28-30)

Do you see what it says there? Jesus knew "all things had *already* been accomplished." The Bride had been redeemed! A mystical work of union between heaven and earth had been consummated! The blood dripping down the mercy seat of the cross was the seal and proof of this. Since all of this was accomplished, Jesus asked for wine. He could have just given up His Spirit, but He had something more to do. The words *I thirst* were a request. He knew very well what would be offered to Him if He said those words because He had already been offered something similar (Mk. 15:23). Yet now, all things were *accomplished*. Jesus was ready for the fruit of the vine.

And so, the Lord was given sour wine to drink and the mystery of the Ages played once again. For what appeared to be sour on earth was actually sweet to heaven. What were instruments of pain and sorrow became carriers of the Song of all songs, the declaration of God's heart and the everlasting union between Him and humanity. Jesus drank from the fruit of the vine because the Kingdom He talked about at the Last Supper had come!

Two Cups of Wine

This facet about the wine gets a little bit more radical when you understand more of the Hebrew culture in Jesus's day. During that time, Jewish marriages were marked by two important cups of wine. The first cup of wine was poured during the betrothal period. This is something that happened well before the actual wedding ceremony,

The Song of the Ages: Part III

when a young man would ask for a woman's hand in marriage and offer gifts to her and her family. They would then drink a cup of wine to signify the completion of this betrothal and the guarantee of its promises.

But then there was a second cup of wine, which wouldn't be drunk until the actual wedding itself. Once the consummation had come, the couple would drink the second cup of wine, which sealed the marriage and declared it as finished. This would signify the two were now one and they should begin to live in the joy and blessing of their new union.

In the same way, there were two main encounters with wine during Jesus's wedding procession from the Last Supper to Golgotha. The first was when Jesus celebrated Passover with His disciples and made the promise of the New Covenant. But then Jesus stopped and could not drink the next cup until the "ceremony" had been consummated. This happened through the shedding of His blood, after which He was given wine on the branch of a hyssop (see Ex. 12:22). This was the "second cup" of wine. And so, after receiving it, Jesus cried out something of eternal significance.

Kalah!
Bride!
It is finished!

13
Like Thunder and Dawn

*Who is this coming up from the wilderness
Leaning on her beloved?
(8:5a)*

For a long time, the world has peered out into the dusty landscape of religion and asked an important question: *What is this?* What is coming up from the wilderness of our separation—our exile from Eden? Something *is* emerging, but what is it? Is it something that can connect us back? Maybe it's a system of spiritual rules and regulations? Or maybe it's a holy box surrounded by strange commandments to a distant God? Perhaps it's a religious organization of some sort, defined by countless creeds and required deeds?

Or is it something more?

Ever since human civilization moved east of Eden and set up camp in a spiritual desert, God has been resurrecting something out of the ashes of our foolishness. For a long time, *what is emerging* has remained hazy, but through the Song of Songs it is becoming clearer and clearer.

Ultimately, what is coming forth is Jesus Christ and Him crucified. It is His glorious and harsh cross. But there is something else in the midst of that. There is also a Bride; one who has somehow emerged from that unspeakable event with Him.

The Bride is the after-effect of Christ's work on the cross. She is the growing rumble of thunder coming from the lightning strike that cracked Calvary's hillside. Thunder, of course, comes after a strike since sound is much slower than light. It is the consequence of lightning's immense power after it heats the atmosphere around it and expands outward. In the same way, the effects of the cross have been slowly expanding as the Sound of the Ages reverberates throughout space and time. The cross was a complete and finished work, but its effects are travelling outward and slowly reaching the ears of the nations, causing hearts to tremble and eyes to open.

In the coming of Christ, a blast of light struck the wilderness of humanity, and people have questioned its meaning ever since. We just looked at the first time this question was asked, but the thunder has expanded outward. Now, in the eighth chapter of the Song, the question is being asked a third and final time. The tapestry of revelation is almost complete and the full picture of God's divine purpose is coming together. But before we finish the picture, we have to now look back at the second time this question was posed. This additional look will provide yet another key thread that will join up with all the other pieces, revealing to everyone exactly *what is* coming up from the wilderness.

House of the Rising Sun

In the sixth chapter of the Song, we reached a divine turning point. It was then that the Bride's eyes were opened as she beheld her union with Christ more deeply and intimately than ever before (Sgs. 6:2-3). Her simple awareness of this, born after a season of persecution and worship, led to a glorious manifestation of its truth in her life. The glory of Jesus Himself began to radiate from

Like Thunder and Dawn

within her. From there, the people of the world took serious notice of her. They asked the question, *"Who is this that grows like the dawn?"*

At first glance, this may seem unrelated to the first question about one coming up from the wilderness. The daughters of Jerusalem are now talking about a sunrise and don't even mention the word "wilderness." But there is a deep connection here between these questions. Sunrises happen in the east, and for the daughters of Jerusalem this is the same direction as the wilderness. The people of Jerusalem associated the wilderness with the eastern regions beyond the Jordan River where their ancestors had wandered for forty years. Therefore, it appears as though the people are still looking out in the same direction; still seeing the same thing unfolding before their eyes. It is the same musical light but with a growing thunder behind it.

At first, Israel and the world only saw Solomon's mysterious chair, and with that, a crowned and bloodied Messiah. But now they see more, and they get even more specific with their question. They want to know, "What is this sunrise that's also emerging?"

The queens, concubines, and maidens of humanity are looking at the Bride this time around. They are seeing the one who has taken hold of her union with the King. Because of this, they can now behold more of what they were seeing and sensing earlier on. Through the life of the Bride, Solomon's sedan chair is getting closer and the true meaning of Moses's Ark is opening up to them. What's essentially happening is *the Ark of the Marriage Covenant is being unveiled to humanity as the Bride rises into her true identity.*

Now there's a powerful connection between this part of the Song and a particular story about Moses's Ark found in the book of 1 Samuel. Much earlier in Israel's history, before human kings had been established, when the Ark was the main thing seated at Israel's capital, something horrific occurred. The Ark was captured by Israel's worst enemy at the time, the Philistines, who had carried

The Song of the Ages: Part III

it into their own land. In other words, the Ark had been brought into the *wilderness* of enemy territory. This was a national tragedy that unfolded after a serious failure of leadership by the High Priest, whose sons had defiled their priestly roles (1 Sam. 3-4).

The story very much parallels the failure of leadership found in Adam. Adam was called to be like a High Priest, a caretaker and overseer of the land, but he and his children squandered this great calling. As a result, the enemy came in and stole the truth and power of our union with God—just like the Philistines stole the Marriage Ark from Israel. Thankfully, God brought the Ark back to Israel and the event became a prophetic sign of what was to come for the entire world.

After being held in the wilderness for a season, the Ark was returned on a wooden cart pulled by cows that had been separated from their offspring. (Later in the story, these cows would be sacrificed, just as Jesus was sacrificed to deal with our own separation from our heavenly Parent.) The first people who saw the Ark returning to Israel were from a town in the territory of Judah. The town was named Beth-Shemesh.

> *Now the people of Beth-shemesh were reaping their wheat harvest in the valley, and they raised their eyes and saw the ark and were glad to see it.*
> *(1 Sam. 6:13)*

Here's where the story crosspollinates with the Song. The name Beth-Shemesh can literally be translated as "House of the Rising Sun." So, the Ark was re-revealed and restored to Israel in a place named after a sunrise. This connects with the lyrics of the Song, where the daughters of Jerusalem (Judah) were watching the coming of Solomon's sedan chair as it emerged from the horizon like a new and hopeful sunrise. As we've seen, this pointed to the restoration of marriage between God and man. And this was fully revealed in Jesus, who is in Himself the restored marriage between God and humanity. But all of this was meant to be thunderously manifested through His awakened Bride.

Now notice how all of this happened while "the people of Beth-Shemesh were reaping their wheat harvest." The harvest of wheat is a significant image throughout the Bible. It speaks to the "Christ-in-you" harvest manifesting through humanity. This image goes hand in hand with the rising of the sun. Before dawn, when you look out in the east, all you see is darkness. This is not unlike the darkness of humanity's exile, an apparently hopeless state of separation where we seem very far from exhibiting the original life of Christ. But when the sun rises, there comes the hope of a glorious new light that will soon fill the entire sky. In the same manner, the glory of Christ will fill the whole earth before the story of human history is over. Christ will reign supreme and every knee will bow and every tongue confess the beauty of who He is. Therefore, every morning when the sun comes up, the Gospel is being declared to the earth—though most people have no idea.

The Direction of the Promise

Let's go back then to this ongoing dialogue throughout the Song. In a way, the onlooking world has been seeing both the crucifixion and resurrection of Jesus. They saw His bloody crowning first, but now they are seeing the rising of the sun. They are seeing the hope of Jesus's resurrection. And yet there's more to this scene because we find they were specifically talking about the Shulammite this time around. She is the one who is doing the "rising." The reason for this is that Jesus's resurrection is meant to be revealed *through us*. We are the witnesses of His resurrection. We are the radiance of His brightness, just as Jesus is the radiance of the Father's.

The Song of the Ages: Part III

So, in the story of Beth-Shemesh, when the people of the village saw the Ark, they "raised their eyes" and "were glad." The joy of this scene reveals the joy that will come upon the poor and weak of the earth when they see the Bride of Jesus manifesting His nature—when they see us laying down our lives just as He did when He took up the sedan chair of the cross. And this is our destiny: to make the world "raise their eyes" and become wonderfully "glad" as they behold the overflow of our blissful, sacrificial love!

Now, all of this leads to an important question of our own. If we are rising from the east, then in what direction is the world watching us from?

If they are being described as the daughters of Jerusalem, that means there is only one direction they can be watching from—the west. This leads to a stunning revelation; another truth that has been unfolding over time. The position of the onlooking world suggests they are in the territory of the Promised Land. In other words, the onlooking world *is* the Promised Land!

Remember, the Ark itself was designed in the wilderness, but it was never meant to stay there. God told Moses that the Ark was to be carried into the Promised Land of Canaan. In the same way, the Bride was born out of the wilderness of Christ's death, but through our resurrected life in Him we are to now reach the Promised Land of humanity! And just as the western sky is promised to get lit up before the day is over (and in fact, the day can't end until this happens), so too are there people in the world who are *promised* to get lit up by an ignited and awakened church.

We need to say it again and again. All of humanity is the Lord's Promised Land. The nations are Jesus's inheritance! And since we are united with Him, they are *our* inheritance as well. This is the beautiful and prophetic tapestry coming together to unveil the greater plans of God. With His Bride at His side, the Lord is

Like Thunder and Dawn

moving ever westward, gathering up the fruits of His labor at the cross—the great wheat harvest of humanity.

A Reason for the World's Resistance

Now there has obviously been much resistance to the church's move westward, which goes back to the poor witness the church has exhibited along the way. Over the centuries, and throughout Solomon's Song, the world has looked out into the east and seen a mixture of wilderness and sunlight. In other words, they have seen too many similarities between themselves and the church. Worldliness has infiltrated the witness of the Bride, fogging up the vision of who she truly is. So the world looks at us and while they may see fragments of Christ's nature, this is too often enmeshed with the elements of control, superstition, and performance. Hence, the answer to the question *"what is this"* has remained cloudy.

Thankfully, the true church is destined to emerge in the complete likeness of Jesus (Eph. 4:12-14). The Son's light will cover the entire earth and it will be reflected off of a radiant Bride. This is what will bring true clarity to the world. The promise of this emergence is breathtaking and sure, and its truth deepens the colors within the Song's tapestry, making even clearer another key theme from its lyrics:

Only an awakened church can wake up a sleeping world.

The Bride is the one called to bring Christ to the nations. For some reason, Jesus has chosen to use broken human instruments to play His Song to the world, knowing it might even take over two thousand years to bring the full orchestra together. The Bride has been chosen for this purpose, to reveal the mystery of the ages. And by His grace, she will be successful. When the truth of this mystery consumes her own vision, the rest of the world will see and believe for themselves.

The Song of the Ages: Part III

Another way to say all of this is that the cross of Calvary—the true Ark—is meant to be revealed through our earthly lives. Without the Bride manifesting selfless love and divine grace, the world will not see the true meaning of Jesus's personhood and work.

Rise of Sleeping Beauty

There's an interesting parallel to this facet of the Song in Walt Disney's version of the classic tale *Sleeping Beauty*. In the film, the princess falls asleep and the entire kingdom ends up being put to sleep as well. No one is allowed to wake up until the princess herself awakes. Walt Disney didn't know it, but he was prophesying to the coming generations through this story. God was continuing to speak Kingdom parables through the medium of film.

In the story, the prince comes to rescue the one he loves; whom he also desires to wed. At the end, he approaches a strong fortress where this princess is locked away, having to first cut through a thick barrier of thorns to get there. He then goes to strike down the evil dragon guarding the princess, doing all of this with a weapon specifically called the "sword of truth." Once this is accomplished, he goes to his beloved princess, lost in a deep sleep, and there he kisses her. She awakes, and soon the rest of the kingdom wakes up as well. Upon this awakening, the first thing the people see is the prince and princess walking side-by-side. In a way, the princess is leaning upon her beloved as this magical tale comes to a close. Together, the two of them dance before the onlooking world and the story ends in the midst of a triumphant song. This all paints such a wildly accurate picture of what we're seeing unfold throughout the Song of Solomon!

In the fulfillment of all our fairy tales, Jesus came to rescue us from the fortress of our spiritual sleep. Through a heavenly warfare, Jesus defeated the thorns of the curse and pierced the

Like Thunder and Dawn

ancient satanic dragon of deception. He did this by taking the thorny curse upon His own head and allowing Himself to get pierced by the sword of the accuser (see Zech. 13:7). Jesus essentially took the sword of Eden upon Himself and experienced death on our behalf. Through this, He destroyed the power of the curse and released the kiss of His love to the Bride. Now, as the true Bride awakens to the splendor and power of this kiss, the rest of the sleeping world will be stirred up as well. And, like the end of *Sleeping Beauty*, they will fully wake up when they behold the mystical dance between the Bride and her Bridegroom, the two now walking as one.

Watering Adam

There's another fascinating picture of this truth found in the book of Genesis, which brings us back to Song of Songs 8 and the main question at hand—*who is this coming up from the wilderness?* The Hebrew word for "coming up" has to do with rising and the first place it shows up in the Bible is Genesis 2. There, the Scriptures talk about a mist that would "come up" from the ground. This mist would rise from the earth and from there it "watered the whole face of the ground" (Gen. 2:6 KJV).

In a moment, we'll look at the spiritual implications of this passage, but first there's a few more words that are important to understand here. The Hebrew word for the "ground" that the mist would water is very significant. It is the word *adamah* and it comes from the root word for Adam. So, the mist would rise up and water "the whole face of *Adamah*." Now remember, the face represents identity. Hopefully, you can follow all the revelatory puzzle pieces hidden in this one simple passage. Let's put them together and see if a clear message emerges.

Through our union with the Spirit, we as the church have *become* that healing mist. The water "coming up" from the earth is a picture of the church "coming up" from the wilderness. Christ was buried in the earth and we were co-buried with Him. But like water from an underground spring (or like the sun in the east), we arose with the triumphant Christ! Now, as we rise from the wilderness of His death, we are called to water the *identity* of Adam's children. In other words, we refresh and enliven *the whole face of Adamah!*

That alone may need a brief *selah* before moving forward.

From Glory to Glory

Before we press on, let's take a step back and soak in the full view of revelation that has been slowly filling our vision. The first time the question about the wilderness was asked, the world only saw a crowned Man. This was "on the day of his wedding." But the Bride was not yet in their purview. Thankfully, that changed in the sixth chapter. A new clarity began to dawn, and the world asked the question a second time as they began to see more of the Gospel manifesting through the King's spouse. No longer burnt-out, weary, and fluttering back and forth between religion and grace, they now saw one who was shining with resurrection power.

And yet there was still so much more to come. Remember that this was only the "dawn." This was just the beginning of her story and of the light of Jesus breaking out into the world around her. The Scriptures tell us the righteous will shine brighter and brighter until the full noonday sun (Prov. 4:18). Noon is when the sun shines highest in the sky, removing every opportunity for opposing shadows. This connects to the words of the apostle Paul who told us we are to go "from glory to glory" (2 Cor. 3:18). Greater glory is the destiny and promise upon the church as her story unfolds throughout time.

So now in the eighth chapter this question is being asked for a third and final time, and it appears that the glory is approaching its noontime position. We can infer this by the way this question

Like Thunder and Dawn

differs from the previous two. In the first instance, the world looks and sees a "sedan chair." As we explained before, sedan chairs were royal carriages. The word for sedan has an Egyptian origin and it speaks to a very specific type of carriage—a carriage with only *one seat*, built for only one person. Thus, the world only saw the King sitting on the chair at that point.

As the Song progressed, they continued to stare in the same direction and watched as the same thing unfolded before their eyes. As they continued to look, the world saw a Bride rising like the early sun. Therefore, in the first instance, the world only saw the Messiah. In the second instance, they only saw the Bride. Here, in this third moment of questioning, the world is still looking out in the same direction and staring at the same thing. They are still seeing the approach of a royal carriage equipped with only one seat for one person. Yet despite the seating arrangement, the world is seeing the King and His Bride together.

They are finally seeing the two as one!

The reason for this, of course, goes back to that recurring note and melody of union. We are seated at the right hand of the Father *in Christ*. This doesn't mean there are countless rows of extra chairs adjacent to the right hand of God. There remains only one chair for one person—the King of glory who is united to His treasured Bride. Here, at the end of the journey, the world is beginning to see this in action. To put it in different words, they are seeing the Bride "leaning upon her Beloved," which is actually much more than leaning. This is a complete embrace of her oneness with the Messiah. It's a posture that allows the Lord to do the heavy footwork in her life.

This is what the entire church has been slowly wooed into. "Leaning" in this way is not possible without total confidence in His love. How can you completely lean into something you feel might be unstable or even slightly hostile? Trust (as well as the

The Song of the Ages: Part III

elimination of self-effort) is the key to seeing this happening. But trust of this nature cannot be established in the false shadows of religion. Demonic doctrines about the nature of our Father and the work of the cross will never allow this kind of trust to fill our hearts. If such lies remain unchecked, there will always be sneaking suspicions and subconscious concerns about the intentions of God. True "leaning" will not occur.

Therefore, the Father, Son, and Spirit have been actively engaged in eliminating lies from the heart of the church. Over the centuries, the Spirit of God has been doing a deep work of both deconstruction and reconstruction. He is deconstructing fear and religion even as He reconstructs the foundations of abiding confidence. This is why Paul prayed the way he did in his letter to the Ephesian church when he asked that they be completely established in God's love (Eph. 3:19). It was *so that* they would be filled with all the fullness of God! Apparently, the fullness of God cannot manifest in our lives without a deep trust in His pure and perfect love—another way of saying *"leaning on our Beloved!"*

From the beginning, a trust-building love has been kissing the heart of the church—God's royal princess—and calling her to wake up and lean into His grace. On that note, there is one more mystery to unfold from this question at hand. It is perhaps one of the greatest mysteries hidden within this verse, and it centers around the word *wilderness*. Come away a little bit more into the heart of God as we look at this scene even more closely…

14

Whales, Deserts, and the Head of Creation

> *Who is this coming up from the wilderness*
> *Leaning on her beloved?*
> *(8:5a)*

Once again, we are dealing with a homonym. Words of this nature are like keys in the hands of God, having multiple teeth and notches at their ends. Depending on which way you turn them, different doors are opened up, each of which lead to different realms of revelation. Like so many other words we've picked up and examined along the Shulammite's trail, the word for "wilderness" is another such key. It comes from the Hebrew word *midbar* and its alternate meaning opens up a particular door that will bring this entire expedition full circle.

Besides wilderness or desert, *midbar* can be translated in some circumstances as "mouth." So, this verse could be translated as, "Who is this coming up from *the mouth*, leaning on her Beloved?" Now that translation is awkward and seemingly irrelevant, which is why no English translator would ever suggest translating *midbar* in this way. It makes much more sense to leave it as is. However, when you go back to the beginning of the Song and think through the entirety of its melodic tapestry, this alternative translation unlocks something incredible.

Think again of the Shulammite's first request to God. The one that launched her into this whole journey in the first place. It came up again when we recalled the story of Sleeping Beauty. What did the young maiden from Shulam desire and cry out for?

> *May he kiss me with the kisses of* **his mouth**...
> *(Sgs. 1:2)*

Though lost in spiritual sleep, this weary child of God called out for the Prince of Peace to come and kiss her into awakening. We saw this right in the first chapter of the Song when the Shulammite sought after what we interpreted as the kisses of His Word. But now, in the final chapter, we see her coming up from out of a *mouth*. This imagery that strangely bookends the Song leads us to some remarkable conclusions.

In the Belly of Trust

First of all, the kind of trust that fully leans into the Beloved is the result of receiving a divine kiss. This kiss, which came over and over again, built trust in her heart, leading her to worry less and less about her own life. This meant she gave less and less thought about herself as she blissfully handed over her life to the care of her Beloved. Eventually, this kiss consumed her entire soul with trust. No longer did she live, but Christ lived from within her (Gal. 2:20). You might say she was swallowed by the kiss of God, like when Jonah was kissed by the mouth of a whale—to put it lightly.

Think of that story for a moment. Jonah was swallowed up into the belly of a whale (another picture of the wilderness) and there he learned to surrender and lean into God (Jon. 2:9). Three days later, the prophet emerged from that giant mouth and went

Whales, Deserts, and the Head of Creation

on to declare the grace of God to the "queens, concubines, and maidens" of Assyria. The same exact thing is happening with the Shulammite. She is re-emerging from the "mouth" of the Father with a mission of transformation and mercy!

But there's even more to this revelation than that. In reality, the Bride has become the very thing she was seeking after in the first place. By coming out of the mouth, it appears as though the Shulammite has actually *become the kiss of God!* She has literally become God's mouthpiece to the nations. She is His earthly thunder. To say it differently, she has become God's love-poetry. Her life proceeds from His lips like a glorious poem told by the wisest, smoothest, and most intense Poet in all of heaven and earth. This is something Paul captured in his letter to the Ephesian church:

> *We have become his poetry, a re-created people that will fulfill the destiny he has given each of us, for we are joined to Jesus, the Anointed One...*
> *(Eph. 2:10a TPT)*

Of course, Jesus Himself was the forerunner of this. He was the first one seen coming up from the *midbar*—the wilderness *and* the mouth. Jesus wrapped Himself in the dust of our humanity and arose out of the wilderness as the true King of the earth. But in coming out of this wilderness, Jesus was also coming up from the mouth of the Father. He is the incarnate Word who came to us with a very specific mission—to kiss and awaken our sleeping hearts. He is God's greatest love-poetry, written before time and delivered right to our doorstep through His miraculous incarnation.

Unfortunately, many do not realize that this work of incarnation continued beyond the birth of Jesus Christ. The Word of God, which is the *kiss* the Shulammite longed for, is now becoming incarnate through her own life as well. We are the ones who are

The Song of the Ages: Part III

now rising with Christ from the mouth of the Father, bringing refreshment and grace to a weary world. And this is the destiny of God's Word—not only to become incarnate through the earthly life of Jesus, but to be made flesh in each and every one of us!

A Better Word

This insight and revelation we're pulling from *midbar* is not isolated to this one line of Scripture. There are many other instances throughout the Bible where the wilderness and mouth tie together. Indeed, the wilderness is the place where God often chooses to *speak*. Think of these words from our friend Hosea:

> *Therefore, behold, I will allure her,*
> *Bring her into the **wilderness***
> *And **speak** kindly to her.*
> *(Hos. 2:14)*

Ideally, to speak is to reveal what's going on inside of you. Communication gives substance to what's happening in the unseen places of your heart. It seems then that God has chosen to use the wilderness as the place where He reveals the contents of His heart to us. And thankfully, what's going inside of God is breathtaking and beautiful. God has spoken "kindly" to us and His communication *is* Jesus! "The kindness and love of God appeared" through a perfect expression of thought communicated in God's Son (Tit. 3:4).

This is immensely encouraging because the wilderness has many things to speak to us as well. Usually, its message is one of death and decay. The wilderness reminds us of our exile from Eden, including all the guilt and regret that came with it. It's a dry and arid land that makes all of us long for "a better word" (Heb. 12:24). And praise the living God, it's in our decrepit dryness that a better Word has come! Jesus has come as the living Word,

Whales, Deserts, and the Head of Creation

announcing to each and every one of us the true and original glory still hidden within the dust of our flesh. He comes with a word of kindness that gives us the power to repent (Rom. 2:4). In other words, He leads us back to Eden as the dust of our lives is turned back into a rich and fruit-bearing soil.

The Blossoming Desert

There's a powerful picture of this hidden right within the natural world involving the largest desert on the planet. The Sahara Desert is a barren stretch of sand and rock that fills almost all of northern Africa. It's an enormous swath of infertile ground that leaves little room for human beings to thrive. As a result, the area has historically been filled with heartbreaking amounts of poverty and death. But despite this, we have discovered this was once a plentiful land filled with lush valleys and sprawling greenery. This is why the area is very much connected to the cradle of civilization where the earliest people groups gathered. Sadly, something happened here that caused the lushness of this region to wither up and die at an alarmingly fast rate. During a major shift in the climate, a rapid desertification took place leaving everything dried up and dead. Interestingly enough, scientists date this devastating event to about 6000 years ago, which corresponds to the biblical timeline of when human sin began to intensify and grow.

Today, the Sahara remains one of the most barren parts of the earth; however, something quite amazing happens with all the dust this desert conjures up. Fierce dust storms grow from its bleak terrain and end up billowing across several African nations until they reach the western shorelines of the continent. From there, they spill out over the sea and travel on the wind across the Atlantic Ocean where they eventually end up in South America. There, the dust settles back into the ground and becomes fertilizer, creating an incredibly rich soil that goes on to produce the most complex

The Song of the Ages: Part III

and oxygen-rich forest in the world—the Amazon rain forest! And so, what began as a violent storm of dust arising from the ashes of an arid land, ends up transforming into something that helps create the most life-filled place on the planet.

There's another parable of the Gospel here; one that spans continents and seas. Right within the region where so much of our brokenness originally multiplied, a promise of restoration lies hidden. Thousands of years ago, the "dust" of human flesh transformed into an enormous desert, producing an abundance of poverty and death. Like the Sahara's ancient past, this happened at an alarming rate. But Christ came to our spiritual desert and wrapped His own Spirit up with our dust. He faced the hopelessness of death head on and conquered its seemingly undefeatable power. After this, He ascended into the clouds in a furious storm of love, and now pours His Spirt back upon the earth in order to re-awaken the true purpose of human flesh—the purpose of being lush and fertile soil that brings forth the diverse fruits of holiness, prosperity, and grace.

In this scientific parable, the rain forest is much like the Promised Land of an awakened humanity. Like the Amazon, humanity has looked out to the east and beheld the approaching march of smoke and dust. But what at first glance has seemed like the approach of something dry and deadly has now been transformed into a message of good news. Through Christ, hope has come to us in the form of something that previously looked hopeless—the *adamah*—the dust of flesh and bone. This message of hope now travels across the sea of humanity on the winds of the Spirit with the ultimate goal of restoring everything that's been lost. This is a wondrous parable of God's kindness in Christ who has come to transform our biggest wastelands into the richest sources of life and diversity. It's the great promise of seeing

Whales, Deserts, and the Head of Creation

the desert blossom once again; a promise that is as literal as it is spiritual (see Isa. 35:1-2).

This is also a picture of God's ability to birth something out of a very infertile situation—which leads us to one last point. Hopefully you won't mind being swallowed up just a little bit more by the Word of God as we unearth one more piece of revelation from this tiny verse about the wilderness...

Womb of the Dawn

Just as the Bible talks about God transforming deserts, it also has a lot to say about the transformation of barren wombs. There is indeed a deep biblical connection between the wilderness and the womb we cannot miss. Like a womb, the wilderness was seen as a birthing place for something new to emerge; something free from confine and restriction. When God delivered Israel out of Egypt, He was "delivering" a baby—a new nation—who would go on to live in the Promised Land of fruitfulness (Deut. 32:18). The transition between Egypt and Canaan was much like a birth canal into this great promise, and thus it was only meant to be a temporary juncture.

Similarly, life in the womb is only temporary. If a baby stays there for too long, it will eventually grow too big and both itself and the mother will die. In like fashion, Israel was told they would experience death if they stayed in this wilderness-womb for too long. Instead, they were told to break through the amniotic fluids of the Jordan and enter into the wide and open spaces of Canaan.

In this regard, the law of Moses was also like a wilderness and a womb. It was specifically given to the people while they were in "the wilderness of Sinai" and provided them with temporary guidelines and restrictions for their future life together (Ex. 19:1-6). The law gave the people a kind of incubational protection, for the nation of Israel was pregnant themselves with something beyond

The Song of the Ages: Part III

imagination. The people were carrying the hope of a redeemed humanity, which was really about human flesh bearing the fruit of God again. Thus, before the birth of Jesus, the people were hidden under the shadows of the law, much like a baby remains hidden in the shadows of the womb. And in the same manner as the wilderness, the people were not supposed to stay there too long. For the exterior rules of the law, which guide and restrict behavior, were never meant to be a long-term solution to the enormous problem of our spiritual infertility. Instead, we are meant to break out of the law into the open air of sonship, living from our natural DNA as God's image-bearers.

So again, Jesus Christ was the forerunner and first-fruit of this. The lush glory displayed in His own flesh was meant to be multiplied amongst a whole body of people, both Jew and Gentile. In light of this, look at the prophetic words of Psalm 110, the most quoted Psalm in all of the New Testament:

> *The Lord says to my Lord:*
> *Sit at My right hand*
> *Until I make Your enemies a footstool for Your feet.*
> *The Lord will stretch forth your strong scepter from Zion,*
> *saying,*
> *"Rule in the midst of your enemies."*
> *Your people will volunteer freely in the day of Your power;*
> *In holy array, from* ***the womb of the dawn****...*
> *(Ps. 110:1-3)*

This Psalm speaks of all that follows the death of the Messiah; the One who rose like the hope-laden dust of Africa. It says He was seated at the right hand of Yahweh and given authority to rule and reign from that place. But in this Psalm, a prophecy is given of a certain "people" who will come after this. "From the womb of the dawn," this group will "volunteer freely" and do extraordinary

Whales, Deserts, and the Head of Creation

things. These are those who have emerged from the womb—the wilderness. These people are much like the Shulammite, emerging from this wilderness-womb like the coming of a new day. In fact, the people of this Psalm are not *like* the Shulammite—they *are* the Shulammite.

Solomon wrote about one rising like the dawn and compared her to "an army with banners" (Sgs. 6:10). In Psalm 110, David wrote about a people rising from the womb of the dawn in holy array, serving an enthroned King. Both the Song of Solomon and the Psalm of Solomon's father are prophesying the same thing. They are speaking of an awakened people who will serve God bountifully and freely; not because they have to, but because they have come into the maturity of love. It's their heart's desire to honor and serve the Lord their King above everything else. Therefore, they will come from the wilderness in holy array, shining like the Son of Man and doing the same works as Him, and even greater. They are a radical army of love who will emerge in the day of God's power; a day that has been here ever since the bloody coronation of the King.

Jesus is the One who stands at the head of this great love army. And literally, Jesus is the *Head* of His people. That then brings us back to the metaphor of the womb. For when a baby is delivered, its head is typically the first thing to come forth from the confines of its mother. Ironically, the beginning of this process is called *crowning*, where the head of a baby starts to emerge. Afterwards, the head finally breaches the womb and is out in the open, having passed through blood and water. So too, the bloody crowning of Jesus was the starting point of a new birth for humanity! Three days later, Jesus fully emerged in the resurrection, just like the literal head of a human body emerges after its own painful crowning.

Jesus Himself experienced this quite literally as an infant before He ended up embodying the spiritual fulfillment of it.

The Song of the Ages: Part III

His literal head had once come forth from a virgin womb. Then, thirty something years later, His entire body came out of a virgin tomb—a grave that had never been used before (Jn. 19:41). This was the moment when the new Head of humanity breached the birth canal of death's wilderness—or the *womb of the tomb*, you could say.

In view of this, look at some of the verses that specifically teach this part of Christ's identity and role:

> *He is also **head of the body**, the church; and He is the beginning, **the firstborn from the dead**, so that He Himself will come to have first place in everything.*
> *(Col. 1:18)*

> *...and He is **the head** over all rule and authority.*
> *(Col. 2:10b)*

> *But I want you to understand that Christ is **the head of every man**...*
> *(1 Cor. 11:3a)*

In the resurrection, Christ emerged as this glorious "Head of every man." The first part of a new humanity was now out in the open, forever free from the confines of the wilderness. And now He is calling the rest of the "body" to follow Him out into the same open air.

The Creation Itself

Now this is where things get really fascinating. In the delivery process, the shoulders naturally come next, and the Bible also has something important to say about the shoulders of this Messianic King. It is found in the words of Isaiah, the prophet who probably spoke more directly about the Messiah's incarnation than any

Whales, Deserts, and the Head of Creation

other Old Testament writer. He wrote that "the government will rest on His shoulders" (Isa. 9:6). According to the Scriptures, the government of God on earth *is* the church. We are His "royal" priesthood (1 Pet. 2:9). Moreover, we are the ones who are intimately connected to the Head, like the shoulders on a human body (Col. 2:19). Therefore, we, the awakened church, are His shoulders! *We are the next thing to emerge from the wilderness and womb!* This Song is unveiling the birth of a redeemed humanity. A humanity of which Christ is the Head and the church is His governmental shoulders.

Remember, it is *one body* seated on that approaching palanquin of glory. As the dead and sleeping world looked out to the east and saw the rising of smoke from a barren landscape, it turns out they were seeing a birthing take place. This was not another dead religion coming out of the desert, but rather a living organism emerging from a dark womb. They were seeing humanity reborn—or re-awakened—to our original nature of Love. In the third chapter of the Song, the world looked and only saw the crowned One coming forth. In the sixth chapter, they saw the Bride rising like the dawn. This was the beginning of the King's shoulders breaking through the wilderness. Now, in the eighth chapter, both of them are out together. And together, they are the forerunners of an even greater redemption.

And that brings us to the most exhilarating part of this whole metaphoric journey of birth and new life. For after the hard work of contractions and crowning is finished—and once the head and shoulders have breached the birth canal—the rest of the baby's body easily follows. This all speaks to what comes after the true awakening of the church. Something else is on the horizon, which has to do with the universe itself. The rest of creation will emerge in fullness once the awakened church rises in the glory of Christ. And like a baby's body following its head and shoulders, this will happen quickly and easily.

The Song of the Ages: Part III

This is not some strange rabbit trail of theology spun out of random metaphors and symbols. This is the direct prophecy found in the eighth chapter of Romans:

> *The entire universe is standing on tiptoe, yearning to see the unveiling of God's glorious sons and daughters! For against its will the universe itself has had to endure the empty futility resulting from the consequences of human sin. But now, with eager expectation, all creation longs for freedom from its slavery to decay and to experience with us the wonderful freedom coming to God's children.*
> (Rom. 8:19-21 TPT)

This "slavery to decay" is the wilderness we've been discussing. It is this slavery that has turned the landscape of northern Africa into dust and the song of human hearts into a bitter refrain. But remember, in Psalm 110 we find the declaration that all of God's "enemies" are being put under "the feet" of our victorious Messiah. This includes the enemies of slavery, death, and decay. And so, this is also quite fitting with our birthing metaphor since an infant's *feet* are the last things to emerge from the womb. This means when the fullness of this new humanity arises, there will be no more enemies left. Everything will be under the feet of Christ and His Body. To put it in different terms, the Last Adam and His Bride will have finally subdued the earth in love (Gen. 1:28). At last, they will have brought about Eden's return…

A Swift Awakening

We've spent a lot of time looking out to the east. The rising of one in the wilderness has filled our gaze and submerged our eyes with light. Now we must draw this part to a close and move forward in the Song. That being said, there is a thread left hanging here that needs to be addressed. It's an important distinction about

Whales, Deserts, and the Head of Creation

God's role in the wilderness itself; specifically the fact that He is *not* the Creator of it... We are.

David's prophecy in the Psalms reminds us that evil is God's enemy. There's no friendship, kinship, or partnership between the two. God is neither the author nor the initiator of anything wicked that has taken place in the "womb" of human history. Rather, He is the One challenging it and overcoming it. And more than overcoming it, He is redeeming it. Even in the midst of continent-sized sins, God is at work in reversing everything that's been lost. In fact, He's turning all of it around and fashioning something even greater than what was there in the beginning.

In the beginning of God's creation there was Eden, the place of unhindered union and fellowship, a rainforest of overflowing joy and cohesive diversity. But in our departure from grace, this joy withered and the diversity turned to division. Dry bones and barren fields crisscrossed the earth like suffocating spiderwebs and Saharan sand. Yet despite this, God took the threads of evil and spun them in the opposite direction. Through the life of Christ, He turned all of it into a cocoon from which a new creation would emerge. With dust-covered hands, God reached into our world through the person of Jesus and knit together a new beginning in the womb of our darkness.

Our heavenly Father is weaving together the tapestry of the ages. It's a living tapestry of awakened children who have been reunited with the King of grace. This tapestry will be revealed more and more in the days ahead with an incomprehensibly stunning design. Though we haven't seen the full picture of it yet, all creation is groaning and even prophesying of its emergence. In dawning sunrises, in deserts and rainforests, in the female anatomy, and even throughout Hebraic history, the promises of God's redemptive plans are being shouted to us all the time. This

The Song of the Ages: Part III

is a message the whole universe is heralding, and it is summed up beautifully in the eighth chapters of Romans and Song of Songs.

Thankfully, the real important work of this tapestry is finished. The full emergence of the new creation is upon us. Ever since the Head broke forth from the womb in Christ's resurrection, this emergence has been utterly assured. Any remaining birth pangs are now just the result of a Bride who has not yet come into the full light of who she is.

But that is quickly changing. The Bride is awakening, and as that continues to happen, the rest of creation's awakening will be swift and sure. Like Sleeping Beauty, the rest of the kingdom will wake up once the King's royal daughter comes out of her imprisoned chambers, freshly kissed by her Beloved and Friend. Then, just as quickly as everything turned to a sleeping desert, so will everything's return to Eden be—with even more splendor than before. And all the time we've spent in this temporary womb will become a far and distant memory.

Eighth Selah

Let us return briefly to the description of one who has learned to *lean on her Beloved*. Let that image settle into your soul...

This leaning of blissful trust is the trajectory of the entire global church. We're not reading something else into the text when we talk so much about the Bride's ultimate awakening to grace. The completion of the Great Commission—the work of resurrecting Eden out of the dust of human deserts—cannot and will not happen through human strength. This is put succinctly and famously in the words of the Old Testament prophet Zechariah:

> *So he answered and said to me: "This is the word of the Lord to Zerubbabel: 'Not by might nor by power, but by My Spirit,' Says the Lord of hosts.*
> *"Who are you, O great mountain? Before Zerubbabel you shall become a plain! And he shall bring forth the capstone with shouts of 'Grace, grace to it!'"*
> *(Zech. 4:6-7 NKJV)*

This passage is talking about the construction of God's temple, which is really about the building of the church. The "capstone" is the final celebratory piece placed upon the finished construction

The Song of the Ages: Part III

project. So, it says this final piece of the spiritual temple will be put on with shouts of *"Grace, grace!"* This is the reason why this book is a message for the "end-time" church. *The capstone of church history will be marked by shouts of grace!*

Think about that. Every sector of the church must heed this call and understand we are on a collision course with our Beloved's immense love and power. Too often the church has tried to accomplish the work of the Kingdom on her own—which is like forcing the petals of God's garden to blossom before their time. But true and organic blossoming is upon us, and it flows only from the place of rest.

Let's pause and take this in for ourselves. We are called to lean—and all that this means is that we are to be swallowed up by God's glorious kiss of grace.

God, consume us with this kiss. Swallow us like Jonah until we lean completely into our union with the Son of Man—the One who went into the belly of the earth and raised us into the heavenly realm.

Amen.

15
The Kiss of the Ages

Beneath the apple tree I awakened you;
There your mother was in labor with you,
There she was in labor and gave you birth.
(8:5b)

A lot can happen underneath a tree. Dead leaves fall to the earth and crumble into life-giving soil. Seeds drop and burrow into the ground to produce new trees after their own kind. Animals find shelter. Lovers find shade. Roots hug the earth like a baby grasping its mother's breast to draw out nutrients and life. And something else can happen according to the Song.

One can be awakened.

Traditionally, the lyrics in this part of the Song are interpreted as Jesus's message to the Shulammite, as though they are meant strictly for the church. Though this interpretation works, we want to stay with the overall flow of what's unfolding in the Bride's story. The Shulammite is coming up from the wilderness. She is rising from the mouth of God. This means her life has become a vessel for God's Word to be made flesh. Through the poetry of her being, Jesus is revealing His word of grace to the world—the people that symbolically lie westward as His promised inheritance.

The Song of the Ages: Part III

The words in this passage are now the words of Christ spoken through His ambassador Bride to the onlooking world. This entire section is the kiss of Christ coming upon the nations. Because of this, the lyrics in this portion of the Song make up *its most significant part*. For in a few lines of simple poetry, the entirety of the Gospel—including all the ingredients for worldwide restoration—is summed up. The Shulammite is taking everything she's learned and bringing it back to the world. For that reason, we'll be moving slowly and contemplatively through these timeless verses.

The Kissing Shade

The kiss of the Gospel begins like this:
Beneath the apple tree I awakened you.

The Shulammite discovered this kiss for herself when she first found rest under the canopy of an apple tree. Among all the other "trees of the forest," this was the only place to find relief for her weary soul—or a true kiss for her lovesick heart (Sgs. 2:3). With its red fruit bursting from hanging limbs, the apple tree paints a picture of something very specific. It's an image of Calvary, the blood being the red fruit of love that sprouted from the outstretched limbs of Jesus. No other hiding place on earth can match the peace and protection that flows from this blood. For it's under the shade of the cross where we find both the majesty and tenderness of God's heart revealed.

This majestic love has been hidden behind man's interpretations of the divine and surface-level readings of the Bible. But when one sits under this otherworldly tree, all arguments about the true nature of God are settled. Beneath the limbs of Jesus, God's infinite goodness is manifested once and for all. And this comes as the sweetest and most refreshing surprise to the striving, guilt-ridden heart. Though it was a dark and shadowy scene, the suffering of

The Kiss of the Ages

Jesus Christ is the only shade that casts true light. It's a life-giving kiss from God upon the human soul.

In order to keep all of this from becoming just a theoretical idea in our minds, let's run through a few stories in the Bible that give a very practical picture of this experience. These stories will help us understand what being kissed by God is like. For ever since our departure from Eden, this kiss is the only thing that will wake up our tired souls from the desert of exile.

Beautiful Reunions

One story comes from the life of Joseph, a man who embraced and kissed the very people who had betrayed him earlier in his life. In Genesis 42, we find the sons of Jacob re-encountering their lost brother whom they had tricked, beaten, and sent off to slavery in Egypt. When they first saw him, however, they were completely unaware it was their brother. They had come to Egypt during a famine and were desperately in need of food. Upon their arrival, they met the most highly ranked official in the entire kingdom, one who stood at the right hand of Pharaoh himself. This was their long-lost brother, yet his true face was hidden from them. Instead, he appeared to be an unappeasable, wrathful, and strict ruler whom they were constantly offending.

After only a few encounters with him, the sons of Israel absolutely feared and trembled before this mysterious man. They worried about the punishment of crossing an Egyptian prince and felt constant terror in his presence. This was a terror not only for themselves, but also for their frail and aged father. They believed this Egyptian was going to take away one of their other brothers and that their father would die from the grief this would cause. The fear of the future, the tension of the present, and the guilt of their past had combined into a cesspool of heartache and regret.

The Song of the Ages: Part III

The experience provided quite a picture of what life in a spiritual desert is like.

But then the kindness and grace of Joseph was revealed and a beautiful shade formed over the hearts of these fearful men. Joseph decided to unveil himself. He showed his *true face* to them. He showed his trembling brothers that even though he was indeed a ruler who carried all the authority of Pharaoh himself, he was still in fact their brother—their flesh and blood. And not only was he family; he was also their friend, for he had chosen to completely forgive them of their sin. He openly declared his love for them and expressed this by literally weeping for joy over their reunion (Gen. 45:14 NLT). And this weeping soon turned into a showering of kisses and hugs.

It was not anger bubbling up from Joseph's soul that day, but an eruption of warm and tender affection. His brothers were fully embraced and accepted. On top of this, they were then provided with a new home in a prosperous region of Egypt, leaving them free from any fear of famine and hunger. This was the greatest day of their lives. As they were given one piece of too-good-to-be-true news after another, it must have felt like coming to rest under the most glorious shade imaginable. The whole experience was a picture of the wondrous, over-the-top, and surprisingly relieving kiss of the Gospel. It is what the Gospel is meant to feel like when we truly take in its full implications.

There's yet another image of this kind of love in the Bible found in a story that also happened during the life of Joseph, though it was from when he was very young. It was when Joseph watched as his own father re-encountered an estranged brother. Such an encounter probably laid the groundwork in Joseph's heart for what would be expressed between he and his brothers decades later.

The Kiss of the Ages

We looked at some of this story in the previous volume. Jacob had betrayed his brother Esau, having tricked him out of a birthright and a firstborn blessing. Such things were supposed to set up Esau for life, both financially and spiritually. Yet, through manipulation and deceit, Jacob robbed his brother's future and left the relationship on an extremely bad note. Years later, Jacob came across his brother as he made his way back to his homeland. From a distance, Jacob saw Esau coming with hundreds of armed men. Panic and terror filled Jacob's heart at the sight of this and he began devising anxious strategies to minimize any casualties in his own family (Gen. 32:13-21). He was under the false assumption Esau would unleash absolute retribution upon him and his family. (Quite fittingly, Jacob was also in a literal wilderness when all of this transpired.)

When the moment came for Jacob to encounter his brother, he was greeted not with swords and wrath, but with tears and affection (Gen. 33:4). Esau displayed nothing but forgiveness and love for Jacob. He simply missed his brother and desired a restored relationship between the two of them! Although Esau had an intimidating amount of power—even a small army at his disposal—the most powerful thing he brought forth that day was a heart of overwhelming compassion. Without hesitation, Esau embraced his lost brother and blessed him. And of course, he kissed him. And therein lies the beautiful Gospel once again.

Now, just put yourself in Jacob's sandals—and in his twelve sons' as well. Think of all the anxiety and fear leading up to these welcoming kisses. Can you imagine the utter relief that would come to you when receiving that first kiss? Can you picture the sudden departure of trembling fear as it rushed out of your mind in such a way that even your physical body felt transformed? Can you envision the utter "shade" this would provide to your guilt-ridden and burnt-out heart? All the planning and plotting on how

The Song of the Ages: Part III

to avoid punishment and how to control outcomes would instantly vanish. Seeing these powerful men and realizing all along they were on your side would be intoxicating! An inebriating joy would settle into your heart, not only as you realized they were on your side, but that they were also filled with a real affection and warmth toward you.

This is the revelation of the Gospel told through wonderful stories of reuniting families. It shows us what can happen under the apple tree of grace.

A Third Witness

But perhaps the greatest biblical story of this nature was told by Jesus Himself when He spoke at a dinner table to a mixed crowd of religious leaders and outcasts. The story of the prodigal son is one of His most famous parables. It's the tale of a young man who did something unspeakably dishonoring to his father. The son asked for his inheritance money early, which in that culture was akin to wishing his father dead. He then left the house and completely walked away from the relationship. Before long, the young man was squandering every penny of his father's hard-earned funds in utterly selfish ways.

Soon enough, a famine came into the picture (much like the one Joseph's brothers encountered in their story). The prodigal son had spent all his money and had nowhere to go. He was hungry and desperate and decided his only option was to go home and face his dad. But before doing this, he prepared himself a shameful repentance speech, rehearsing it on the long and anxious journey back home (much like Jacob heading back to his long-abandoned homeland where Esau dwelled). As the famine-inducing sun beat on his brow and the shame of his past coursed through his blood, this young fellow embodied yet another image of humanity's travel-weary journey through the desert of exile. Imagine the strange and

The Kiss of the Ages

burdening mixture of fear and self-loathing in the prodigal's heart, especially as he thought about the possibility of his dad rejecting him and leaving him to die. His best-case scenario was to beg that he be made a slave in his father's house and never again be called a son.

But then he came to the outskirts of the property and saw his father running toward him. This too must have been somewhat similar to Jacob seeing Esau in the distance and wondering what his intentions were. Perhaps he thought his father was running to him in anger, ready to uncap all the pent-up fury that had been "justly" brewing all these years. But as he got closer, this worry proved to be utter insanity as the son started to see the face of his father. He began to see the expression in his father's eyes with newly cresting tears. The father was running toward his son with nothing but love and gratitude. And soon enough, this prodigal son was hugged—and kissed. And he didn't even get to say his full repentance speech.

Of course, this was then followed up by quite the extravagant display of blessing. Like Joseph's brothers, the prodigal son was not only greeted with unconditional acceptance, but with an incredible home safe from famine! He was given a fattened calf in sheer celebration of his return, revealing that this place was obviously not worried about a lack of food. On top of this, the young man was given three gifts—sandals, a ring, and a robe—all of which restored him to his full place as a son. This wasn't a picture of someone being tolerated with tokens of forgiveness that come with strings attached. This was a beloved child being celebrated and completely brought back to a position of honor within the home. This was a display of undeniable affection.

What an otherworldly shade that our true Father provides for us! We need to put ourselves in *these sandals*. These are the shoes of the Gospel of peace. And they hold way more than a rich display

The Song of the Ages: Part III

of forgiveness. There is also a lavish and scandalous flood of blessing that comes as the greatest surprise to the human heart. For the heart that has wandered through a dry and weary land, this is nothing but shelter and relief. Each of these stories from Scripture are like "two or three witnesses" to the revelation unfolding in the Song (2 Cor. 13:1). Put together, they reveal why the Gospel is truly a life-giving kiss and a relaxing, nourishing shade. This is now the message pouring out of the mouth of the one rising from the wilderness in joy and celebration.

And that is our segue back to the Song. As the Bride brings the kiss of the Gospel to the world, we realize the cross not only provided a restful shade for humanity; it was also the place where we were "awakened." On behalf of Jesus, the rising Shulammite tells the world, *"Under the apple tree I awakened you."* There was indeed a great sleep covering the eyes of man that was decisively dealt with under the tree of Calvary. It was there that mankind was awakened specifically from the nightmarish hypnosis of an angry, distant, and retributive God.

Like Jacob in Mahanaim or the prodigal son on the boundaries of his old home, mankind had only seen their Father from a distance. Like Joseph's brothers, we had seen the intimidating power and royalty of God. We surveyed His holiness and came to understand certain truths about God, like His omnipotence, omniscience, and omnipresence. *But we had not seen His full face.* Thus, the cross came into our sleeping world like the opening of thick blinds on a very sunny morning. There at Golgotha's hill we were stirred up from our dark slumber as the true face of our Father was finally unveiled. In the coming of the Gospel, under the shade of a cutdown tree, the actual tears in His eyes were made visible.

Before His crucifixion, Jesus explained that He was surrounded by legions of angels He could have called upon at any moment.

The Kiss of the Ages

Like Esau and Joseph, He had an unbeatable show of power at His disposal. Yet the true might of God was revealed when He rejected the use of violence and opened wide His arms instead. This was the moment when both our Father and Brother, through the Spirit, hugged us and kissed us. It was there they wept over us with joy. It was indeed joy that brought Them there in the first place (Heb. 12:2). This was a full display of divine tenderness and compassion. And more than that, it was also the display of unimaginable riches and blessing. For under that same tree of Calvary, we were showered with every spiritual blessing in the heavenly places (Eph. 1:3). This was freely given to us and now it is available to all who would simply take hold of it. This is the appeal of extravagant grace and scandalous love now being made known to the entire world. Through His Bride, the Beloved is declaring the overwhelming Gospel of peace.

And because of this, we learn once more the Gospel is an invitation to realize an awakening that has already happened in Christ. In fact, it was at the cross that Jesus *woke up* for us...

Already Awake

Now that may be a strange statement to some, but it involves another clear connection between Adam and Christ. We've probably overdone the parallels between these two, but you'll need to bear with several more. The Song is revealing a *new beginning* for humankind, and so this entails many connections and fulfillments to our first beginning. There's an especially strong link between what's happening underneath the apple tree and the Genesis story of Adam and Eve.

Following Adam's divine rib surgery was a literal awakening. Since he was in the lush and canopied region of Eden, there's a good chance Adam woke up in some proximity to a tree—perhaps even right underneath one. Either way, this awakening was different than

The Song of the Ages: Part III

other times he'd woken up in the Garden. This time was followed by the most wonderful surprise. He opened his eyes to behold someone who was like himself, and yet uniquely beautiful. He awoke to see someone so stunning that he immediately overflowed into an ecstatic burst of poetry (Gen. 2:23). In that instant, Adam beheld Eve and the sting of loneliness was swiftly removed from his heart. We can probably infer that he fell in love pretty quickly. It also wouldn't be any stretch of the imagination to say his poetry was followed up with a kiss or two. Or three. For it was not long after this that the two became one.

Here's the point. Upon coming back to consciousness, Adam was *awakened to love*—literally. Now keep in mind that Adam was "a pattern of the one to come" (Rom. 5:14 NIV). So, in the same way, Jesus went into the deepest kind of sleep on our behalf—the sleep of death—even to the point of being buried. Soon after this, He awoke from the grave in resurrection power. When He awoke, the stain of sin that had veiled the apple of His eye—the one uniquely created as His beautiful image and likeness—was totally and utterly removed. Thus, Jesus awoke to a redeemed and stunning beauty—*us*. In other words, He too awakened to love!

It turns out the greatest awakening already happened 2000 years ago. True awakening is not found in some future revival, or at a special event, or in the mystical teachings of some super-spiritual guru. Awakening is found in no other place but the cross of Christ. All true revival and spirituality flows from this one place. This is so vital to understand because people all over the planet are looking for a spiritual awakening. To some degree or another, people recognize they're living in a Matrix-like dream world. They can identify a false heaviness to life, a type of subpar existence from which they long to break free. This is the driving force behind both drugs and suicide. People feel they must die to their normal consciousness whether through chemical substances or literal death. And ironically enough, this is the drive behind religion itself. Whether it's an organized thing or an individualized pursuit, the same underlying push for death and transcendence creates the appeal of religion. The Old Covenant was actually the epitome of this self-attained awakening (or you can substitute the word "awakening" with "salvation"). But of course, that covenant was given in order to expose the futility of our self-effort. We couldn't wake ourselves up. We still can't. Someone else had to do it for us—and *as us*.

So again, the cross came to us like the sweetest shade on the hottest day. It was there Jesus *already* fulfilled man's desire for awakening! He did this by falling into our sleep and breaking its power from the inside out. In Christ, mankind received everything we've pursued in our own strength or imagination. Every ideal of perfection was already attained through our union with Christ. Through Him, we ascended the holy mountain and reached nirvana, enlightenment, and heaven all at once—simply because we were included in His life, death, and resurrection. This is a vital part of the Gospel-kiss coming out of the mouth of the Bride.

On Eagle's Wings

This brings us to another important element about awakening. The word Solomon uses for "awakened" here can also be translated as "lifted up." In fact, more often than not, this is the way the word is usually written in the Old Testament. It's a phrase reminiscent of something Jesus said a few days before His fateful crucifixion. He said, "If I am *lifted up* from the earth, I will draw all men to Myself" (Jn. 12:32). This is another beautiful facet of the Gospel; a facet we've examined many times. Through His Bride, Jesus is now speaking to the whole world, telling them they too were *lifted up* at the cross.

The Song of the Ages: Part III

One major place this word "awakened" shows up is in Deuteronomy 32, which, providentially, contains lyrics to another famous song in the Bible. This is the Song of Moses where we find a powerful description of how God came to His fallen children in the wilderness. Look carefully at its lyrics:

> *He found him in a desert land and in the wasteland,*
> *a howling wilderness;*
> *He encircled him, He instructed him,*
> *He kept him as the apple of His eye.*
> *As an eagle **stirs up** ("awakens" or "lifts up") its nest,*
> *hovers over its young, spreading out its wings,*
> *taking them up, carrying them on its wings.*
> *(Deut. 32:10-11 NKJV, parenthesis mine)*

Though this is speaking of God's dealings with Israel, the lyrics resound with a message for everybody. In this passage, God is comparing Himself to an eagle circling around its immature offspring who are unable to leave their nest. This nest is found in the "wilderness" and it parallels an immature humanity stuck outside of Eden, unable to fly in the mature heights of the Spirit. Yet the Lord is enveloping them as the "apple of His eye" (the "daughters" and "villages" of humanity). Along the way, it says He has been "instructing" the people. Indeed, through Israel, God first instructed humanity through the law of Moses. This was the schoolmaster that would lead us to something greater. It was preparing us for a time when we would learn to soar upon the wings of grace.

Moses's song then prophesies how this mature soaring would come about. It says the divine eagle "stirred up" or *lifted up* its nest. The poetry points to when God literally swooped down into our barren nest by becoming a man. Then, when He spread out His arms on a Roman cross, this was the same moment God "spread

The Kiss of the Ages

out His wings." On that day, according to John 12, Jesus drew all of fallen humanity to Himself, bearing us on eagle's wings. In His resurrection and ascension, all of us were *lifted up* into the heavenly air, restored to our identity as divine eaglets.

So, as you can see, a lot happened underneath this particular apple tree. Not only was the human race woken up from the sleep of an angry and distant God; we were also lifted up with Christ into heavenly places. This is the true awakening and ascension humanity is striving after. But it is something hidden and unseen, a *mystery* that must be received by faith in order to encounter it (which sums up the entirety of the Shulammite's poetry).

This dynamic of the Gospel shouldn't come as a shock to people, for the world is filled with many pursuits toward spiritual secrets and mystical transcendence. Yet there is only one true mystery, and it is not a secret reserved for a select few. The Bible has been openly declaring it for a very long time. It was poetically hidden in both the Song of Moses and the Song of Solomon, but it has been blatantly expressed in the New Testament for nearly 2000 years. One of the clearest expressions of it is found in the third chapter of Ephesians. There, Paul writes:

> *By revelation there was made known to me the mystery…*
> *to be specific, that the Gentiles are fellow heirs and **fellow***
> ***members of the body**, and fellow partakers of the*
> *promise in Christ Jesus through the gospel.*
> *(Eph. 3:2, 6).*

This statement might seem a little perplexing, but there's a joyful simplicity to what's being communicated here. The "Gentiles" are the nations of the world. To Paul then, the great mystery is *specifically* that the nations are part of the very body of Jesus. Therefore, what happened to Him, happened to all of us. What is true of Him is true of us as well. Just as He is loved and

The Song of the Ages: Part III

precious to God, so are we. Just as He was raised to life, so were we. For the truth is, the whole world is within Him—part of His very being. Or, you could also say it like this:

The whole world is part of the ribs of Jesus.

Like Eve was hidden within Adam before His divine sleep, the entire world has been hidden in God even before Christ's death. Only a few verses after he talks about the nations being "fellow members" of Christ's body, Paul says, "For ages this mystery has been *hidden in God* who created all things" (Eph. 3:9). Elsewhere, Paul wrote that *in Him* we live and move and have our being (Acts 17:28). So too, Eve lived and moved and had her being around the heart and lungs of Adam. The ribs surround these two organic containers holding the life and breath of the body. Eve was at the center of Adam's being, and when he went to sleep, that hidden part of him was brought out into the light. Eve was revealed. You could also say that she was born. Yet in a *mysterious* way, she had already existed near the heart of her beloved.

In the same manner, humanity's origin is in the heart and breath of God, even before the foundation of the world. Before we were clothed with flesh in our mother's womb, God knew us (Jer. 1:5). But the fullness of this revelation was hidden until the coming of Jesus. When He said *"it is finished"* and exhaled that last bit of oxygen in His lungs—along with a final beat of His heart—this mystery of humanity's true identity was made visible. The God of the entire universe had given up everything for us. There's no greater proof of the infinite weight of glory God has placed upon each one of us. That final exhale was His undying kiss that brought this truth out into the open. In that one moment, humanity was truly born.

Or reborn. For though we came into being under the trees of Eden, our full nature and true identity was released under the apple tree of the cross.

The Kiss of the Ages

Already Reborn

"There your mother was in labor with you. There she was in labor and gave you birth."

This is the next part of the Gospel's poetic kiss. Its divine lips are targeting a world that is not only striving after spiritual awakening, but after a form of rebirth as well. People may not put it in these exact terms, but this is at the heart of multitudes of spiritual pursuits and ideologies. For ages, people have looked to be reborn, which often involves a philosophy (and methodology) of suffering and death. The teachings of reincarnation are a perfect example of this. They involve ascending the cosmological ladder through personal sacrifice and morality; one of the many ways man has dreamed up salvation in his spiritual sleep. Yet all of this is actually a recurring nightmare keeping us in bondage to systems of self-effort. And so here again we find the over-the-top, refreshing joy of the Gospel. The suffering and dying we feel must happen *already happened*. Beneath the suffering limbs of Jesus, which held up the weight of our sin, there was a rebirth that already took place.

We began to look at this in the last chapter when we examined the crowning of Jesus; however, this element of birth comes out even clearer when we look at the moment right after Jesus pushed out His last bit of breath. After He died and His side was pierced and opened, two of the main things that issue from a woman's womb during birth were released from Jesus's body—water and blood (Jn. 19:34). This signified the crucifixion was indeed a moment of birthing.

Now even though this birthing took place at the cross, the contractions and labor pains had begun a long time beforehand. This will explain why the Song speaks of the Shulammite's "mother" giving birth under the tree. It was Mother Israel as a nation who carried this messianic seed long before the actual death of Jesus.

The Song of the Ages: Part III

From the time of Abraham to Jesus's incarnation, there were many contractions leading up to the birthing that occurred at the cross. Like a pregnant woman going in and out of pain and discomfort, there were intermittent periods of exile and hardship for Israel as her womb grew larger and larger. But these labor pains intensified when the Messiah showed up and Israel began to "push" out the very seed of promise that had been hidden inside of her for thousands of years. When Israel initiated Jesus's suffering, she was accelerating her own labor pains in that moment. Then, under the apple tree of the cross, she was at last giving birth. It was there the darkness of her womb gave way to the dawning light of promise.

Curiously enough, there was a strange darkness that settled over the entire land of Israel on this day of the Roman apple tree. Matthew tells us that during the crucifixion "darkness fell upon all the land *until the ninth hour*" (Matt. 27:45). This is more significant than it seems because the number nine is very much symbolic of birth due to the nine months involved with gestation. So, like a womb surrounding Israel, darkness covered *all* the land, and this lasted specifically until the "ninth hour." It was during this hour Jesus's work would be completed. As Israel pushed Him into death, Jesus took their sin upon Himself and pushed out the last bit of life within His chest. As a member of Mother Israel Himself, it was ultimately Jesus who would give birth to a redeemed humanity at the cross.

Now here is where it's important to remember Israel is a representative for the nations. In reality, all humanity was participating in this all-important birth. It wasn't only the Jews taking part in the suffering of Jesus on that day—Gentiles were there as well. In fact, they were the ones who actually put the thorns on His head and the nails in His hands. Indeed, before Abraham carried the seed of the Messiah, his pagan ancestors carried it as

The Kiss of the Ages

well. And before them, this seed went all the way back to Eve, which brings everything full circle once again.

Under the shade of a different tree—one called the Tree of Knowledge of Good and Evil—darkness was brought into the world. It was at that moment God foretold of labor pains that would come upon Eve and her children:

> *To the woman He said, "I will greatly multiply your pain*
> *in childbirth; in pain you will bring forth children."*
> *(Gen. 3:16)*

In a way, all the painful "labor" humanity would experience was wrapped up in this one statement. Yet in that same statement was also a word of hope, for the very idea of labor pains suggests an ending to that pain—through birth. Thus, it was in this same conversation God also gave the promise of a "seed" that would come forth to crush the power of darkness:

> *And I will put enmity between you and the woman, and*
> *between your seed and her seed; he shall bruise you on the*
> *head, and you shall bruise him on the heel.*
> *(Gen. 3:15)*

Because of this promised seed, the darkness that came over our world was instantly transformed into a temporary womb. Though this womb would spread across the planet, multiplying into hatred, division, and war, so too would the seed of promise grow and develop. This growth would continue until finally Mother Israel and her Roman conspirators would crown the Head of humanity with thorns. In so doing, they would participate in giving birth to the true destiny of humanity. For this seed was not only about the Messiah, but about the birth of a totally new humanity Jesus was inaugurating at the cross.

The Song of the Ages: Part III

Under the shade of the apple tree, our mother gave us birth. There, the darkness of humanity reached a boiling point as we collectively murdered God's Son. But in the pinnacle of our deception—at our absolute worst moment—love crushed the power of evil as our Father poured out His healing love upon us. In that same instance, the seed of a victorious and restored humanity was birthed. We see here at the end of the Song the stunning sovereignty of God over the pain of human history. This is not a sovereignty of force and control, or the type that insinuates God is the initiator of evil. Rather, it is sovereignty of complete and utter love. It is the kiss of an all-encompassing plan that was determined to overcome our darkness right from the beginning.

You can draw these same conclusions about God's loving sovereignty if you look at Eve's story from a biological point of view. The moment a female is born, the eggs holding her children are already inside of her. So, when Eve was created, the seed of the Messiah already laid within her physical being. Before she ever sinned, the promise of salvation was present. Even when she ate from the wrong tree and was encumbered by shame, God saw right through her naked body and beheld the glory radiating from within. God knew the darkness we would embrace and had implanted a time bomb of unfailing love into the world. Even when our original mother embraced deceptive shadows, light was already destined to shine out of that darkness. This light would lead to our true and final birth, with Christ as the Head. Again, we were conceived in Eden, but our true birth didn't happen until the day of the apple tree—the true Tree of Life.

Wonderful Grace!

Solomon's strange poetry about a tree—and the awakening and labor that happened underneath it—only makes sense in the context of the cross. It was there mankind's pursuits toward divine

The Kiss of the Ages

awakening and spiritual rebirth were already accomplished. In Christ, humanity was forgiven, kissed, and lifted up into heavenly heights. As Paul says, this happened "while we were yet sinners" (Rom. 5:8). Or better yet: "Even when we were dead and doomed in our many sins, he united us into the very life of Christ and saved us by his wonderful grace!" (Eph. 2:5 TPT) This happened before anyone believed it or said yes to it. Such is the kiss of the Word rising from the wilderness. This is the full message of the Good News, the eternal Gospel of peace, which the awakened Bride is finally unleashing to the world.

But of course, not everyone has embraced this kiss… And that leads us to the next part of the Song of the Ages. Even though humanity has been united with the glorious life of Christ, people are still called to say *yes* to this love and receive it for themselves. For though He is wonderfully sovereign, God will not force relationship upon anyone, for then it would cease to be love. That's why the next few verses are of great significance. The kiss of truth must be embraced, which is what the "seal" is all about.

16

The Royal Seal

Put me like a seal over your heart,
Like a seal on your arm.
(8:6a)

In Genesis 24, the great patriarch Abraham sends one of his servants to find a bride for his beloved son—the one born supernaturally from a barren womb. Abraham asks his servant to find this bride from among his own relatives and then makes him keep an oath that he will stay true to this all-important task. This is followed up, however, with a caveat: "But if the woman is not willing to follow you, then you will be free from this my oath" (Gen. 24:8).

It's not hard to see the connections between Abraham's request and the call of the Gospel. Abraham's son Isaac is a clear representation of Christ, perhaps one of the clearest in the entire Old Testament. Christ is the true beloved Son and His Father is preparing a Bride for Him. Through divine servants and ambassadors, God is extending the invitation of marriage to the entire world. Just like Abraham, the Father wants Jesus to have a Bride from among His own relatives—which would be the whole world since every person shares the same flesh and blood as Him!

The Song of the Ages: Part III

Now we just looked at what took place under the apple tree, including its effect upon humanity. Before anyone knew about it or believed it, God finished the work of reconciliation under the glorious tree of Calvary. The Scriptures teach us that by the blood of the cross, God reconciled all things back to Himself and made peace both with things in heaven and on earth (Col. 1:20). This is *the finished work* of Christ. Through Jesus's death and resurrection, the world has been brought back into union with its Creator and there is no escaping this reality. Even if someone wants to make their bed in the realm of death, the all-consuming presence of God cannot be escaped.

> *If I ascend into heaven, You are there;*
> *If I make my bed in hell, behold, You are there.*
> *(Ps. 139:8 NKJV)*

And yet, all that being said, true reconciliation is a relational thing. Relationships by their very nature must go two ways. So, even though God has washed away the separating sins of the world and now fills all things with His love, each person must be willing to receive this love for themselves. Hence the reason we started with the profound story of Abraham and his pursuit of a *willing* bride for his son. In the same fashion, God will not have a forced Bride for Jesus. It is this issue that will take us into the next part of the Song.

The Evangelist's Kiss

One of the Father's greatest messengers and bondservants was the apostle Paul. Like the Shulammite at the end of the Song, Paul arose from a literal wilderness in Arabia and *went west* to bring the kiss of the Gospel to the nations (Gal. 1:17). In one of his letters, Paul summarizes this kiss in the clearest of terms:

The Royal Seal

*For the love of Christ controls us, having concluded this,
that one died for all, therefore all died; and He died for all,
so that they who live might no longer live for themselves, but
for Him who died and rose again on their behalf.*
(2 Cor. 5:14-15)

Paul had become convinced of something in the wilderness; something that compelled him, like the Shulammite, to go into the world of God's promised inheritance. He had come to the full and stunning conclusion that when Christ died, *all died.* The entire world was crucified under the apple tree of Calvary. In 2 Corinthians, Paul is giving an evangelistic declaration of what Solomon poetically foreshadowed. And this evangelistic kiss goes on:

*Therefore from now on we recognize no one according to
the flesh; even though we have known Christ according
to the flesh, yet now we know Him in this way no longer.
Therefore if anyone is in Christ, he is a new creature; the
old things passed away; behold, new things have come.*
(2 Cor. 5:16-17)

Paul says here we should recognize *no one* according to what is seen on the outside. This is because the apostle understood the deeper truth of a world that had already been reconciled through the blood shed at the cross. He looked beyond the separating veil of sin and beheld the face of each beloved son or daughter of God. This was now the way he viewed everyone, whether they were Greek or Jewish, barbarian or educated, male or female, slave or free (Col. 3:11).

Paul's next statement then—*therefore if anyone is in Christ, he is a new creature*—is a declaration, not a condition. It is similar to another statement he made: *"If God is for us, who is against us?"* (Rom. 8:31) Paul is not really posing a question there. He is stating a triumphant fact. The same goes with his words in 2 Corinthians.

The Song of the Ages: Part III

After saying that he recognizes *no one* according to the flesh, Paul concludes with, *"Therefore **if** anyone is in Christ, he is a new creature."* He is making a declaration of the true identity of all people. It is the kiss of the Good News—the bright announcement of a new creation already come.

Yet, the apostle's message continues with something of immeasurable importance:

> *Now all these things are from God, who reconciled us to Himself through Christ and gave us the ministry of reconciliation, namely, that God was in Christ reconciling the world to Himself, not counting their trespasses against them, and He has committed to us the word of reconciliation.*

> *Therefore, we are ambassadors for Christ, as though God were making an appeal through us;* ***we beg you on behalf of Christ, be reconciled to God.***
> *(2 Cor. 5:18-20)*

Paul is being very clear here. God had *already* reconciled the world to Himself. From heaven's perspective, this work was fully accomplished. There is no separation between God and His children. Paul and every other messenger of grace is now compelled to bring this "word of reconciliation" to the nations. Similar to Abraham's servant, this involves bringing Jesus's flesh and blood relatives into a fully restored relationship with God; a relationship akin to being His very *Bride*. But like Isaac's bride, this can only come through a willing heart. So with that, we come to this marvelous verse in the Song of Songs:

"Put me like a seal on your heart, like a seal on your arm."

The Royal Seal

The Divine Proposal

Over the millennia, a countless assortment of songs, poems, and sermons have arisen from this one tiny verse. Combined with unending studies and biblical expositions, this has left us with a wide array of interpretations and perspectives on its meaning. But despite all of it, there's a simple interpretation to this verse that isn't that difficult to discern. This is a case where the Bible interprets itself. In the New Testament, the meaning of Solomon's poetic seal gets unveiled with stunning clarity. Here are three verses that lay out its treasures very succinctly:

> *Now He who establishes us with you in Christ and anointed us is God, who also* **sealed** *us and gave us* **the Spirit** *in our hearts as a pledge.*
> *(2 Cor. 1:21-22)*

> *In Him, you also, after listening to the message of truth, the gospel of your salvation—having also believed, you were* **sealed** *in Him with* **the Holy Spirit** *of promise.*
> *(Eph. 1:13)*

> *Do not grieve* **the Holy Spirit of God**, *by whom you were* **sealed** *for the day of redemption.*
> *(Eph. 4:30)*

What is the seal? It is clearly the Holy Spirit of God.

Of course, the Spirit is also the very flame of love, which Solomon will go on to describe with unparalleled beauty—but we'll get to that later. For now, let's put this truth into its immediate context within the Song.

Through His awakened Bride, the Lord has been speaking out the message—the kiss—of Christ crucified: One died for all, therefore all died. By the hand of a loving and generous Father, the

The Song of the Ages: Part III

old order is taken care of and a new one has opened up. Now, in this new era of grace, the Father is urging humanity to wake up and say *yes* to it all. Through His bridal ambassadors, God is pleading with people to receive this love for themselves. Receiving this love is the same as receiving Him, because *He is Love* (1 Jn. 4:8). And so, to receive Him is to receive the most precious gift imaginable.

Now let's go back to the apple tree for a moment, because we're witnessing yet another stunning facet of what transpired there. We're discovering that it was at the cross *God knelt down and proposed to the world*. With everything in Him, God came and asked for our hearts in marriage. This is the essence behind the words, "Set me as a seal on your heart!" Through the person and work of Jesus, God tangibly knelt down on one knee before a sin-weary world. The book of Philippians describes this when it declares that Jesus "humbled Himself by becoming obedient to the point of death, even death on a cross" (Phi. 2:8). Humbling Himself, Jesus knelt down and became a servant to us, kneeling even into our dusty wilderness of death. As He did this, Jesus offered up His entire being to us. This was His divine proposal. Then, with nail-pierced hands, Jesus held out a gift worth more than all the treasuries of heaven and earth combined. To each and every person, He held out a luminous ring—one that was made both for the "heart" and "arm," according to Solomon. This wedding ring is of course the gift of the Holy Spirit.

During the days of the Old Covenant, the prophet Joel declared this gift would soon be poured out upon all flesh (Joe. 2:28). Centuries later, on the day of Pentecost, this remarkable prophecy was fulfilled according to Peter (Acts 2:14-22). The words of Joel are no longer a coming reality, but something that was already released after the day of Calvary, when the sun turned to darkness. The Spirit of God has now been poured out upon all

The Royal Seal

flesh, which enables us to no longer view humanity according to the flesh. This gift has been released to all, and has redefined all.

Yet, like a ring held out in a proposal, the Holy Spirit must be willingly taken. *Like any other gift, the Spirit must be received and unwrapped.*

Now at this point, we're touching on things that may sound elementary to some readers. You may have come to the end of the Song expecting some deeper truths to arise from its final burst of divine vocals. But there's a simplicity at the Song's end that equips us with what we need to bring this kiss to the nations. This equipping is desperately needed, for there's a world in dire need of this divine love. Unfortunately, throughout her time in the wilderness, the global church has either skewed or lost complete sight of some of these truths. Basic teachings on salvation, baptism, and the gift of the Holy Spirit have often been distorted, bringing a flood of confusion and complication to these precious topics. Yet now we are seeing an awakened Bride rising with a clear and pure message. This triumphant Shulammite is where the church is headed. She is right on the horizon. Therefore, in the days ahead, we should expect the church to be filled with the greatest clarity ever regarding these matters. This clarity is so important, for the world will not experience a true awakening of its own without the *truth* shining its clearest and brightest.

In light of this, let's press through any remaining distortion and discord and hear again the crystal-clear notes of heaven blasting through the Song...

A Ring on the Heart

Let's first return to those New Testament verses about the "seal" of the Spirit. If there was any doubt the cross was a divine proposal, the following should settle the matter.

The Song of the Ages: Part III

In the beginning of 2 Corinthians, Paul wrote: "Now He who establishes us with you in Christ and anointed us is God, who also sealed us and gave us the Spirit in our hearts *as a pledge*" (2 Cor. 1:21-22). The Greek word we typically translate as "pledge" or "down-payment" is the word *arrabōn*. In Greek culture, this word was used to describe something very specific. It was used—even to this day—for when a man presents a woman with a gift and asks her hand in marriage! Today, this gift would be an engagement ring, but in Paul's day this was something way more binding and official than the modern engagement. Though the full wedding ceremony wouldn't happen right away, the *arrabōn* was a complete commitment and "sealing" of the marriage. It was more like an actual wedding ring. To receive this gift was the same thing as saying, "*I do.*"

Understanding this word makes it quite clear that when a person says *yes* to the Gospel, it is actually an *"I do"* to a covenant relationship with Jesus. And with that comes the Spirit as a seal and wedding ring upon the heart. This sealing is an incredible gift, and it comes only by believing in what Christ already accomplished. The second New Testament verse we mentioned before will help confirm this even further. Look at it again, very closely:

> *In Him, you also, after listening to the message of truth, the gospel of your salvation...*

Let's pause there for a moment. Paul is reminding the people of Ephesus of how they first heard the Gospel of their "salvation." At one point, a group of Ephesian pagans and unbelieving Jews had heard *good news* about what Christ had done for them. In other words, they learned they were already included under the apple tree. Paul recalls how they heard this simple message of truth and then he says this:

The Royal Seal

*...having also believed, you were sealed in Him with the
Holy Spirit of promise.*
(Eph. 1:13)

Though they already had salvation in Christ, it still needed to be announced and demonstrated, which is the true purpose of ministry. In the case of the Ephesians, Paul came as an ambassador-servant of God and announced this glorious proposal of love to them. Paul came to them with many blessings from his heavenly Master. This was just like Abraham's servant who came to Rebekah and her family with camels loaded with rich blessings and "a variety of good things" (Gen. 24:10). In Paul's case, he carried and released gifts of healing, demonstrations of mercy, proclamations of truth, and a variety of other good things to the people of Ephesus. Thankfully, many of the people saw these things and accepted his message—just like Rebekah's family did at the coming of Abraham's servant. Then, *having also believed*, the Ephesians were *sealed in Christ with the Holy Spirit of promise.*

All they did was say *yes* to what Paul presented. Faith is not something we can boast in, even slightly. Faith is an awe-filled realization. It is a divine awareness that quickens something within us. There's no work other than to joyfully and wonderfully come alive to what's already been done for us. This is why faith comes simply *by hearing* (Rom. 10:17). A servant of God comes and tells you the beautiful Good News and you become aware of it and gleefully accept it. That's faith! And according to this follow-up letter to the Ephesians, simple faith leads to a person being "sealed" with the Holy Spirit of promise.

This Spirit is the *arrabōn*, or the wedding ring, that a person takes upon themselves. Like a wedding ring, the Spirit guarantees a full and rich life of marital bliss within the family of the Trinity. This is way more than a "pledge" or "down-payment." The Spirit

The Song of the Ages: Part III

of God is the emblem and doorway into tangibly enjoying our union with Christ right here and right now.

That brings us back to the objective and subjective tension we find throughout the Bible. Objectively, the Spirit has been poured out upon all. All have been given the gift of the One who fills and sustains everything everywhere. No living person can utter their next breath without the Spirit's influence in their being. And yet, not all have *received* this glorious gift in a relational way—the subjective way. Not all have been *sealed* with the Spirit of God. As a result, not all have become a true part of the Bride. Some still live in the false identity of a harlot, and bear fruit accordingly.

The word used for "receive" throughout the New Testament helps us understand this even further. It's the word *lambanō* and one of its main definitions is "to take what is one's own."[1] It's to take something that already belongs to you! In view of this, look at this word when it shows up in Romans 5:

> *For if by the transgression of the one, death reigned through the one, much more those who **receive** the abundance of grace and of the gift of righteousness will reign in life through the One, Jesus Christ.*
> *(Rom. 5:17)*

The abundance of grace and the gift of righteousness belongs to all of Jesus's flesh and blood relatives—the entire human race. But it is those who take hold of it who experience its transfiguring truth in their lives. As a result, they return to their original identity as the sons and daughters of God called to reign as kings and queens upon the earth.

---

1. G2983 - lambanō - Strong's Greek Lexicon (NASB). Retrieved from https://www.blueletterbible.org//lang/lexicon/lexicon.cfm?Strongs=G2983&t=NASB

The Royal Seal

But all of this raises a question. Throughout the Shulammite's journey, we've talked a lot about how all people are the beloved children of God and included in Christ's saving work. However, if some people have been sealed with the Spirit and others haven't, can we really say this is true?

We'll answer this very easily by looking at an important event from Jesus's life. This event will open up a much greater understanding of the "seal," including its place in humanity's ultimate destiny.

Jesus and the Spirit

Did you know that Jesus "received the Spirit" as well? After being baptized by His relative John, the heavens were opened and the Spirit of God came upon Him. It was after this experience that the Scriptures say Jesus was "filled with the Spirit" (Lk. 4:1). This was also the moment when Jesus was publicly declared as the beloved Son of the Father (Mk. 1:11). In light of this event, someone could then ask the question: Did Jesus *not* have the Spirit before His baptism?

The answer to this seems easy, but there's a few things to consider. On one hand, Jesus obviously had the Spirit from the moment of His conception. He was God Himself made flesh. Long before this public declaration, Jesus was already the beloved Son of the Father. And yet, the Scriptures explain that the Spirit descended upon Christ and remained in a clear, substantial way. It was this moment that He was "anointed with the Holy Spirit and power" (Acts 10:38). Something real happened between Jesus and the Spirit that hadn't occurred until that point. Jesus was not just going through the motions when He asked John to baptize Him. This was an eternally significant event where Jesus received a divine confirmation of His identity. Yet more than that, it is also where He was empowered to manifest that identity before the world.

The Song of the Ages: Part III

Before His baptism, Jesus had not operated in the fullness of His divine abilities. The reason for this goes back to something explained in Philippians 2, where it talks about Jesus becoming a servant on our behalf. It says there that the Lord "emptied Himself." The orthodox consensus of this passage over the centuries is that Jesus laid aside His divine powers in becoming a man. It doesn't mean He stopped being God. He was still fully God, but He laid aside His "right" to utilize His divine privileges and abilities. (And remember that word "right" because we'll come back to it in a little bit.)

As such, Jesus walked completely as a human being while on earth. He experienced the human life one-hundred percent, including all of its trials and difficulties. However, when He was baptized and filled with the Spirit, Jesus began to manifest the divine side of His identity as a Child of God. He was not *attaining* or *gaining* this divine side—it was simply manifesting. And this manifestation came through the help and power of the Holy Spirit. Through all of this, Jesus demonstrated what each and every human being is called to experience. This is where we'll look more closely at the imagery of a "seal," which will bring everything we've discussed into beautiful harmony.

The Sealing of Christ

A seal was a vital part of people's lives during biblical times. Typically, it was an engraved ring or some other object that could mark an impression into clay, wax, or some other moldable material. A seal played several roles. Its primary purpose was one of authentication. In ancient times, no document was considered valid without the mark of a seal on it. A person's seal could also make purchases or close deals in their name. This is also why it would be used to authenticate letters and messages from people.

The Royal Seal

Consequently, a seal was used to confirm someone's identity and back up purchases, agreements, and communications.

Solomon, the author of the Song, would have been very familiar with seals. The king's seal was a key part of his day-to-day responsibilities. Let's say that Solomon wanted to deliver a message—*a word*—to a certain group of people. He would put this message into a vessel of some kind, a type of ancient envelope. Both the message and the envelope would objectively belong to the king, for the "word" within that envelope came from his own hand. However, people would not take this message seriously until the envelope was marked with the royal seal. It could contain the most important message in the world, but unless it was sealed the message would not get far, especially in the ancient world. Thus, the seal would do two things:

First, it would *confirm* the message truly belonged to King Solomon.

Secondly, the seal would *empower* that envelope with a royal authority.

Because of the seal, people would now take seriously the envelope and its inner contents. Even though it belonged to the king beforehand and carried the essence of his authority, this truth was now validated and outwardly (subjectively) manifested.

Now let's connect all this back to the truths coming out of the symphony of the rising Bride. Christ is the *Word* of God born into the earthly envelope of Jesus of Nazareth. He was always the Word, even from before His birth. Because of this, Jesus already had all the essential power and authority of heaven behind Him. Yet it wasn't until He was baptized and thus "sealed" with the Spirit of God that these realities were outwardly manifested. Thus, two things happened on the day of Jesus's baptism:

First, God *confirmed* that Jesus was indeed His beloved Son, the Word made flesh. When the Voice of God burst forth from

The Song of the Ages: Part III

heaven, saying, "This is My beloved Son in whom I am well-pleased," it was like the royal seal of heaven being placed upon Jesus of Nazareth.

Secondly, Jesus was *empowered*. Being one-hundred percent Man, Jesus was now endowed by heaven with the power to manifest the true glory inside of Him. Beginning with the miracle of turning water into wine and then moving into acts of divine healing, Jesus began to demonstrate the power of God. Again, that power was always latent within Him, but it was not subjectively unleashed until after His baptism and His reception of the Spirit.

Now let's shift the focus back onto humanity. Remember, Jesus didn't *have* to be baptized. He did this to demonstrate something for us. As the book of Hebrews teaches, Jesus came to be a forerunner for His lost brothers and sisters (Heb. 2:10-11 & 6:20). He came to show us the Way, the Truth, and the Life (Jn. 14:6). Human beings had become estranged relatives from God. We were still "little Christs," sons and daughters of the same Father, but we had lost the *way* to this *true* and divine *life*. Thankfully, when a person discovers the good news of their restored union with God—including their forgiveness and redemption—something changes. We come back to the Father's house and to our true selves. When we believe, it is then God's pleasure to release the seal of the Spirit upon the clay vessel of our lives!

You can think of every human being as an envelope—a vessel—that is also filled with the Word of God. Hidden within all people is the mystery of God's image, which is Christ Himself (compare Gen. 1:26 & Heb. 1:3). The redemption of this original Word was accomplished under the apple tree. At the cross, the separating veil between our hearts and the Father was permanently removed. The false identity of sin was conquered and washed away. There at the tree, we saw who we are and Who our true Father is. We were thus given complete access to step back into our original

The Royal Seal

relationship with God as His divine children—the little brothers and sisters of Christ.

And yet, for the thousandth time, love cannot be forced. Relationships are all about love. A person must be willing for this relationship to happen—and it is by hearing the Gospel that people are invited back into this truth. All a person has to do is believe. By believing and receiving, we can then begin to manifest these truths—*through the Spirit*. The seal of the Spirit comes to us and does the same two things for us that it did for Jesus at the Jordan River:

First, the Spirit confirms who we are.

To see this, you can look no further than Romans 8:

> *The Spirit Himself **testifies** with our spirit that we are children of God.*
> *(Rom. 8:16)*

The Spirit testifies that we *are* the children of God. We always were, but the Spirit is the stamp and seal of this reality. He authenticates that we are beloved sons and daughters, and confirms God's love for us deep within our own hearts. As Jesus said to His disciples, "I will not leave you as orphans; I will come to you" (Jn. 14:18). He then spoke of the Spirit who would come and awaken us to the unfailing love of our Abba Father.

But then there is the second element to the Spirit's seal upon a person. It is not just a confirmation of identity; *it is also an empowerment to live according to that identity*. This is explained very clearly by John during the opening words of his gospel:

> *But as many as received Him, to them He gave the right to become children of God, even to those who believe in His name.*
> *(Jn. 1:12)*

The Song of the Ages: Part III

Many have used this verse (and other parts of John's writings) to say that some people are the children of God while others are not. But that is not what John is insinuating. Though some live like children of the devil, that is the false identity of the harlot. The devil can beget no one. Jesus died for lost sons and daughters, not demonic progeny. So when someone *receives* Jesus—when they say *"I do"* to His proposal of grace—they are given the "right" to become who they truly are. The Message Bible does an excellent job with this particular verse. We quoted it earlier in our discussion on the maturing of nations, but it is worth looking at again:

> *But whoever did want him,*
> *who believed he was who he claimed*
> *and would do what he said,*
> *He made to be their true selves,*
> *their child-of-God selves.*
> *(Jn. 1:12 MSG)*

Here is where we come back to that word "right." Throughout the New Testament, this word is more often translated as "authority" or "power." The term shows up particularly in connection to Jesus—but only *after* His baptism! It was after that event that people around Him began to notice the "authority" and "power" on His life (Lk. 4:26). This is because He was now walking in the empowerment of His Father's seal!

This is now the inheritance of every single person. All of us are called to be "empowered" by the Spirit to *become* the children of God in a subjective, manifested way. This is where the gifts and fruit of the Spirit come into play as well. Such things cannot be experienced by our own strength. It is only through the Gospel that we can be empowered like Jesus to manifest the ancient glory hidden inside of us.

The Royal Seal

So let's get our bearings here. We're in the eighth chapter of the Song of Songs and the Beloved is proposing His love to the world. He is calling people, even pleading with them, saying: *"Set Me as a seal on your heart, as a seal on your arm!"* Therein lies the two key things that the Spirit of God does:

The seal comes on the *heart* to confirm that we are the children of God, beloved and treasured.

Then, the Spirit comes upon the *arm*, which represents our strength and ability. This is where the Spirit comes upon us to empower us to walk out our true identity as a little Christ—to do the same things Jesus did, and even greater.

Water and Spirit

This also gets at the reason why there seems to be two separate types of baptisms in Scripture. On the one end, you have the baptism of water, which many would say corresponds to being "baptized in the name of Jesus" (Acts 2:38 & 8:16). Then there is the baptism of the Holy Spirit. This has become a contentious issue over the centuries, with Christians on different sides of the aisle using Scripture to argue whether or not these are two different things. In many sectors of the church, there are those who focus on the differences between the two, using phrases like "the second blessing" to describe a separate baptism of the Spirit. But the other view is that a person receives the Spirit upon their initial faith. For them, only one baptism is necessary.

Obviously, we're significantly overgeneralizing here. There are a lot of details and arguments in between these two points, but we won't be getting into any of that. Humans are very good at complicating things and we're going to steer clear of the religious clutter surrounding this issue. In reality, both sides of the aisle are embracing different parts of the truth. On the one hand, people are correct in saying that we receive the Spirit through our simple

The Song of the Ages: Part III

faith in Christ. When a person believes, they are receiving God Himself. You are breaking apart the Trinity if you say someone can receive Jesus and not the Holy Spirit. The two are eternally undivided. This corresponds with the objective side of the Gospel, which also reminds us that a person has God even before they believe. Faith simply opens their eyes to what (Who) was already theirs!

But then there is the subjective side, which is where things get a little messier. In several accounts of Scripture, there are individuals who clearly experience a separate "filling" of the Holy Spirit after their initial faith in Jesus. The first time this dynamic shows up is with Jesus's own disciples. At first, the disciples "received the Spirit" by the Lord Himself. Jesus breathed upon the disciples and told them to receive the Holy Spirit (Jn. 20:22). But then something different seemed to happen a few weeks later. On the day of Pentecost, the Spirit fell upon each one of them like fire, bringing a divine empowerment to their lives (Acts 2:3-4). And that's far from the only example. Other accounts show people embracing the Gospel and being baptized in water before they actually "receive the Spirit." One of the most glaring instances is from Acts 8, when Phillip went to preach the Gospel in Samaria. The people there received his message with gladness and were baptized in water; yet soon after this, the other apostles heard about what happened and decided to go down to Samaria to pray for them to receive the Holy Spirit. The text says that *"He (the Spirit) had not yet fallen upon any of them; they had simply been baptized in the name of Jesus"* (Acts 8:16). So, they prayed and the people visibly received the Spirit of God into their lives.

Several other accounts in Acts give us more detail as to what this reception of the Spirit looked like. Usually it involved supernatural manifestations and outward signs such as "speaking in tongues" and "prophesying" (see Acts 10:44-46 & 19:6). Sometimes this

The Royal Seal

occurs right at the very moment a person believes when at other times it happens at a clearly separate point from their first embrace of the Gospel. But again, this is not always as clean and clear-cut as some would like it to be. There are instances in Acts where people experienced an outward manifestation of the Spirit *before* they get baptized in water and make their official *"I do"* to Jesus (Acts 10:44-48). In that case, it seems some people get their "second blessing" first!

Then you have to consider something else. There are other accounts where the Spirit comes and fills an *already filled* group of disciples (see Acts 4:31 & 13:52). What do you do with that? Perhaps this is reminding us of other Scriptures that suggest we are to be *continually* filled with the Spirit (Eph. 5:18). It seems then we may not be talking about a one-time thing or a second-time thing. Rather, it may be that God wants to keep confirming our identity and giving us an ongoing empowerment to live it out!

Of course, receiving this empowering gift has to start somewhere, and that is where we come back to Jesus Himself who was our great forerunner and example. As the Child of God, Jesus of Nazareth took hold of all that was already His. There in the Jordan River, Jesus received both the baptism of water and Spirit, an experience that culminated with these joyous words: "This is My beloved Son, in whom I am well-pleased!" Jesus received a gift from His Father, which was one single seal of love.

Accordingly, the Beloved in the Song of Songs doesn't tell us to set His *seals* upon our heart and arm. There is one wedding ring—one Holy Spirit—whom we receive freely as a gift from the Father when we say *"I do"* to His love. Yet this single gift carries a *twofold purpose*. In touching both the "heart" and the "arm," it awakens us to love on the inside and releases us into power on the outside. Like Jesus and the disciples who followed Him, this empowerment comes so that we would be supernatural witnesses of this heart-changing Gospel.

Wild Wind

The problem is that man has consistently tried to put God in a box by affixing rules and laws as to how His Spirit works. But this is like establishing a single code for how the wind blows. Jesus reminded us of the foolishness of such a perspective. The wind moves as it pleases (Jn. 3:8). God can move upon the world however He chooses. Certainly, there are key laws of nature guiding the movement of the wind—so too, there is a key law behind the Spirit's movement throughout the world. According to Galatians, this law is very simple: it is the law of faith in what Christ accomplished at the cross (Gal. 3:1-5). But exactly *how* the wind moves from this springboard of grace will change from person to person, and even season to season.

Sadly, the church has too often built up walls of division that keep people from understanding what Paul originally spoke to the Ephesians—*the message of truth, the good news of our salvation*. As a result, there have been misguided teachings stating that if someone doesn't get baptized or speak in tongues then they are not saved—or that they don't really have the Holy Spirit in their lives. In reality, a lack of certain "signs" doesn't mean a person lacks the Holy Spirit. They may not have unwrapped all the blessings the Father has prepared for them, but that doesn't mean the Spirit of Christ is not with them.

In the same way, the physical act of baptism is not what saves a person. Jesus *saved us* under the apple tree. This is a finished work, once and for all. Going into water doesn't somehow accomplish salvation, as though Jesus cries out again and again "it is finished" after every new believer gets dunked in a baptismal tank. Going into the water is simply our embrace of our co-crucifixion with

The Royal Seal

Christ. Coming up from the water is then our personal step into a life of co-resurrection. But upon believing, it is the Spirit who comes to make all of this real and subjective in our lives. Through His influence, a person washes the robes of their old name and takes on the new and true name of the Triune God.

Teachings that exclude people from who they already are and what Christ has already done for them arise from an orphan mentality. They come from the mindset of a people stranded in the wilderness and unable to see the glad face of their Father. They can't see the One who would give everything He has to rescue His kids. Such a Father is not standing on the porch waiting to see if His children dunk their heads in water or pick up an angelic dialect before He determines to let them in the house or not. This is a Father who is standing on tiptoe waiting and watching for the slightest opening of the heart. And better yet, this is a Father who has already come into our mess and died our death for us in the person of Christ.

But please understand something else. This is not meant to minimize the absolute significance of baptism. When Jesus released His disciples into the Great Commission—the global calling to bring humanity back to their Triune family—He made baptism a central part of the journey. Baptism is very much like putting a wedding ring on the finger to demonstrate your acceptance of God's love. If someone believes in Jesus but refuses baptism, it's like a person saying *"I do"* to their spouse and then refusing to wear their wedding ring publicly. They may be legally married, but that missing ring raises serious questions as to where their heart lies.

In addition to this, a full encounter with the Holy Spirit is crucial. When a person gives their simple *"I do,"* there is a wonderful gift of supernatural empowerment made available to them. The apostles were very passionate about people receiving this part of the seal with its impact on the *arm*. They would travel miles into uncomfortable territory like Samaria to make sure this part of the gift was received. Essentially, they wanted to make sure the wedding ring was shining bright enough for the whole world to see.

Unfortunately, the desert has not been kind to our understanding of the waters of salvation. Right from her birth in the book of Acts, the church went back into the wilderness and, with a parched throat, preached a Gospel filled with the waterless notes of separation and lack. She established outward rituals and prayers as requirements for entrance into membership within Christ's body, denying the very "mystery" that all nations are already hidden within that very body (Eph. 3:6). Yet despite the fact that man has continued to focus on the exterior, God continues to look within. He looks at the image of Christ still buried within all people, and He waits patiently for hearts to awaken to this magnificent truth. When that happens, a confirming surge of power is given to help them walk in that reality.

A Transformed Message

In the end, people really only "lack" one thing, which is the same thing the Shulammite lacked in the very beginning of her journey. It's "the lack of knowledge" Hosea and other prophets warned about. This is the lack of *knowing* and trusting the Father's love, revealed most clearly at the cross. It's a knowing that goes beyond the mind into the depths of your being. To use the biblical vernacular, it's akin to *knowing* one's spouse. This lack of knowledge is serious, for the prophet said, "My people *are destroyed* for lack of knowledge" (Hos. 4:6). The prodigal son may have been a beloved child with a mighty estate waiting to be restored to him; however, if he stayed in a foreign land there was only famine and death to be experienced. (And that death would be his own doing, not His Father's.)

The Royal Seal

It is because of this global lack the Father sent His only begotten Son into the world. God gave us the kiss of His Son so that we would not perish, but rather walk once more in the ways of Eden. Therefore, the joy and severity of the Gospel remains. All people are children of God, loved by the Father and given the Spirit in a hidden way. Because of this, Eden is already hiding within the ground of humanity. *Yet it only breaks through the soil by faith*. When that *"I do"* comes, people receive what is already theirs and heaven manifests on earth a little bit more.

Such is the call of the Gospel rising from the east. As the church comes up from the wilderness leaning on her Beloved, we can expect her message to triumphantly transform. It's not that the Gospel will change, but that her appreciation and understanding of it will deepen. Her message as an ambassador and servant of the King will not carry any of the previous notes of fear, lack, or ritual. Rather, it will carry the purest harmonies of love and power. This pure Gospel of Christ's finished work and the Father's love will not lead to apathy or passivity. Rather, when truly understood, it will compel people into a greater passion and a stronger witness than any other message can produce. Messengers of this Gospel will not hold forth a shallow, lackadaisical word about love that is devoid of fire and zeal. This is a love that will lead us to plead, even to beg our lost brothers and sisters to come home—even if that means some of us who carry the message must go down the path of martyrdom. For true love is as strong as death, as we'll see soon enough.

But before we go there, there is one more element of the Spirit's seal we have yet to uncover.

17
Ring Within a Ring

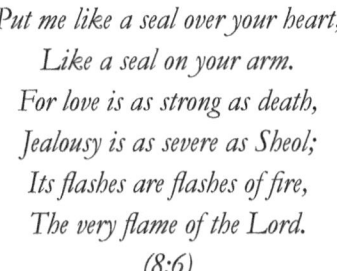

Put me like a seal over your heart,
Like a seal on your arm.
For love is as strong as death,
Jealousy is as severe as Sheol;
Its flashes are flashes of fire,
The very flame of the Lord.
(8:6)

There's a word that carries one of the most remarkable and yet least understood aspects of the Holy Spirit's work on planet earth. It's found in the opening of Ephesians where Paul expresses a divine plan laid out from the beginning of time. The details of this plan so burned in the heart of God that it erupted out of His mouth like a fire from the chest, forging the first burning atoms of creation. The elements were then weighed out, arranged, and coordinated according to the end purpose of this plan. Paul explains it as follows:

> *He chose us in Him before the foundation of the world, that we would be holy and blameless before Him. In love He*

The Song of the Ages: Part III

*predestined us to **adoption** as sons through Jesus Christ to Himself, according to the kind intention of His will.*
(Eph. 1:4-5)

Before time, God *pre-destined* something—a reality that could be summed up by the word "adoption." Understanding this term is vital. Besides explaining our own destiny, this will also complete the revelation of the Song's eternal seal. For the Scriptures tell us that when a person receives the seal of the Spirit, they are also receiving "a Spirit of adoption." The ideas are one in the same.

Today, most people read the word adoption and think of the legal process whereby a child is placed in a family that is not of their biological origin. This is a beautiful thing and perhaps one of the best expressions of love found in the world. However, it does not convey the deepest meaning behind this ancient terminology. Paul is using a common Greek word here that often meant something very different to the people of his day. It is the word *huiothesia* and it described something that happened to a young boy who already had a family.

A Rite of Passage

In order to unpack this word, let's look at one of the other key verses that introduces us to this concept:

> *For all who are being led by the Spirit of God, these are sons of God. For you have not received a spirit of slavery leading to fear again, but you have received **a spirit of adoption** as sons by which we cry out, "Abba! Father!"*
> *(Rom. 8:14-15)*

Paul is writing to the heart of the Roman Empire. As such, he's using a phrase that would have meant something very specific in the mind of a Roman. In that culture, there was a particular path laid

Ring Within a Ring

out for young boys when they were ready to enter into manhood. This was determined by their father and typically happened around the age of fourteen. A boy would undergo a formal ceremony involving other adult males from his family, during which he would remove the toga he wore throughout his entire childhood. In its place, he would be given a new, larger, and more expensive toga—the *toga virilis*. "The toga of a man." After being clothed with this new garment, the young man would be publicly acknowledged as an adult son in his household and then given new privileges. He was now allowed to marry, conduct business in his own name, and was given the right to join the local assembly and vote. This was the moment of *huiothesia,* or "adoption," as our English translators put it.

The ancient world was filled with many such rites of passage. For the most part, these pathways into adulthood have been stripped away from our modern world. The awkward in-between phase from child to adult now known as "the teenage years" is a very recent idea. For a vast portion of the world's history, teenagers were simply considered adults. Their transition into adulthood was a serious thing, marked with ceremonies and tasks that created a powerful and affirming experience for a child. Through this process, the boy would be *confirmed* as a mature son and *empowered* with certain rights and privileges that come with that title.[2]

The Roman concept is not far from the modern Bar Mitzvah, a Jewish ceremony where a twelve-year-old boy is acknowledged as a "son of the Torah." This dates back to older Hebraic rites of passage where young boys would be recognized as a man in front of their community. They would then begin to be more involved with their father's trade, taking the first steps toward eventually

---

2. Harrill, J. (2002). Coming of Age and Putting on Christ: The Toga Virilis Ceremony, Its Paraenesis, and Paul's Interpretation of Baptism in Galatians. *Novum Testamentum, 44*(3), 252-277.

taking it over. Hence you have Jesus in the temple at twelve-years-old telling Mary and Joseph He needed to be about *His Father's business* (Lk. 2:49).

While the modern process of adoption can be applied to the word *huiothesia* as well, the context of Paul's use of this word would suggest something much different in the minds of his readers. Paul was not writing about how we become God's kids through a legal process. Rather, he was speaking about how we rise up into the full stature of spiritual adulthood. This becomes even clearer when you read how he used this term in a letter sent to a different region of the Roman Empire:

> *Now I say, as long as the heir is a child, he does not differ at all from a slave although he is owner of everything, but he is under guardians and managers until the date set by the father. So also we, while we were children, were held in bondage under the elemental things of the world.*
> *(Gal. 4:1-3)*

Paul is talking about life before Christ. He says that before the revelation of grace, we were like "children." The word here is *nēpios*. Remember this word, for it will reveal many decisive things before our journey is over. This word was used in reference to infants and minors. Thus, before the coming of grace, we still belonged to God but were in a type of spiritual infancy. This is what we started to unpack at the beginning of this volume.

Since we were like infants and minors who can seriously hurt themselves without external boundaries in place, we were placed under the guardianship of the law to protect us during this season of immaturity. This protection, however, became a type of slavery in and of itself, for it says we were "held in bondage." In this way, we were no different from ancient slaves on a rich estate who had no access to the owner's inheritance, even though in reality we

Ring Within a Ring

owned everything in our Father's Kingdom. But this was not the end of our story. All of it was leading toward that magnificent destiny—*huiothesia*.

> *But when the fullness of the time came, God sent forth His Son, born of a woman, born under the Law, so that He might redeem those who were under the Law,* ***that we might receive the adoption as sons.*** *Because you are sons, God has sent forth the Spirit of His Son into our hearts, crying, "Abba! Father!" Therefore you are no longer a slave, but a son; and if a son, then an heir through God.*
> (Gal. 4:4-7)

The destiny of man was never to stay as *nēpios*—spiritual children—but to become mature sons reflecting the full image of our Creator. This is the process Paul is explaining in Galatians whereby a son finally gains access to what had always belonged to him yet was out of his physical, emotional, and spiritual reach. He's explaining that this is exactly what happens in salvation when the Spirit comes upon a person and stamps their heart like a seal. However, he notes something very important. *Because you are sons, God has sent forth the Spirit of His Son into our hearts.* Once again, the Spirit confirms what was already there. We were always sons, but we needed to be empowered to rise up and walk in the full stature of that identity, including all the rights that come with it. This again points to the seal upon the heart and arm. An earlier edition of the New International Version translates this verse accordingly:

> *...to redeem those under the law, that we might* ***receive the full rights of sons.***
> (Gal. 4:5 NIV 1984)

The Song of the Ages: Part III

Obviously, this is not speaking of a modern adoption. People do not become God's kids through a legal process. Such conclusions are the fruit of a legalized Gospel that strips away the true identity of humanity. Salvation is simply a person embracing who they truly are as God's child. In that embrace, they are marked and clothed with a new *toga*—a robe of spiritual adulthood woven together in the fires of love. This garment is the very Spirit of Christ. Before God breathed forth the elementary atoms that would one day clothe our physical bodies, this was the true clothing we were destined to wear. It goes hand in hand with the royal seal.

And not only does this confirm and empower us—this clothing and seal also gives us access into a crucial part of our destiny as the mature and *adopted* children of God.

Legislative Assembly

In Roman culture, when a young man received his adult toga, one of the immediate privileges he gained was access into the local assembly. This was a legislative gathering where men would cast votes and influence larger community matters. This element of Roman adoption is another connection to the seal of the Spirit, for when a person is baptized and receives the Spirit, they become part of a legislative assembly as well. This assembly is known as the *ekklesia*.

Another radically misunderstood Greek term, *ekklesia* is where we get the word "church." Today this is thought of in religious terms, but Jesus borrowed this word from secular culture when He first used it in Matthew 16. In His day, this referred to a type of legislative body that made important decisions for the community. It's often been translated as "called out ones," but it needs to be understood in its legislative context. The people who formed these ancient assemblies were *called* to go *out* to the city gates to render decisions and provide wisdom for their fellow community members. They were not called to be separate from the community,

Ring Within a Ring

but rather to be specially positioned to influence society toward a wiser and healthier way of life.

In the same way, the awakened child of God is still a member of the human race. In fact, they are now a truer member. Like Jesus, they are demonstrating what humanity was always supposed to look like. With this, they are called to spiritually "legislate" the Kingdom of our Father upon earth, guiding humanity toward greater health and more abundant life. Earlier we pointed out how we are called to take what's already ours, and that by receiving this abundance of grace we will *reign in life*. This "reigning" is beyond the territory of our own personal lives. Whether we realize it or not, our baptism into Christ is a baptism into kingship. This puts a whole new spin on joining the church! Through word and deed, every saint is now invited to enact the policies of heaven on earth. This is also what comes with our adoption into sonship.

Naturally, this speaks of a different kind of reign than man's *nēpios* ways of leadership. And so, when Jesus came to earth, He revealed not only what a true child of God looks like, but also what a true king looks like. As the "firstborn of many brethren," Jesus modeled the mature leadership man was destined to walk in from the beginning (Rom. 8:29). He showed us the *toga virilis* in action. It would do us well to look a little closer at how He wore this clothing, for each of us are destined to get quite comfortable in the same attire.

Difficult Words

After His resurrection, Jesus declared that all authority in heaven and on earth had been given to Him (Matt. 28:18). In order to appreciate and learn from the way Jesus utilized this authority, let's first think about what *He didn't do* with it. The first thing to recognize is His avoidance of any opportunity to sit on an earthly throne. This is something He could have easily done right after walking out of the garden tomb.

The Song of the Ages: Part III

Imagine something for a moment. Picture Jesus meeting up with Mary Magdalene for the first time. After the shock of that initial encounter, let's say that Jesus told her to gather the disciples and bring them back to the garden instead of telling them to wait in Galilee. This would seem like an appropriate place to start. He could have gathered them together right then and there to go out and "subdue the earth." Imagine then, Jesus and His small band of disciples marching back to Pontius Pilate's praetorium. The look on Pilate's face would have been priceless. Perhaps after getting slapped by his wife with a good *I told you so* (see Matt. 27:19), Pilate might have apologized to Jesus. He might have even bowed his knee to Him. However, judging by his heart three days earlier, there's a good chance Pilate's apology wouldn't have had a lot of depth to it. Remember, Jesus said on one occasion that even if someone were to rise from the dead, there would still be those who do not repent (Lk. 16:31).

Pilate was a man deeply concerned about his seat of power and would see a new opportunity before his eyes—a new Caesar to serve. To make up for his mistake, Pilate might have ordered some of his soldiers to go and displace the obviously inept high priest of Israel. Caiaphas would be out of power and Jesus would be offered his position as the true "teacher of Israel." Then let's say that Pilate sent more soldiers to challenge Herod's seat as well. In a couple of days, Jesus could have been made both the physical High Priest and King of the nation. This could have all been done with time to spare before Jews from all over the world gathered at the upcoming feast of Pentecost. When the big day finally arrived, people from the surrounding nations would meet this death-conquering leader of the Jews. And from there it wouldn't have taken long for Rome to get involved.

At this point, boundless possibilities exist. There may have been a split amongst soldiers loyal to Jesus and those loyal to Caesar. Factions

Ring Within a Ring

would quickly form. Amongst those who followed Christ, some would do so out of love, but many would Him follow out of fear or for the desire for power. And there would definitely be those who wouldn't follow Him at all. In light of that, war would erupt in one way or another. There would be those who would try to physically attack Jesus. If He didn't fight back, He might have had to keep dying and resurrecting. Or perhaps He'd just walk through their swords like He walked through walls. If He did fight back, Jesus would have to explain to His disciples why He was not doing the things He had just told them to do—such as turning the other cheek. Remember, a disciple is supposed to be like his rabbi. That teaching would go right out the window if Jesus took up the physical sword. (Unfortunately, many "disciples" today are still waiting for their Rabbi to renege on this command when He physically returns to earth.)

We'll stop the thought experiment there. We simply don't know how things would have gone down if Jesus didn't ascend to heaven forty days after His resurrection. These are just some educated guesses based on the way of the world, and particularly how people treated the Lord before His crucifixion. In reality, it's not that important to know how things would have unfolded. What's important to know is why Jesus avoided all of this in the first place. This leads us then to the statement Jesus made to His disciples on the night before His crucifixion:

> *But I tell you the truth, it is to your advantage that I go away...*
> *(Jn. 16:7a)*

These words are perplexing at best and infuriating at worst. Why in the world was it to our advantage that Jesus left? Think of all the pain, corruption, and unbelief He could have stood against if He stuck around. Most of us who are steeped in Bible knowledge are quick to jump to Jesus's next statement about the Holy Spirit; but

The Song of the Ages: Part III

this is often done in a way that minimizes the real pain in the heart of the disciples, whether it's the eleven in that room or the millions who have asked similar questions throughout the centuries.

Let's just stay in the difficulty of this statement for a moment. How has the past 2000 years been to our advantage? Consider all the terrible evil and suffering that has taken place since Jesus left the earth. Think of things like the dark ages, the inquisitions, cancer, the holocaust. How many of these circumstances and events could have been altered if He physically remained with us? And furthermore, why couldn't the Holy Spirit just come to us while Jesus remained on the planet? The Holy Spirit was certainly active while He physically walked the earth. And of course, when Jesus does come back, the Holy Spirit isn't going to leave to make room for Him.

If we're honest with ourselves, this is a profoundly difficult statement the Lord made. Yet the fact remains that He said it. He told us His physical departure was for our good—and He never lies. Understanding the reason and intention of His heart then is absolutely vital. The answer certainly has to do with the seal of the Holy Spirit, but this goes much deeper than we can imagine. It is an answer that will bring us from the wilderness to the apple tree to the *toga virilis*. It will also take us from the first fiery atoms of creation spouted from the mouth of God to the last apocalyptic blast of flame destined to consume everything around us. Let us look then a little bit further into these things…

The Helper

> *…for if I do not go away, the Helper will not come to you.*
> *(Jn. 16:7b)*

Jesus gives His reason for leaving with these simple words. He talks about a Helper, which is the Greek word *paràklētos*, defined as "one called alongside to help." Though sometimes translated

Ring Within a Ring

as Comforter or Advocate, the word "Helper" is very fitting and has a lot of weight and history behind it. To fully appreciate the word—and to see where it coincides with the fires of Solomon's Song—we must go back to the beginning of the Word, again.

We saw earlier that when Adam came out of his death-like sleep under the trees of Eden, he woke up to love and this love became his "helper" (Gen. 2:18). But before we look at the connections between the Helper of the New Testament and the helper in the Garden, we first need to see what happened right before Eve's arrival. Before his love awakening, Adam was engaged in a monumental assignment given to him by the Lord—the naming of the animals. This task held a purpose that went way beyond creative nomenclature. God was teaching Adam something of immeasurable importance here. He does this with all of us. As we're led through different assignments and experiences, God is always unfolding deeper realities beyond the surface of what we're immediately experiencing.

As Adam went about this work, he would have quickly noticed how each animal had its own counterpart. If he was spending any significant amount of time observing these different creatures, it would not take long to see the strange things these counterparts would do with each other. Adam would behold an act that led to the female of the pair growing a belly and producing a new animal on the inside. As he beheld the marvels of multiplication, a stark realization would come into Adam's heart. He would recognize that while he could bestow the identity of a name to an animal, Adam could not multiply or reproduce that identity. Such a thing could only happen if two of those creatures came together in an act of physical union.

As the first man walked with God and looked at this strange dance of creatures, he might have also looked down and discovered that his own "parts" were made to connect with something else—or

The Song of the Ages: Part III

someone else. It would be like walking around your whole life with a strange piece of jagged cardboard inside one of your pockets, to one day realize it was actually a puzzle piece, and that all along there was a much bigger picture to discover—one that you get to play a role in creating. There was indeed someone else for Adam to connect to, both biologically and spiritually. So, as he surveyed the multitudes of creatures walking about Eden, this issue would deepen. Intense longings would be stirred within his physical being (especially if his reproductive system was already in working order). Throw in the emotional longings for companionship, and you have quite a combination of intensifying desire. A passionate fire would have been kindling within the deepest places of Adam's heart.

Stunningly, as these desires grew inside of his chest, the very thing he longed for was hidden in that same spot! Adam's true desire would end up coming from one of the ribs protecting his heart. Many believe Adam was created with an extra rib and that it was from this additional piece of bone that Eve was fashioned. Perhaps over time this extra rib had grown physically uncomfortable within his chest. Maybe it pressed against tissue and muscle and caused a literal pain in his body that matched the painful desires growing in his soul. This is all conjecture based upon a literal interpretation of the text, but it points to something much richer in the story. There was a growing and pressing desire building right in the midst of Adam's chest.

We don't know how long it was that Adam walked with God before this desire manifested. Maybe it matched the time the disciples walked with Jesus through the Promised Land of Israel—*when He was preparing them for their Helper*. Perhaps Adam walked with the Creator for three-and-a-half years through the Promised Land of Eden, unlocking identity within the animal kingdom. Whatever the timeframe was, we know that before Eve came forth Adam walked with God in the Garden of *Eden*. Now the Scriptures tell

Ring Within a Ring

us, "Delight yourself in the Lord and He will give you the desires of your heart" (Ps. 37:4). Incredibly, the Hebrew name Eden means "delight." Think about that. Adam was walking in the Garden of *Delight*. He was literally delighting himself in the Lord and soon enough the desires within his chest were released!

The manifestation of this desire was certainly beyond what Adam could have imagined. Before Eve came about, his only frame of reference for companionship were things like giraffes and bugs. His best hope for a friend was perhaps something a little less hairy or smelly than the creatures he was observing. Regardless, Adam had no clue as to the fullness of what God was planning in this quest for a helper. Adam's eye had not seen, nor his ear heard, nor his mind imagined what God had been preparing along the way (1 Cor. 2:9). But one fine day, he awoke under the trees and beheld one who would not only fulfill the physical longings within him, but the emotional and spiritual ones as well. In a moment of prehistoric surgery, God brought forth a companion out of Adam's own triune being of body, soul, and spirit. This companion was made in Adam's own image and likeness and yet carried a unique and undefiled beauty. This was someone with whom he could share his dreams and hopes. Indeed, she was one with whom he could share his entire life. Such a person would be both a friend and a lover, bringing an intimacy to Adam that no other creature in all of the Garden could provide.

Triune Longings

This brings us back to the great plan of heaven, the royal seal of *huiothesia* that gave way to the elements of creation. For just as it was not good for man to be alone, so it was for the Son of Man. In a similar fashion to Adam, there were deep desires for intimacy burning within the heart of Christ before time and space came forth. Now this is not to insinuate Christ's fellowship within the

The Song of the Ages: Part III

Trinity was empty or lacking, or that Jesus was melancholy and lonely. Rather, the nature of divine Love is such that it carried an intense desire to multiply and expand. Growing within the eternal chambers of Christ's heart was the longing for unique companionship. And in a display of Their perfect union, this longing within Christ coincided with a similar desire churning in the heart of His Father. For within the Father was a desire for multiplied sons and daughters, children who would grow up into *huiothesia*—adoption—and reign at the Trinity's side. Both these desires collided and birthed the explosive plan that set into motion an extremely vast and specific design called the universe—the womb for which "life" would emerge.

So herein lies the mystery of creation. The Father and Son were walking together in the eternal garden of Their fellowship in the Spirit. In the place of intimacy, They joined Their desires in ecstatic union and out came an eruption of creative power. Human sexuality, as an act of creation, is a living metaphor for this original act. The seed (*sperma* in the Greek) of the Word was released through the union of passionate Love within the Trinity. In the midst of Their eternal pleasure, the seed of life came forth and the dream began to grow. Like bone and flesh being extracted from Adam, the Triune God brought a three-dimensional universe out of Their side. This was then bent and molded in such a way that life could come out of it. Though this life would be frail—an intricate carbon-based jar of clay—it would somehow become host to the divine vision. It would lead to the emergence of creatures who would fulfill the burning desires within the Father and Son. For God the Father, this would look like mature sons and daughters who would inherit His Kingdom. For God the Son, this would be an eternal lover and friend.

Ring Within a Ring

Therefore, God the Father dreamed up children who could inherit a ring of sonship. For God the Son this would be a ring of marriage.

The ring itself was God the Holy Spirit.

Holy Spirit is the living bond between the Father and the Son. In creating us, the Father, Son, and Spirit were simply expanding Their circle. They were adding another into Their fellowship.

All this brings us back to Jesus's words to His disciples on the night of His arrest—that it was to our advantage He leave. Hopefully, the bigger picture is coming into focus here. Humankind was made for something so much grander and more glorious than we could have possibly imagined. It was certainly more than the disciples envisioned. The disciples would have been content with Jesus remaining on earth and taking His seat upon an earthly throne. Even after forty days of teaching about the true Kingdom, the disciples still remained clueless, evidenced by their question in Acts 1: "Lord, is it at this time You are restoring the Kingdom to Israel?" Like the crowds that followed Him earlier on, the disciples wanted Jesus to sit on a literal throne of government and administer a new type of law and order throughout the land. And evidently, they wanted the nation of Israel to be the supreme center of this new empire.

But Jesus had a vision that went back to the fires that forged the first stars. This vision involved a much different throne, one that Christ and His Father had always intended to sit upon.

The True Throne

As usual, there is something within God's creation that will help us understand this particular aspect of His purposes. Indeed, there's a powerful connection between human anatomy and what's revealed in Scripture about the throne of God—specifically, the anatomy of the human heart. This all-important organ is essentially

The Song of the Ages: Part III

a muscular pump that releases a steady stream of blood from its chambers. If you were to look into a person's chest, zooming in extremely close on the heart and seeing through its valves, you would find this stream is like a literal river of blood going out into the body. If you were to zoom closer, you would see this river carries oxygen—the substance behind our *breath*. Traveling through the circulatory system, this coursing stream brings vitality and empowerment to every other organ in the body. It is literally a river of life.

Amazingly, when the Scriptures reveal the throne of God, we see a river of life proceeding out from it:

> *Then he showed me a river of the water of life, clear as crystal, coming from the throne of God and of the Lamb.*
> *(Rev. 22:1)*

Remember, Scripture teaches that *life is in the blood*. John, the one who received this vision of water coming from the throne, is the same person who saw a stream of water and blood coming from Jesus's side. As such, this "river of the water of life" can also be seen as a river of blood coming from the throne. As the vision progresses, John remarks that this river goes out into the city of the New Jerusalem. In its watering paths, the river breaks the curse and brings health and vitality to the entire area. Now we know that this city is the Bride of Christ. That means the city is also *the Body of Christ*. So, just as the human heart produces a river of life-giving blood for the body, so does the throne of God in Revelation! This tells us the human heart was designed to mirror the throne of God. And indeed, the true throne of the Creator is the human heart. This is where He always intended to sit down and reign (see Eph. 3:17 & Col. 3:15).

But there is one more connection between the human frame and the mystery of God's Kingdom we have to explore. Surrounding

Ring Within a Ring

the physical heart is something of great importance—the ribcage. Everyone, going all way back to Adam, has two sets of ribs, both of which are bowed around the heart. Incredibly, each set is supposed to be comprised of twelve ribs. This means our entire ribcage is made up of 24 ribs *bowing* around the heart. When you go to the book of Revelation and look again at the throne of God, you discover that it too is surrounded by the number 24. Surrounding the throne are 24 elders, each of which are bowing before it!

Around the throne were twenty-four thrones; and upon the thrones I saw twenty-four elders sitting, clothed in white garments, and golden crowns on their heads.
(Rev. 4:4)

This is not a coincidence. This is the careful crafting of God's design with a message of eternal substance. Before the fiery birth of the universe, the Trinity dreamed up a holy jar of clay that would host Their presence and become Their true dwelling place. Within all the wonders of creation, the seat of God's authority would lie within this tiny jar in the place of its physical and spiritual command center—the heart. This is why Jesus said *the Kingdom is within*. Accordingly, when the apostle John went through an open door in Revelation 4 and beheld God's throne, he was actually going into an internal Kingdom.

After these things I looked, and behold, a door standing open in heaven...
(Rev. 4:1)

John was going through the door of communion with the indwelling Christ. This was the same door Christ knocked upon only a few verses earlier, when He wanted to come in and dine with His church. It is the door of the heart!

The Song of the Ages: Part III

Behold, I stand at the door and knock; if anyone hears My voice and opens the door, I will come in to him and will dine with him, and he with Me.
(Rev. 3:20)

But to gather up all the revelation we're uncovering in this chapter, we now want to focus in on those 24 elders. These are the ones who metaphorically connect to the human ribcage and thus bring us back to the mystery of Eve. Thus, they help unveil the true meaning of the Helper—and of Solomon's fiery seal. Hopefully, you haven't lost track of where we are in our journey with the Shulammite. This will all come together with ordered beauty as we look even closer at these 24 individuals.

First of all, it's very probable that the elders of Revelation are not literal people. If they are, they speak to something much bigger than themselves. They are part of John's visionary encounter, something we've amply studied through its many parallels to the Shulammite's travels. Just as the seven-headed dragon is not a literal creature, nor are the stars in Jesus's right hand actual balls of fire, the same can be said of the literal nature of these crowned men.

One piece of evidence for this is the symbolic importance of their number. In his writing, John mentions the twelve tribes of Israel (Rev. 7). Later on, he brings up the twelve apostles of the Lamb (Rev. 21:14). The number 24 brings both of these realities together—like two sets of twelve ribs joined together as one. It is speaking of Israel and the church—Jew and Gentile—coming together as *one new man*. Thus, the 24 elders would represent the same thing as the *New* Jerusalem. They speak to the entire Body of Christ; a Body surrounding the beating heart of the enthroned Lamb—the One who is constantly releasing life through the breath of His Spirit!

When John writes that these elders were "around the throne," the word for "around" comes from the Greek term *kyklō*. This is

Ring Within a Ring

where we get the words "cycle" or "circle." This imagery connects with a similar vision of the throne given to the prophet Ezekiel. In his encounter, Ezekiel looked at the enthroned God and said he saw "a wheel within a wheel" (Ez. 1:16). In John's vision, the 24 elders would create this exact image because they formed a circle around a throne that already had a circle around it—a halo of light (see Rev. 4:3).

For both Ezekiel and John, God was giving prophetic images pointing to the greater dream hidden within His heart. Fittingly, the word *kyklō* can also be used for "ring." And so, we see how all of this comes together in the unity of the Holy Spirit's seal! As Jew and Gentile come together in a unified, covenantal circle around the slain Lamb, we find the vision of the Trinity being fulfilled. As a result, the 24 elders represent the fully mature children of God. The word "elder" can be plainly defined as someone advanced in years—which then connects us back to that remarkable term *huiothesia*. These are the mature sons of the Father who are also the radiant bride of Christ, united in the Spirit of God.

Still, the connection to the human ribcage goes even deeper. John sees these 24 elders sitting on their own magnificent thrones, and yet all of them fall down and bow before the one throne of God. They also cast their golden crowns before that same throne. This here is a picture of the "ribs" of humanity returning to their Maker. If you think about it, this is what happened with Eve and Adam. Eve was taken from Adam's ribcage and fashioned into a distinct and separate individual; but afterward she was called to return to Adam as his wife. In this return, she was made one flesh with him again. In the same way, man was taken out of God and made into a distinct and glorious creation. Great authority (represented by crowns and thrones) was given to mankind. Yet the invitation of the Gospel is to submit our crowning glory to the glory of the Lamb. This means we are return to our origin in the beating chest of God. Yes, each of us are a rib from God called to come back to His heart.

The Dream Fulfilled

There's one last parallel between Christ and Adam that shines further light on what we're seeing here. When Jesus awoke in a garden from His own sleep of death, the first person He beheld, like Adam, was a woman. The first human being Jesus saw was Mary Magdalene. Just as Eve became Adam's helper in Eden, so did this precious disciple of Jesus right outside the garden tomb. Mary became the first evangelist, the one sent to tell the rest of the disciples the wonderful news of Jesus's resurrection (Jn. 20:10-18). In this act, Mary was essentially carrying the seed of Jesus's Word to others. Like a wife bearing her husband's seed, she would be the first to multiply the good news of His finished work. This was the beginning of Jesus's own *helper* coming forth, which would multiply into John, Peter, and countless others.

The gospel of Luke tells us that Mary of Magdala was delivered from seven demons. In the footnotes of The Passion Translation, Dr. Brian Simmons points out the following: "The number seven means completeness. Mary was completely possessed by demons, but Jesus restored her true self and cast out her demons." Mary demonstrated what all creation is predestined and called to embrace. We are *all* divine ribs invited to return to our Creator and Source. A rib has no meaning nor does its marrow have any vitality apart from the body. It is like a branch on a vine. If we as individual ribs do not abide in God, we will not experience true life. Mary was someone who had returned as a rib to her Maker. She bowed before the Lord and surrendered to His Word, and her meaninglessness and darkness was turned into transfiguring light. This was the beginning of the *ekklesia*, the fulfillment of everything Eve pointed to, and the great dream burning in God's heart.

Ring Within a Ring

So again, this all explains why Jesus's physical departure was necessary and vital. The Lord said He had leave in order for *the Helper* to come forth. It turns out this statement was as much for Him as it was for us! You see, the Lord is our Helper and we are His. *We are our Beloved's and He is ours!* Jesus left so that the true Eve—the Father's sons and Jesus's bride—could come forth in the great seal of the Spirit's love!

The world did not understand this hidden purpose in the heart of God. People were (and still are) looking for a completely different kind of kingdom. Well before his "Revelation," even the apostle John wanted to know who would have secondary power in the Kingdom (Mk. 10:37). But this question was met with one of Jesus's most important teachings as He flipped the idea of authority upside down and unveiled the reality of divine servanthood. While the world wanted Jesus to establish a pyramid-like system of control, God wanted a ring-like circle of love—a true uniting bond of peace. This would ultimately look like "elders" from all nations reigning in spiritual adoption and coming together as a loving Bride. It would look like people surrendering their own crowns to the love flowing from God's heart. And herein lies the mystery of creation once again: The Triune circle of self-giving love was expanding Their Kingdom through human flesh.

Now this leads us to another statement in Scripture, one that is even more difficult than what Jesus spoke at the Last Supper. A look into this will begin to set us toward the finish line of the Shulammite's journey.

18
Transfiguration of the Cosmos Pt. 1

———•◆•———

Put me like a seal over your heart,
Like a seal on your arm.
For love is as strong as death,
Jealousy is as severe as Sheol;
Its flashes are flashes of fire,
The very flame of the Lord.
Many waters cannot quench love,
Nor will rivers overflow it;
If a man were to give all the riches of his house for love,
It would be utterly despised
(8:6-7)

Going through the Song of Solomon is like ascending a spiral staircase that encircles a pillar of billowing fire. As we travel through its lyrics, we come around the same burning revelations, but with different vantage points and ever-increasing perspectives. Now we are nearing the pinnacle of this staircase where a singularity of glory converges at the top. We are approaching the white-hot tip of its flame, the essence of the entire

The Song of the Ages: Part III

Song. This is wrapped up in the revelation of divine love, which is all found in the Holy Spirit Himself. He is the gift and treasure we are called to receive and embrace. He is the wedding ring and the seal of God's greatest purposes for man.

When God breathed forth the cosmos and all the elements emerged, everything was fine-tuned for this reality to take place. Today, scientists and philosophers are talking more and more about an infinite number of universes—a multiverse—simply because they're discovering how impossibly perfect our universe's design is, and how it seems tailormade for our *specific* kind of DNA to exist. They assume we must be living in the perfect version of an infinite number of imperfect universes. But the truth is, our universe was purposefully bent, shaped, and molded so something very tiny and yet eternally significant could come forth—a living vessel that could host the glorious flame of God's Spirit. It was so that a Bride and helper could emerge, one who would reign alongside the King of glory. This is the one rising from the wilderness, calling the whole world to this same flame. She sings of it as a seal and says, *"Its flashes are flashes of fire, the very flame of the Lord! Many waters cannot quench love, nor will rivers overflow it!"*

John the Baptist, another one of God's instruments chosen to play the Song of the Ages, proclaimed the coming of this fire when he spoke of One who would baptize the nations in it. Actually, he spoke of One who would *flood* the nations with fire (Mk. 1:8). The English word "baptize" was not invented until the days of the King James Bible. It has since turned into a religious term, but before that it was a commonly used word that could be simply translated as "immerse." John was telling the people of Israel about One who would *immerse* them in flame. He spoke of this right before Jesus came into the Jordan River and demonstrated once and for all what it means to receive the fiery seal of adoption.

Transfiguration of the Cosmos Pt. 1

Of course, global immersion of a different kind had happened once before. In the days of Noah, the nations were immersed in water that covered the entire planet, annihilating everybody except for righteous Noah and his family. Yet it turned out Noah's flood was a prophetic picture, an inverted image of something utterly wonderful to come. It spoke of another flood that would immerse the entire planet in salvation—one involving a different Man of righteousness (who, as an inversion of Noah, would be the One to die in our place). This Messiah would release a love stronger than the floodwaters of judgment. This time around, the flood of many waters would be overcome by a flood of fire. *The Holy Spirit and fire*, according to John the Immerser.

Some three years after Jesus's baptism, the Holy Spirit came with tongues of fire upon His disciples, leading to the awakening of 3000 people. This was another inverted image from the Old Testament, for during the time of Moses 3000 people were swept away in judgment, an event that many believe happened on the same exact day as the awakening in Acts—the feast of Pentecost (Ex. 32:28). There are many similar upside-down images throughout the Old Testament pointing to something greater to come. What seems like the fires of retributive judgment in the Old Covenant turn into the fires of restorative grace in the New.

Even so, there are passages in the New Testament that are still immensely intimidating, especially ones that talk about fire. One of the most intense is a prophecy about the heavens and the earth being burned up in flame. That is something much bigger than a worldwide flood of water. That is a universe-wide flood of unparalleled heat. Yet perhaps there's a way to read this without the old inverted lens of law and fear. Maybe there's a purer path toward the interpretation of that prophecy; one that involves the "very flame of the Lord" from the end of Solomon's Song? It's

The Song of the Ages: Part III

important we explore this possibility, for it will lead us into the crescendo of the Song's fiery lyrics.

Burning the Elements

On the day 3000 people received the fires of grace, somebody in particular was preaching. Interestingly, this is the same person who went on to write the prophecy about a cosmic flood of fiery destruction:

> *But the day of the Lord will come like a thief, in which the heavens will pass away with a roar and the elements will be destroyed with intense heat, and the earth and its works will be burned up…*
> *(2 Pet. 3:10)*

The apostle Peter spoke of an all-consuming fire that will specifically destroy two things: the "elements" of the heavens and the "works" of the earth. As if for emphasis, the word "elements" shows up again two verses later when he reiterates, "The heavens will be destroyed by burning, and *the elements* will melt with intense heat" (2 Pet. 3:12).

Throughout the centuries, many have assumed Peter is speaking of a literal destruction of the universe's physical elements—those elementary atoms breathed out from the mouth of God. Now we'll ignore the fact that there are many other Scriptures contradicting the literal interpretation of a scorched universe. We'll also ignore the bad fruit that has come out of these interpretations, such as a poor stewardship of the earth, or an escapist mentality that longs to leave and go to a far-away heaven instead of staying and bringing heaven to earth (*since it's going to be burned up anyway*). Instead, we'll just jump right into a different way of seeing this passage.

As always, Scripture interprets Scripture. Important biblical truths are confirmed by two or three (or a hundred) other witnesses

Transfiguration of the Cosmos Pt. 1

in the Bible. Using other Scriptures then, we can come to some stunning conclusions about this fiery prophecy. In another part of the New Testament, we learn something very insightful about this particular word "elements." We actually looked at it in the last chapter when discussing *huiothesia*. We haven't departed from that topic just yet. It fits right in with where Peter's prophecy is taking us.

In the book of Galatians, when Paul speaks about man's season of immaturity as *nēpios*, he says, "So also we, while we were children, were held in bondage under the *elemental things* of the world." This phrase "elemental things" is the same exact word Peter uses when talking about the elements that will be melted away with intense heat. When Paul uses this word, he is speaking about the law. He refers to the law and other external works as the elementary things to which mankind has been in bondage. At its most literal level, this word can be translated as the "first things" or "elementary principles." In the New Testament, it is a reference to the elementary principles of external rules that were meant to lead us toward the freedom and maturity of sonship.

Like the cocoon for a butterfly or the placenta for an unborn child, these first principles of the law served an important but restrictive purpose. They showed us the futility of our self-effort and independence, and were meant to eventually be cast aside. And this makes sense when you connect more Scriptural dots. The writer of Hebrews brings up this word "elements" as well, and he actually does this after mentioning *nēpios*—spiritual children! The writer of Hebrews rebukes Jewish believers for going back to the law system and calls them to move beyond "elementary principles" (Heb. 5:12). Again, this is the same word Peter used for the "elements" destined for the flame.

Now remember, Peter said the elements of the heavens will be burned up and the *works* of the earth will be destroyed as well.

The Song of the Ages: Part III

Incredibly, the same word Peter used for "works" also shows up in these same passages in Galatians and Hebrews! In both letters, believers are rebuked for going back to the *elements* and *works* of the law.

> *For as many as are of the **works** of the Law are under a curse...*
> *(Gal. 3:10)*

> *Therefore leaving the **elementary teaching** about the Christ, let us press on to maturity, not laying again a foundation of repentance from dead **works**...*
> *(Heb. 6:1)*

We can now piece together a few things. It seems quite evident the "elements" and "works" of Peter's prophecy have to do with man's elementary season of immaturity; a season where our identity and righteousness were based on performance, effort, and independence. Peter is giving the prophetic imagery of a soon-to-be-complete destruction of these things. Paul, in his epistles, is then unpacking the deeper meaning of what exactly is being destroyed by the fires of grace. On that note, it's incredible to realize that after the prophecy of destructive fire, Peter specifically mentions Paul. This is one of the only times a writer of the New Testament affirms another writer by name. Peter says the writings of Paul are hard to understand and "the untaught and the unstable distort" them (2 Pet. 3:15-16). Indeed, those who are unstable in the grace of God have distorted many biblical truths. They have focused on literal interpretations of judgment (which often brings us back under fear and performance) and have missed the hope-filled realities of the Gospel.

According to these Scriptures, mankind has been stuck in a type of spiritual immaturity that is centered around the elements

Transfiguration of the Cosmos Pt. 1

of law and fear. But all along, love was "the mark of true maturity" and "the goal of fulfilling all the commandments" (Col. 3:14 & 1 Tim. 1:5 TPT). While the law focused on our external lives, love is about an internal freedom, the likes of which can be entrusted with the very reins of creation. Thankfully, the immature works of fear that run this planet and harmfully affect creation will be quenched by the flame of the Lord. As the *nēpios* life of our spiritual infancy is burned away, the entire universe will be transformed. According to Paul, the creation will be set free from corruption. According to Peter, there will be a new heavens and a new earth. They are both talking about the same thing—the manifestation of God's mature sons.

> *The creation itself also will be set free from its slavery to corruption into the freedom of the glory of the children of God.*
> *(Rom. 8:21)*

> *But according to His promise we are looking for new heavens and a new earth, in which righteousness dwells.*
> *(2 Pet. 3:13)*

The burning of the universe is not about the burning of *atoms*, but *Adam!* It is the destruction of the *nēpios* life making way for mature sons and a unified Bride of Christ.

But do not miss this one point. This all-consuming flame has already been released upon mankind. The elements and works are already melting away. As people set the flame of the Spirit upon their hearts, more and more of the heavens and earth will be transformed from a spiritual desert to an awakened rainforest, as we saw earlier. This is our destiny. For according to Peter (and many other biblical prophecies), this glorious fire will soon

The Song of the Ages: Part III

consume the entire creation. And when it does, love will be the only thing remaining...

When the Perfect Comes

This is something expressed in the Bible's great "love chapter." As we close up the Song with its billowing celebrations of love, we would be amiss not to bring 1 Corinthians 13 into the conversation. Besides its focus on love, this famous passage also contains a surprising connection to this issue of adoption and maturity.

Once again, Paul is the one who penned these timeless words about love, describing some of its qualities and then ending his thoughts on how everything else will pass away except for faith, hope, and love (1 Cor. 13:13). Love is truly the crescendo of space and time. It's where the entire universe is headed. On that note, it's quite fitting that the word "universe" literally means *one song*. Though there have been some difficult verses along the way, love is the chorus and finale of creation's music, planned well before God opened His mouth and sang out it first notes—*let there be light!*

In 1 Corinthians 13, Paul speaks of this "perfect" way of love and explains how this is the destiny of creation. But in the midst of that discussion, he makes an interesting comment about himself. Look carefully at his words:

> *But when the perfect comes, the partial will be done away. When I was a child, I used to speak like a child, think like a child, reason like a child; when I became a man, I did away with childish things.*
> *(1 Cor. 13:10-11)*

Can you guess what word Paul uses to talk about being a "child"?

Nēpios.

Transfiguration of the Cosmos Pt. 1

This is the same revelation hiding within the famous love chapter of the New Testament! Like the Shulammite, Paul is a first-fruit of this reality. Through a revelation of the Father's kindness and the finished work of His Son, Paul experienced what it meant to leave behind the wilderness ways of law and fear. It's in this context he then speaks of all other things passing away except for love. As we know now from Peter and the Song of Solomon, this is because the intense heat of grace—the flame of the Lord—will melt away everything else. The cocoon will shrivel up and the perfect way of love will fill the cosmos. The same stars we see today will shine in the new heavens, but their glow will meet purified eyes that behold the glory of creation anew. And these renewed stargazers will steward the cosmos with unprecedented grace and wonder.

A New Perspective on Judgment

In this swirl of illuminating fire, Solomon throws a penetrating statement into the furnace. He says, *"If a man were to give all the riches of his house for love, it would be utterly despised."* We're going to spend a good amount of time on these words as they are, in many ways, a summarizing statement for the entire Song—as well as the entire Bible. At its simplest essence, this phrase further establishes the truth that love cannot be bought or forced. It is describing more of the fabric of God's Kingdom, a reality unfolding with greater depth and power as the Song hits its final notes.

Earlier when we examined Solomon's repeating chorus—*do not awaken My love until she pleases*—we saw how buying or forcing love is akin to spiritual prostitution. Prostitutes engage in a form of love, an act of intimate union, through payment. It represents *earning* union, and as such, it has nothing to do with real love. It is a "form of godliness," and thankfully, "the form of this world is passing away" (2 Tim 3:5 & 1 Cor. 7:31). At the very end of

The Song of the Ages: Part III

Scripture, in that climactic dichotomy of two women—the great harlot and the radiant Bride—the latter is established upon the earth like an everlasting city while the former is "burned up with fire" (Rev. 18:18). In Solomon's terms, her ways are *utterly despised*.

Now oftentimes an apocalyptic vision like this is seen as a horrifying judgment against one group of people while salvation comes to another. But what if, like the fires of Peter's prophecy, there is another way of seeing this passage? What if this vision actually has to do with the transformation of the "city" of humanity? A transformation from law to love…from *nēpois* children to mature sons…from a spiritual prostitute to a radiant Bride?

This may seem like a controversial perspective, but there's an Old Testament foundation laid out for this in a book we have come back to many times over. It is found in the book of Hosea. Though he's not the only prophet to do this, Hosea issues a very clear characterization of God's people as prostitutes. He also speaks of God's people like they are one woman. Through the prophet, God tells this woman about the punishing destruction coming upon her due to her spiritual prostitution. His warnings reach a climax halfway through the second chapter:

> *"I will punish her for the days of the Baals*
> *When she used to offer sacrifices to them*
> *And adorn herself with her earrings and jewelry,*
> *And follow her lovers, so that she forgot Me,"* declares the
> Lord.
> (Hos. 2:13)

The prostituting nation with her earrings and jewelry is not unlike the great harlot in the book of Revelation with her prodigious wealth and fine jewels (Rev. 18:16). But now look at the verse immediately following Hosea's indictment of the prostituting

Transfiguration of the Cosmos Pt. 1

nation. Watch especially at how Hosea is still speaking to the same nation—the same people who were just condemned:

> *"Therefore, behold, I will allure her (the prostitute),*
> *Bring her into the wilderness*
> *And speak kindly to her.*
> *Then I will give her her vineyards from there,*
> *And the valley of Achor as a door of hope.*
> *And she will sing there as in the days of her youth,*
> *As in the day when she came up from the land of Egypt.*
> *It will come about in that day,"* declares the Lord,
> *"That you will call Me Ishi (Husband)*
> *And will no longer call Me Baali (Master)."*
> (Hos. 2:14-16, parentheses mine)

God judges the prostitute by bringing her into the wilderness and speaking kindly to her. As we saw earlier, these kind words *are* the Good News. It is the sword of truth cutting through every lie of our estrangement and alienation from God. In the wilderness, the prostitute experiences a fiery transformation of grace. She comes under the divine flame of the Lord. Because of this, she no longer calls God "Master," a word that speaks to a fear and law-based relationship. This word was also synonymous with one of the worst idols of the time—Baal. Instead, she soon refers to the Lord as her "Husband." She ends up speaking as a confident bride. And of course, Hosea lived out this entire prophecy by marrying an actual prostitute and showing her a repeated display of mercy until she could finally become the person she already was—a treasured spouse.

Now it's fascinating to realize that when the apostle John sees the great harlot in Revelation, the encounter happens in a very specific place:

The Song of the Ages: Part III

*And he carried me away in the Spirit into a **wilderness**; and I saw a woman sitting on a scarlet beast...*
(Rev. 17:3)

It's in the wilderness that the destruction of the prostitute ensues. Her judgment comes with burning fire and soon enough the Bride emerges on the scene. Could it be that this consuming fire is the same flame we've been circling around this whole time—the flame of God's Spirit, which no flood of sin can overwhelm?

And with that in mind, could it also be that the destruction of the prostitute is actually the *unveiling* of the Bride?

The Story of the Soul

At this point it's vital we recall something examined in a previous volume regarding the names of the main characters in the Song of Songs—Solomon and the Shulammite. Both names come from the same root word, the first being the masculine version and the second feminine. The feminine Shulammite is the representative for humanity while the masculine King Solomon is a representation of God. We've seen this is not so much about gender but rather a display of the likeness and union we share with our Creator. Like Adam with Eve, Jesus is our root and origin while we are His beautiful counterpart.

As it happens, there are different Hebrew words used for the human "soul" throughout Scripture and each one of them is a feminine term as well. This confirms something we have indirectly shown but never plainly stated: *That is, the journey of the Shulammite represents the journey of the human soul.* The delightful "garden" of the Shulammite is indeed the soul of humanity where God intends to dwell. The human heart, as the centerpiece of the soul, is truly His desired resting place and throne.

Now we bring this up for a very important reason. If you remember, this young woman from Shulam started out her journey

Transfiguration of the Cosmos Pt. 1

by describing herself as *one who veils herself*. This was a direct allusion to the prostitutes of Solomon's day who would cover their faces with a veil, making this a firm symbol of the false identity. This is indeed speaking of that immature *nēpios* life which is enslaved under the "elements" and "works" of human effort. As a representative of humanity, the Shulammite's journey is then a picture of the maturity of the soul—which, at the same time, *is the unveiling of the human soul*.

This dynamic of a veiled humanity is mysteriously hidden within the design of Solomon's temple. We know very well by now that the temple points to human beings, particularly because of its three main sections corresponding to man's body, soul, and spirit. Curiously, the two inner rooms representing the soul and spirit—the Holy Place and the Holy of Holies—were both covered by a veil. Amongst other realities, this speaks of that same veil of prostitution that has covered over the true identity of humanity! But remember, God's glory still resided in the Holy of Holies even when it was covered by a veil. This was a sign that the image and glory of God was still resident within a veiled and idolatrous human race!

We saw this when we looked at the young woman Tamar who covered her face with a veil and engaged in an act of prostitution. Even though she committed that act, Tamar was not truly a prostitute. Instead, she was a carrier of the seed of Christ. And so it is with the human race. Humanity is not truly a prostitute. We participated in its deeds—we engaged in the false forms of love and pseudo-godliness and thereby covered ourselves with a guilty veil—but behind it all was still that precious seed of glory. Thank God, that veil of a false life would be violently judged and overthrown, and what was hidden behind it would be redeemed and recovered.

The Song of the Ages: Part III

A Great Metamorphosis

In his second letter to the Corinthians, Paul teaches how this veil has specifically covered the minds of men (2 Cor. 3:15 & 4:3-4). Interestingly enough, the great harlot of Revelation has something over the place of her mind as well:

> And **on her forehead** *a name was written, a mystery,* *"Babylon the great, the mother of harlots and of the abominations of the earth."*
> *(Rev. 17:5)*

This mysterious name represents something that has impacted all of the world. This is why the woman is referred to as the mother of *all* prostitution. She's a symbol pointing to the very thing that produces evil in the first place. It's no surprise this all comes down to *a false name covering the mind*. This is the mother-root of our brokenness and it goes all the way back to our first mother in Eden who embraced a lie about herself (a false identity) and sought something she already had through personal effort. That was our first attempt at "buying love." And that too was *utterly despised*.

But praise the living God, in the book of Revelation there's another mother who emerges. But in describing her, John doesn't use the word "mother." He mainly refers to her as a city—the *New Jerusalem* descending out of heaven. Yet it's illuminating when you connect some more biblical dots and find out what Paul calls this city:

> *But the Jerusalem above is free; she is our mother.*
> *(Gal. 4:26)*

Within the gates of this other symbolic mother, there are a people who have something else on their forehead. Together, they

Transfiguration of the Cosmos Pt. 1

look into the face of the Father and it says, *"His name will be on their foreheads"* (Rev. 22:4). These are the ones who have been unveiled. They have turned back to the truth, which is the essence of repentance. To reestablish a previous point, this is not about being adopted into a family you never belonged to. It's about turning back to your true origin—the Father of lights and the mother of the New Jerusalem.

Here then lies a marvelous insight as to why we are *transformed* by the renewing of our minds. This famous command from Romans 12 comes after eleven other chapters expounding on the wonderful mystery of the Gospel, which is the theme of the entire letter (see Rom. 16:25). This is the true mystery of grace and of our redeemed identity in Christ (as opposed to the identity of Adam that corresponds to the other "mystery" written on the harlot's forehead). In Romans 12, we're called to renew our minds to the right mystery. In other words, we're to set it like a seal upon ourselves. When we do this, we are literally *transformed*—even in this present life.

Now you may be surprised to find out the word Paul uses for "transformed" is the same exact word the gospel writers use to describe Jesus's *transfiguration*. The implications of this are extraordinary because it shows us this defining moment in the life of Christ is something we're called to experience as well. Moving forward, this will take up a good deal of our focus as we see its association to so many of the things we're uncovering in our study of the royal seal and the fiery purposes of God.

This moment in Jesus's life was when He took Peter, James, and John "up on a high mountain." There, a burst of transcendent glory came from within Him in full view of His three friends:

> *Then Jesus' appearance was dramatically altered. A radiant light as bright as the sun poured from his face.*

The Song of the Ages: Part III

*And his clothing became luminescent—dazzling like lightning. He was **transfigured** before their very eyes.*
(Matt. 17:2 TPT)

It's important to first recognize Jesus wasn't actually changing His essence here. Neither was He receiving or gaining some new glory upon Himself. Rather, the disciples were seeing what was inside of Him all along. The true glory hidden within Jesus of Nazareth was being put on display. Some of the ancient church fathers, such as Maximus the Confessor, taught the only thing that changed on the mountain that day was the three men's perceptions!

This word usually rendered "transformed" in Romans and "transfigured" in the gospels is the Greek word *metamorphoō*. As you might suspect, this is where we get the word metamorphosis, the strange process in nature where a creature changes its form. We've alluded to this process several times throughout our journey, especially in regard to the caterpillar. The emergence of the butterfly is indeed a transfiguration. But it's important to now recognize this process is really where *a creature moves from an immature state into its adult form*. It's a signpost within nature showing our destiny to move from the *nēpios* life to a state of *huiothesia!*

So, a butterfly is really just a mature caterpillar. In a way, the butterfly was always within the caterpillar, yet there was a process of transformation that needed to happen for it to manifest. As the Son of Man, Jesus of Nazareth showed us what was within the sons of men. He was showing us what an adult child of God looked like. In this important moment chronicled by three different gospel writers, Jesus revealed our own destiny of transfiguration, and pointed us back to the eternal plan in the heart of God for having mature sons and daughters.

But again, all of this requires repentance (*metanoia*), which is literally a transformation of the mind. Or you could say that it is receiving a new name—a true name—upon your forehead. And

Transfiguration of the Cosmos Pt. 1

that brings us back to the grand finale of Scripture and the two women found in a book titled *The Unveiling*. It seems this is not really about two women but rather one woman being transfigured *by fire* into something else. Let's look a little bit deeper into this, for the Lord would have us be fully assured of these realities.

The Hour of Judgment

In John's description of the great harlot, he makes a clear delineation between people of the world and the prostitute herself:

> *And he said to me, "The waters which you saw where the harlot sits, are peoples and multitudes and nations and tongues."*
> *(Rev. 17:15)*

The harlot is sitting *over* the nations. This is more evidence that she does not represent the wicked people themselves, but rather the distorted forms and systems people have adhered to. On the other hand, the "multitudes and nations and tongues" are those Jesus purchased by blood, their destiny being sealed and announced earlier in Revelation:

> *After these things I looked, and behold, a great multitude which no one could count, from every nation and all tribes and peoples and tongues, standing before the throne and before the Lamb, clothed in white robes, and palm branches were in their hands.*
> *(Rev. 7:9)*

Again, Jesus came to restore what was covered over and hidden by our great harlotry. This is where Solomon's temple is especially insightful. We just learned how the veil blocking the way into the Holy of Holies represented this ancient issue of spiritual prostitution. It spoke to the false name covering and hiding the

The Song of the Ages: Part III

true glory of God within humanity. Now let's recall what happened inside of the temple's innermost room. Within the walls of the Holy of Holies was the Mercy Seat, something we've seen as a symbol of the throne of God. More recently, we've looked at how God's throne is also the human heart. This all fits together astoundingly. As the centerpiece of the temple, the Mercy Seat is representative of the center of our souls and spirits—our hearts. And indeed, the Mercy Seat was sprinkled with blood, which is the same thing that would happen to the throne of our hearts!

> *Let us draw near with a sincere heart in full assurance of faith,* **having our hearts sprinkled clean** *from an evil conscience...*
> *(Heb. 10:22)*

To sprinkle the physical Mercy Seat with blood, the High Priest had to first go through the veil that blocked the way to it. This gives us a picture of Jesus coming to *speak kindly* through the veil of our false identities. With His kind words and shed blood, Jesus proceeded to wash the guilt off our hearts. He sprinkled our hearts clean from an "evil conscience." One way to translate and understand the Greek word for "conscience" is *self-perception*. Thus, it was Jesus's joy to cleanse how we see ourselves! His sacrifice was the judgment against the false self—the harlot who sits over the waters of the nations. This is why the book of Hebrews opens by saying that when Jesus made purification of sins, *He sat down* (Heb. 1:2). Jesus is the One who was truly meant to sit over the waters of the world! (See Matt. 13:1-2)

This then helps us understand why the book of Revelation depicts a total destruction coming upon the harlot in *one hour*.

> *"Woe, woe, the great city, Babylon, the strong city! For in* **one hour** *your judgment has come."*
> *(Rev. 18:8)*

Transfiguration of the Cosmos Pt. 1

Those with a more literal perspective of Revelation believe this is about an actual sixty minutes of plagues, famine, and death that will suddenly break out in the former Babylonian regions of the Middle East. But they miss the fact that this book is primarily a *revelation of Jesus Christ*. This "one hour" is the same hour He spoke of right before His death:

> *...But for this purpose I came to this **hour**... Now **judgment** is upon this world; now the ruler of this world will be cast out.*
> *(Jn. 12:27, 31)*

If any of this is hard to believe, then take the following into consideration. In his vision, John specifically sees both the harlot and the beast she rode upon clothed in *scarlet*.

> *And he carried me away in the Spirit into a wilderness; and I saw a woman sitting on a scarlet beast... The woman was clothed in purple and scarlet...*
> *(Rev. 17:3-4)*

When Jesus approached His own hour of judgment, He too was clothed in a very specific color...

> *They stripped Him and put a scarlet robe on Him.*
> *(Matt. 27:28)*

This is the same exact "scarlet" adorning the beast and the prostitute. Such a vision makes total sense when you consider how Jesus took *our sins* upon Himself!

In Revelation, a scarlet-clad woman reigns over the waters of the multitudes, nations, and tongues. But as we just saw, those same multitudes are clothed in white in another part of the book. Yet again, this all speaks to the work of Christ. Before His crucifixion, Jesus was literally stripped of His white rabbinical garments and

The Song of the Ages: Part III

then given a scarlet robe. Gentile soldiers later divided up His white garments into four pieces—a picture of His righteousness being given to the four corners of the earth (Jn. 19:23). All this was the "hour" Jesus took our spiritual prostitution upon Himself and endured a violent and bloody death on our behalf—a death that was actually the bloody overthrow of the great prostitute! When He died, the veil in the temple was torn and the judgment upon that false "mother" was complete. It was the fiery judgment of love! Thus it is written in the book of Ezekiel:

> *"As I live," declares the Lord God, "surely with a mighty hand and with an outstretched arm and with wrath poured out, I shall be king over you."*
> *(Ez. 20:33)*

This "outstretched arm" of "wrath poured out" was indeed the stretching out of Jesus's arms on the cross. This was the passion of the Christ, a fiery act of true love that would eternally win back the hearts of humanity. This was the only way God could become the true King of our hearts. These interlocking truths sprinkled throughout the Bible build an amazing and wonderful picture of what redemption is all about.

And of course, this sprawling network of biblical connections runs even deeper, especially when you look at how the color scarlet shows up in other places. Stunningly, this exact color appears in two stories that just so happen to be about prostitutes! We've looked at both of them already. The first is Tamar—the veiled woman who joined herself with the patriarch Judah. She is the one who gave birth to a redemptive child who had a scarlet thread wrapped around his finger. As you now know, that child was a prefigure of our great Sin-Bearer, Christ.

The second is arguably the most famous prostitute in Scripture—Rahab. She was a veiled woman who carried on her

Transfiguration of the Cosmos Pt. 1

business within the sinful city of Jericho. But when a scarlet cord was tied to her window, she was delivered from the destruction that came upon the city. In that hour of judgment, the walls of Jericho were *utterly despised*. Those walls represented the same ancient system of deception—that Babylonian mother of wickedness. Yet the veiled individual hiding behind those wicked walls was redeemed. Rahab went on to live in a totally new nation and became another ancestor of Christ. She was revealed as someone in the very *gene-ology* of Jesus—someone with the DNA of the Lamb on her forehead!

In other words, the prostitute was transfigured.

But like the butterfly in the caterpillar, this DNA was always inside of her. It was simply waiting for its freedom from the cocoon-like walls of Jericho. Those walls are the "elements" and "works" destined for the eternal flame!

Mercy and Destruction

When we continue to look at the book of Revelation and the mother of all harlots, we find another amazing connection to the work of Christ. After saying she was clothed in scarlet, the description continues:

> *The woman was clothed in purple and scarlet, and adorned with gold and precious stones and pearls, having in her hand* **a gold cup full of abominations** *and of the unclean things of her immorality.*
> *(Rev. 17:4)*

Not only did Jesus take our scarlet stain upon Himself, He also drank a "cup" on our behalf. This was the same cup He asked to be taken away from Him in the Garden of Gethsemane. Jesus was in fact referring to the goblet of our own abominations and uncleanness—and the punishment due to it. Therefore, when

The Song of the Ages: Part III

Jesus surrendered to the Father, He was clothed in scarlet the next morning. This was the proof He had drank the harlot's cup!

Here's the fact of the matter. The judgment of the prostitute is a picture of the Gospel. At the cross, all our systems of elementary religion and false love were judged and forgiven at the same time. Severe judgment came upon the veil while mercy and forgiveness came to the people who participated in its false deeds. This is why John notes that the leaders of the earth were separated from the prostitute when her judgment came. Look at this:

> *And the kings of the earth, who committed acts of immorality and lived sensuously with her, will weep and lament over her when they see the smoke of her burning,* **standing at a distance** *because of the fear of her torment, saying, "Woe, woe, the great city, Babylon, the strong city! For in one hour your judgment has come."*
> *(Rev. 18:9-10)*

It seems strange that when judgment finally comes, those who are arguably the most to blame for the world's wickedness are found "standing at a distance." It even says the same thing about the "merchants of the earth" a few verses later (Rev. 18:15). These are the movers and shakers within the fallen systems of our governments and economies; the seeming producers of the worst evils of humanity. Such a separation doesn't make sense unless your eyes are open to the Good News hiding within the Apocalypse. This is the Song of the Ages once again playing its powerful notes through a glorious and violent parable.

The prostitute is destroyed while those who were impacted by her predominance stand and watch from afar. The distance between them and the actual destruction is due to the One who took our sins upon Himself. He is that infamous "scapegoat" from the law of Moses; the cursed creature that went into the *wilderness* and died

Transfiguration of the Cosmos Pt. 1

there on the people's behalf (Lev. 16:21). It's the same message over and over and over again. The wilderness is the place of both destruction and mercy, death and resurrection. It is ultimately the place of transfiguration and unveiling.

We have much more to say about these things, but let's take a moment to pause and meditate upon the immense kindness of our King. With that, let's also prepare our hearts to bear with a few more words about these prophetic promises. Up and over the lyrics of the Song and through a terrain of many other Scriptures, we have gained a clearer understanding of the apocalyptic flames of love. However, we have not yet finished ascending its burning splendor. To do that, we must go back to the place where Jesus Himself was transfigured, looking more closely at the mountain where this occurred.

19
Transfiguration of the Cosmos Pt. 2

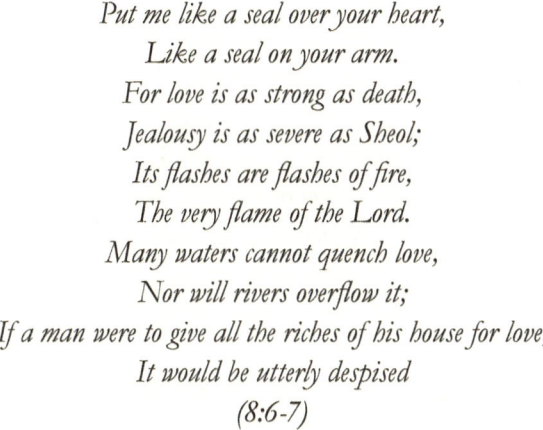

Put me like a seal over your heart,
Like a seal on your arm.
For love is as strong as death,
Jealousy is as severe as Sheol;
Its flashes are flashes of fire,
The very flame of the Lord.
Many waters cannot quench love,
Nor will rivers overflow it;
If a man were to give all the riches of his house for love,
It would be utterly despised
(8:6-7)

We turn our attention now to the actual location of Jesus's transfiguration. Religious tradition tells us this happened on the mountain of Tabor, yet much of our modern scholarship asserts that the real site was Mount Hermon. Tabor was a Roman encampment surrounded by garrisons of soldiers, making it doubtful Jesus would have traveled up its ascent with His disciples. Furthermore, the place

The Song of the Ages: Part III

of transfiguration was described as being a "high mountain" when Mount Tabor is relatively average-sized. Hermon on the other hand is incredibly high. It is in fact one of the tallest mountains in Israel with a snowcapped peak that melts into the Jordan. The biggest problem with Tabor, however, is that it is quite far from the place where Jesus had just been with His disciples right before the transfiguration. The events preceding that moment happened in a city called Caesarea Philippi, which just so happens to be located near the base of Mount Hermon.

Before looking at Hermon's significance, we first have to look at Caesarea Philippi. This was a dark and idolatrous place filled with all the "harlotries" of man. It was a center for demonic worship, having an area within its borders where even human sacrifices took place. This spot was often referred to as the "gates of hell," and it was most likely at this exact place that Jesus made His eternal proclamation, "Upon this rock I will build My church; and the *gates of hell* shall not prevail against it" (Matt. 16:18 KJV). Jesus spoke this after the revolutionary moment when Peter acknowledged His identity as the anointed Messiah and Son of God. Six day later, Jesus would take Peter, along with James and John, up to a high mountain to confirm this confession (Matt. 17:1-13).

Corrupt Origins

Now, if this mountain was indeed Hermon, it was an incredibly purposeful and appropriate choice. According to the Jewish literature of Jesus's day, Hermon was a location of great spiritual meaning. This is especially noted in the first book of Enoch, a text with which Jesus and His disciples would have been very familiar.

A quick disclaimer here before we go forward. We need to be ever careful of using extrabiblical texts in our development of revelation. It's true the disciples were familiar with this book, and it even gets quoted and referenced in the New Testament. However,

Transfiguration of the Cosmos Pt. 2

the New Testament also quotes pagan poets (Acts 17:28). A quote in the Bible doesn't mean the entire source document was on par with the special inspiration of Scripture. There's a reason the hand of God did not allow Enoch to be canonized by the Jewish community nor by a vast majority of the Christian church. There are things to glean from it, but most scholars recognize that many additions were made to the book over the centuries, and some of those additions are contrary to Scriptural truth. Let's also remember Paul's warning to his spiritual sons when he told them not to be distracted by Jewish myths, speculations, and genealogies (1 Tim. 1:4 & Tit. 3:9). Many of those things come into play within the book of Enoch.

All that said, the parts of Enoch that get referenced in the New Testament are quite relevant for us at the moment. In particular is Enoch's account of the wickedness that led to the great floodwaters of Noah. Interestingly, he writes how it all began at Mount Hermon (1 Enoch 6). There, a group of fallen angels gathered together and made plans to sexually unite with the daughters of men, bringing about a great corruption to humanity that necessitated the release of a global flood. It's incredible how this brings us back to our starting place in this entire discussion on the apocalyptic fires of Solomon's Song. In his prophecy of a worldwide flood of fire—which we have been comparing to Solomon's flame of love—Peter was partially referencing the book of Enoch!

We have now thoroughly re-examined this fire in the consummating light of Christ's finished work. If there were shadows in the Old Testament needing Christological interpretation, you better believe there are even murkier shadows in extrabiblical writings requiring the same clarity. We've made the case that these flames are to be spiritually discerned. They are the fires of perfect love; a love that burns away the elements and works of man's immature state. This fire is ultimately the flame

The Song of the Ages: Part III

of the Holy Spirit who brings *transfiguration to the world*, turning the city of humanity from harlotry to purity, from immature children to adopted sons and a mature Bride. It is the judgment of love, greater than the "many waters" running from the fountainhead of man's corruption.

So think about all of this. Jesus first came to a wicked city that had a place within it referred to as the gates of hell. There He was confessed to be the Messiah, the true Savior and Redeemer of corrupt humanity. As the Son of Man, Jesus showed us that the sons of men are also the sons of God. Six days later, Jesus confirmed this glorious confession by ascending a mountain that was most likely the same one His entire culture believed was the *actual gate of hell*. Jesus went up to the place where His contemporaries believed fallen angelic watchers had gathered to corrupt the DNA of God's children. We don't know if this is literally what happened. God did not allow Enoch to be canonized for a reason, and the mention of a similar story in Genesis 6 is open to varying interpretation. Yet the fact remains that this literature was very popular in Jesus's time and He would be making quite a statement by ascending that infamous mountain.

In the writings of Enoch, it is a satanic figure named Azazel who comes to Hermon and gathers a group of fellow angels to populate the world with evil, spurring on the floodwaters of judgment. How marvelous then, that on that same mountain Jesus would gather some of His fellow disciples with a mission of restoration. A mission that would soon lead to a worldwide flood of fiery redemption! But perhaps even more marvelous is how the name of this lead angel mysteriously shows up in the Hebrew canon. While you won't find the name itself in the Bible, the word is used to describe an important creature, one we just brought up in the last chapter. Azazel is the Hebrew word for *scapegoat*, the creature from the Day of Atonement that was released into the wilderness to die. This brings us back to the

Transfiguration of the Cosmos Pt. 2

idea of the wilderness and the "mouth." Jesus truly descended into our wilderness and took on all the ways we were falsely "fathered" into an unclean identity. Like that scapegoat, He then carried it all away and left behind the truth of our original sonship. He reversed the works of Azazel!

This opens up a deeper understanding of what the prophet Hosea said about God *speaking* in the wilderness. If you remember, Hosea said God would "speak kindly" to His prostituting people in the wilderness. When God inspired these words, He was using a common Hebrew phrase that shows up in several other stories in the Bible. One example is when Joseph "speaks kindly" to his guilt-ridden brothers (Gen. 50:21). The phrase is filled with tender compassion and it corresponds beautifully to the Gospel. That said, our appreciation of what these words actually mean are limited by the translation. This is because the phrase gets changed from the literal meaning when it's put into the English. In the pure Hebrew tongue, it simply means *"to speak to the heart."*

It is in this literal wording we uncover the same burning realities unfolding all around us as we scale this heavenly staircase of poetry and revelation. When God brings His veiled prostitute-bride into the wilderness, He does so to *speak through* the lying veil and talk directly to her true heart! In other words, He comes to cut off the demonic identity and redeem her true self. This is the powerful message behind people like Tamar and Rahab showing up in the genealogy of Christ. Ruth is another example, and she might actually be the best one.

Even though she wasn't a prostitute, Ruth was something far worse in the mind of a Jew. She was a Moabite. This was a group of people the Law told the Hebrews to have no dealings with, even to the tenth generation (Deut. 30:3). They were detested by Israel primarily because they descended from a disgusting incident of incest between a father and his two daughters (Gen. 19:30-38). The

The Song of the Ages: Part III

Moabites were thus a completely perverted line within the family of Abraham. However, one of the many daughters birthed from that debauched event ended up meeting a man from Israel named Boaz. This man fell in love with her and became her redeemer. In fact, he was called her "kinsmen redeemer" (Rth. 4:14). Boaz was a picture of Jesus Christ, the One who came as our true *kinsmen*. He is the One who shares our flesh and blood and kindly tells us that our hearts are still His Holy of Holies—even if demonic harlotry has enshrouded it. We see this beautiful message right in the story of Ruth when the Moabite foreigner expresses her surprise at how Boaz treats her:

> *Then she said, "I have found favor in your sight, my lord, for you have comforted me and indeed have **spoken kindly** to your maidservant, though I am not like one of your maidservants."*
> *(Rth. 2:13)*

The enemy has ardently sought to corrupt our DNA—that precious divine code of life which this entire universe was custom-built to sustain. When looking at the exterior of our lives, it seems he has been successful, and many conclude that the cosmos should indeed be burned up with violent fire. But the mystery and good news is that this work of evil has *not* succeeded. Though our exterior lives have become shattered and marred, a scarlet thread of hope covers the broken walls of our being. Behind those walls lies the seed of an incorruptible glory. Transfiguration is simply the tearing down of those walls. Just as Jesus's transfiguration was an uncovering of the resplendent treasure within, so is the work of the Spirit upon the human soul.

Glorious Hindsight

Everything we're currently seeing was shown to us much earlier in the Shulammite's journey. However, we were not able to see it

Transfiguration of the Cosmos Pt. 2

at the time. Thankfully, the eighth chapter of the Song continues to give us an extraordinary amount of hindsight as we look back on previous parts of the story. For instance, the Shepherd King spoke three times about a perfect loveliness that existed *behind the Shulammite's veil* (Sgs. 4:1, 4:3, & 6:7). In each of those three instances, the word used for "veil" was *tsammah*. This one word leads us to something astonishing. It's another biblical connection that should wipe away any semblance of doubt as to the deepening bond between John's Revelation and Solomon's Song.

When describing the fabric covering the Shulammite's face, Solomon uses a word that is found in only one other place in the entire Bible. It shows up specifically in Isaiah 47. The fact that it just so happens to be in that chapter is unbelievable, for that particular part of Isaiah is about *the destruction of Babylon*. John quotes from this very chapter when writing about the mother of all harlots (Rev. 18:7). In the Isaiah passage, God addresses the nation of Babylon and calls out her wickedness, promising to put an end to her controlling influence. One of the first statements the Lord makes is where He says to Babylon, "Remove your veil" (Isa. 47:2).

Take off the tsammah!

The Holy Spirit had Solomon use this same word to describe what is covering the loveliness of the Shulammite's face. The message there is clear. The Shulammite represents the journey of the human soul and its destiny to be unveiled from all spiritual prostitution, revealing an original beauty still intact. This same message is hidden in the relationship between Israel and Babylon. We've already seen how Israel is a priestly representative for humanity. As an invader nation, Babylon is then a representation for the deception that has invaded God's sacred inheritance, the souls of His children. What is being judged and destroyed is that *foreign invader*, a false name covering humanity like a prostitute's veil. Yet the people themselves—the multitudes, nations, and tongues—have been forgiven and bought by blood! They are now invited to *repent* and be unmasked in transformative light.

This gift of hindsight becomes even more precious when we step back and look closely at one of the specific moments where Solomon spoke to the Shulammite through her covering *tsammah*:

> *Your lips are like a scarlet thread,*
> *And your mouth is lovely.*
> *Your temples are like a slice of a pomegranate*
> **Behind your veil.**
> *(Sgs. 4:3)*

Did you catch the color that showed up there?

The Lord compared her to scarlet. A *scarlet thread* to be exact.

This message of a prostitute's transfiguration has been there all along!

Saul's Apocalypse

These connecting pieces of literature, prophecy, and vision can be summed up by the simple testimony of one man. In his letter to the Galatians, Paul makes a brief yet profound statement about his conversion. It would be extremely helpful to look at how Paul described this experience, for it contains an eye-opening relevance to what we're now discovering.

First, recall that Paul wrote this letter to warn believers about not going back to the old "elements" and "works" of the *nēpios* life. He was declaring the fullness of their present identity in Christ as the mature sons of God (Gal. 4:7). It is in the beginning of that letter where Paul talks about his own redemption from the life of enslavement—the time when he went by the name of Saul. In speaking of his salvation, he wrote the following:

Transfiguration of the Cosmos Pt. 2

But when God, who had set me apart even from my mother's womb and called me through His grace, **was pleased to reveal His Son in me** *so that I might preach Him among the Gentiles...*
(Gal. 1:15-16)

Our study has been one long unraveling of the power behind single words and phrases in the Bible. These are the puzzle pieces coming together to form a victorious image; strands of differing thread building the tapestry of Christ and His glorified Bride. This term Paul uses for God "revealing" His Son is one of the primary words we've looked at and unraveled. The letter to the Galatians is telling us God "was pleased to *apokalyptō* His Son" within Saul of Tarsus! In Strong's Concordance, the very first definition of this word is "to uncover, lay open what has been *veiled.*"[3] It is of course the same term that is turned into a noun to make the title for the final book of the Bible. Paul is saying that as a young Pharisee he had an experience where the Messiah, the Son of the living God, was *revealed within him*. What was hidden all along in a dark and broken man was finally uncovered. The veil was torn, and a transfiguration came about!

Think carefully about the implications of this. Saul was a religious terrorist filled with envy and murderous intent. He was viciously thirsting for the blood of the saints. This is one of the hallmark attributes of the great harlot:

And in her was found the blood of prophets and of saints and of all who have been slain on the earth.
(Rev. 18:24)

---

3. G601 - *apokalyptō* - Strong's Greek Lexicon (NASB). Retrieved from https://www.blueletterbible.org//lang/lexicon/lexicon.cfm?Strongs=G601&t=NASB

The Song of the Ages: Part III

Saul was also a legalist to the tee. He built his entire life around those elementary systems of legalism and fear (Phi. 3:6). He was the essence of someone steeped in Babylonian harlotry; a man living under a false satanic name. And yet despite all this, a seed of destiny lay within him from his mother's womb. Though he would grow up under the veiling shadow of the law, the time came for the maturity of sonship and bridal love to manifest. This was the moment when the striving of his false life would meet the unquenchable fires of grace. After this experience, Saul's heart opened up to the Lord and he said *yes* to His love. He allowed himself to be baptized and marked by the empowering seal of the Holy Spirit. Because of this, the scales *fell* from his eyes (Acts 9:18). In other words, the veil *fell* from his face. It was his own apocalypse, a fulfillment of what John saw in parabolic fire:

> "**Fallen, fallen** is Babylon the great, she who has made all the nations drink of the wine of the passion of her immorality."
> (Rev. 14:8)

In the book of Acts, we learn more of what this looked like. The text says a blinding light from heaven knocked the militant Pharisee down to the ground (Acts 9:3). The "light" mentioned in Acts was the same kind described in Jesus's transfiguration. Saul encountered the glory that Peter, James, and John saw on Hermon and this ended up awakening the *same glory* within himself. That should shed more understanding on Paul's words to the Corinthians when he described what happens to a person when they turn to the Lord.

> But whenever a person turns to the Lord, **the veil is taken away**. Now the Lord is the Spirit, and where the Spirit of the Lord is, there is liberty. But we all, with unveiled face, beholding as in a mirror the glory of the

Transfiguration of the Cosmos Pt. 2

*Lord, **are being transformed** into the same image from glory to glory, just as from the Lord, the Spirit. (2 Cor. 3:16-18)*

There is a veil covering the glory of Christ within people and it is only removed by the Spirit of God when a person turns their heart to Jesus. Paul explains that this turning is an experience of "beholding as in a mirror." Hopefully you noticed the term used to describe what happens when we do this. The text says we are "transformed." Once again, this is the word *metamorphoō*. This is saying that the same thing that happened to Jesus in the transfiguration happens to us! A hidden glory is unveiled and released.

Now there's also an interesting thing to glean by looking at how many times this word *metamorphoō* shows up in the Bible. It's actually used only four times. Twice it's used to describe the experience Jesus had on the mountain, then it used another two times to describe our own transformation—once in Romans 12 and then here in 2 Corinthians. So, the first two times is for Jesus and the second two times is for us. This is a subtle but powerful testimony hidden within the Word of God, pointing us to the same conclusions. Jesus's transfiguration was meant to be the mirror of our own.

We can also see this mirroring dynamic of the transfiguration by looking at two different but corresponding events in the life of John. The first is from when he was a young man when Jesus led him "up on a high mountain" to experience the transfiguration (Matt. 17:1). There, he and the two others saw the eternal glory hidden within Christ. Later on, a much older John was again "led" by Jesus (the Spirit of Jesus) to "a great and high mountain." It was there he encountered the same "glory of God" (Rev. 21:9-11). This time, however, the glory was radiating out of a city—a city representing *us*. This is teaching the same thing! Jesus's unveiling

The Song of the Ages: Part III

was the coming attractions for another one. This other unveiling would involve the same glory coming out of a much larger vessel—redeemed humanity.

God's Great Joy

Now did you know there was another man who was led by the Spirit up to "a very high mountain," who then saw the same realities we've been discussing? The man was Ezekiel and his experience takes us even further into the meaning of these things. Much like John, Ezekiel was in exile when he received a vision of a glorious city and temple (Ez. 40-48). This temple brought forth a stream of water that went into the Dead Sea and transformed it into a place of abundant life.

The timing of this vision is what we especially want to focus on. This came to Ezekiel fourteen years after Jerusalem's fall to Babylon (Ez. 40:1). It appears as though this number is spiritually linked with redemption, particularly a redemption from the law—those immature elements and works destined for the flames of love. For example, Jacob had to work fourteen years under the cruel reign of his father-*in-law* before he gained his desired bride (Gen. 29:27). Two generations prior, Abraham had a child named Ishmael who was the product of his own self-effort. It was not until Ishmael was fourteen years old that the son of promise was finally born (Gen. 17:24-25 & 21:5). Furthermore, when the new year on Israel's calendar began, it wasn't until the fourteenth day that the Passover Lamb could be slain and celebrated (Ex. 12:6). This marked the exact day the Hebrews were released from their bitter slavery in Egypt. (As a prophetic side-note, it seems providential that the *14th Amendment* written into the United States Constitution gave citizen's rights to former slaves. And, as we saw earlier, the Roman Empire allowed fourteen-year-old boys to

Transfiguration of the Cosmos Pt. 2

move from the slave-like status of children to mature sons in the adoption ceremony.)

So, after fourteen years of Babylon capturing Israel (a representation of our soul's slavery to law and death), Ezekiel was taken up to a high mountain and shown the true temple of God. He was given his own revelation of a free and mature humanity; a world unencumbered by the elements of law, sin, and death. With this, he saw the "Dead Sea" of humanity transfigured. To put it in different metaphoric language, the great harlot covering the waters of the multitudes was being discarded like an old cocoon, leaving civilization metamorphosized.

When Saul of Tarsus awoke to the transfiguring glory of Jesus, it was like a fish in the Dead Sea coming to life. He then made it his life mission to see the entire sea of humanity transformed in the same way. Look one more time at Paul's description of his salvation. This time notice the last part:

> *But when God, who had set me apart even from my mother's womb and called me through His grace, was pleased to* **reveal His Son in me** *so that I might preach Him* **among the Gentiles***...*
> *(Gal. 1:15-16)*

Do you see the word "among"? It's the same word he just used in saying God "was pleased to reveal His Son *in me.*" The Greek term there is actually the same as the word "in." Paul was literally saying, "So that I might preach Him *in* the Gentiles." This is a huge deal. In the same sentence, Paul is connecting the reality of what God revealed within him to what God wants to reveal *in* the Gentiles. And instead of the Gentiles, we can just as well say "multitudes, nations, and tongues."

Here then is another way to read this:

The Song of the Ages: Part III

God took great joy in unveiling His Son within me so that I might go out and announce the same reality within the entire world!

The Coming of the Lord

As we wind down these reflections on the transfiguration of Christ and humanity, we have to come back one last time to Peter's fiery prophecy. We can't quickly leave the second letter of Peter, for there's something else very important to see there. All this time we've been talking about the transfiguration and how it is the end result of everything Peter prophesied in his letter regarding the transformation of the universe. What we didn't point out until now is that this letter is also where Peter directly discusses his encounter on the Mount of Transfiguration! If that event did take place on Mount Hermon, it's very probable this was on Peter's mind when he went on to reference Enoch and the prophecy of a universal flood of fire. Let's look now at the apostle's actual words about the transfiguration:

> *For we did not follow cleverly devised tales when we made known to you the power and coming of our Lord Jesus Christ, but we were eyewitnesses of His majesty. For when He received honor and glory from God the Father, such an utterance as this was made to Him by the Majestic Glory, "This is My beloved Son with whom I am well-pleased"— and we ourselves heard this utterance made from heaven when we were with Him on the holy mountain.*
> *(2 Pet. 1:16-18)*

Peter is clearly talking about the moment when Jesus was transformed into blinding light; when God's audible voice confirmed what had just been confessed by faith six days earlier in Caesarea Philippi. But did you see how Peter described this

Transfiguration of the Cosmos Pt. 2

moment? He referred to it as *the power and coming of our Lord Jesus Christ.*

Underneath this little remark is another reservoir of reformational insight. For those who believe the "coming of the Lord" is only about a second physical appearance of Jesus in the sky, this is quite a quagmire. Peter is blatantly saying the event on that holy mountain was the coming of the Lord. Though this passage has produced a great deal of debate over the centuries, there's little wiggle room to twist Peter's words, especially when you consider what Jesus Himself said in the verse that comes right before the transfiguration story:

> *"Truly I say to you, there are some of those who are standing here who will not taste death until they see the Son of Man coming in His kingdom."*
> *(Matt. 16:28)*

Jesus said this while still in Caesarea Philippi. After these words, He took the three disciples up the mountain and was changed before their eyes. When Peter wrote about this many years later, it was as though the Holy Spirit wanted to make sure we all knew Jesus's words about His coming were specifically tied to the transfiguration event. The unveiling of that majestic glory *was* the Son of Man coming in His Kingdom.

If the transfiguration was a revealing of the glory already hidden in Christ, then the "coming" of the Kingdom is the same thing. So, when we pray for the Kingdom to come, we are asking for what is already present to be made visible. This is obviously another way of articulating the meaning of *apokalyptō*—the revealing of things covered over and veiled. And this is right in line with what the Son of Man taught about the Kingdom when He said it was "at hand"—*within reach*. Jesus was not speaking of things that wouldn't come about for thousands of years. He was making a declaration

The Song of the Ages: Part III

that was relevant to the actual people around Him. The Kingdom was there *now* and they were to take hold of it by trusting in that reality. This has been a key theme flowing through the music of the Song and its currents course through its apocalyptic sister book as well. In fact, if you listen closely, you'll hear this right in John's opening instructions in Revelation:

> *Blessed is he who reads and those who hear the words of the prophecy, and heed the things which are written in it; for the time is near.*
> (Rev. 1:3)

Many have assumed this is saying the "time is near" for Jesus's physical return. However, there is a much different way of reading this text. Once again, the Passion Translation is helpful:

> *A joyous blessing rests upon the one who reads this message and upon those who hear and embrace the words of this prophecy, for* **the appointed time is in your hands.**
> (Rev. 1:3 TPT)

While this seems like a totally novel way of understanding the phrase "the time is near," this translation is based on a verifiable and simple understanding of the Greek language. The word for "near" is from the Greek adverb *eggus,* and the footnotes of the translation explain it as follows: "*Eggus* is taken from a primary verb *agcho,* which means 'to squeeze' (in your hands) or 'to hold the reins' (or 'throttle' in your hands). There is a sense in which the full understanding of the book of Revelation is ready to be unveiled when the reader is ready to receive it. The time for this revelation is now, not the past nor the distant future."

The vision given to John wasn't to fill people's heads with things that wouldn't be relevant for thousands of years, nor was it

Transfiguration of the Cosmos Pt. 2

given to tell people of things primarily related to the first century. Those are the two main approaches toward Revelation; that it is either a book mostly for the first century (referred to as the preterist position) or for the distant future (the futurist position). Both perspectives have truth in them, for there are things written in the text that clearly connect to the first century and some things yet to be seen. The problem, however, is that these positions (even the "partial" versions of them) are all rooted in *space and time*. Meanwhile, the ultimate message of the book is one that deals with a realm standing outside of time—the realm of eternity. It's in this eternal realm we discover the victory of the Lamb and a Kingdom that has already come. But though it stands outside of time, the mystery is that this realm is "within reach." Every believer from every age is called to tap into it. And when we do, the space around us is filled with more of His glory. Or, you could say that space is rolled back like a scroll to unveil a glory already present.

All this being said, it's essential we acknowledge that this understanding of the Kingdom of God still includes a future hope. There's a physical day yet to "come" when there will be a complete unveiling. God deeply cares about this day, for He still cares about space and time. It is a Gnostic position to completely dismiss and minimize what's currently happening in the world. This is where people can make their theology of Christ's finished work an irrelevant and flowery idea. Right now, there are children being trafficked and abused in space and time who need the Kingdom of heaven to manifest *today*. It's not enough to keep this in the realm of ideology and debate. Faith in this higher reality is meant to blossom into love, which looks like the transformation of society.

Much of the Shulammite's travels has been learning to navigate this tension between the finished work of Christ and the current experience of space and time. What we're finding is that this navigation comes down to communing with the God who

The Song of the Ages: Part III

was, and is, and is to come. For whether it is the past, present, or future—the preterist, futurist, or partial versions of reality—the eternal I Am has spoken a Word of victory that transcends our earthly experiences. Our calling is to feast upon that Word, which then leads us to the "redeeming of time" (Eph. 5:16 KJV). This is why the church is to regularly take communion and "proclaim the Lord's death until He *comes*" (1 Cor. 11:26). This coming is for now. When the church gathers to drink the marriage wine, Jesus indeed *comes* and releases amazing miracles of transfiguring power.

But this takes us to something else in Scripture that is absolutely astounding. We, the church, can actually "hasten" the great and final coming of the Lord. This is taught, not surprisingly, in the second letter of Peter:

> *Since all these things are to be destroyed in this way, what sort of people ought you to be in holy conduct and godliness, looking for and* **hastening the coming of the day of God**, *because of which the heavens will be destroyed by burning, and the elements will melt with intense heat!*
> *(2 Pet. 3:11-12)*

This statement holds everything we're trying to convey. But before we explore the wild and preposterous nature of Peter's words, let's pause and recap a few things:

- First, the burning of the elements is a prophetic metaphor for the destruction of humanity's immaturity. This happened once and for all at the cross, and yet it manifests through our lives when we allow the flame of the Spirit to unveil our true identity as God's sons and daughters.
- Secondly, Jesus's transfiguration was part of the inaugural unveiling—the "apocalypse" of mankind's identity and destiny. This was also the coming of God's Kingdom, a domain flowing from the throne of the human heart.

Transfiguration of the Cosmos Pt. 2

- Putting these points together, the transfiguration of humanity by the Spirit of Christ *is* the coming of the Lord. He has already come and yet He is still coming through a transfigured people.

And so here is the bottom line: The coming of the Lord is something that happens whenever the Kingdom manifests through our lives. And this is not to deny the physical return of Jesus Christ. We've made that point clear before and we'll keep saying it to avoid any misunderstanding. Jesus is going to return physically, as the angels said upon His ascension. Yet think of that story for a moment. In Acts 1, Jesus ascended to heaven and the disciples continued to gaze at the sky for a while. It took an angelic interruption for them to stop their gazing and move on to receive the fires of Pentecost. In a similar fashion, the book of Revelation was an angelic interruption (see Rev. 1:1) written to get the complete sevenfold church to experience the coming of the Lord within.

Today, the church still gazes into the sky waiting for someone to rescue us from evil governments and wicked religious systems. Yet the hidden government of God is waiting to erupt from within our awakened spirits. It's imperative we have the right storyline here, *for we are in the days of a great unveiling.* We are incredibly blessed to be living in the era we are in. Things that have long been "sealed" regarding the last days are now being unlocked and understood anew (Dan. 12:9). Though there is still an abundance of mystery as to how everything will play out, we must know that we have a great part to play in the unfolding of these promises. By receiving the flame of love upon our hearts and minds, we are actually speeding up the appearance of our victorious King!

And indeed, there are some reading this who will not taste death until they see the power and coming of this Kingdom in their own lives.

The Song of the Ages: Part III

The Days of Noah

Toward the end of His ministry, Jesus said something exceedingly important about what the world would look like before the day of His coming. He compared it to the "days of Noah" (Matt. 24:37). It's interesting that we have just now entered into an era when the manipulation of human DNA is at our fingertips. Since the year the first book in this series on the Song was written, there has been an unparalleled advance in genetic technology. Scientists can now manipulate and edit the human genome through a technology that is so simple some are already using it in their personal garages to change the DNA of other organisms. This holds quite the connection to Enoch and the alleged events leading up to Noah's flood.

But this is where we need a New Covenant perspective. Those with a doom-and-gloom mentality would see this from a negative viewpoint and surmise that all of it is leading toward a literal fire that will burn away the physical world. There's indeed a fire coming, but contrary to pop-theological opinion, it is the very flames of Solomon's Song, not the explosions found in conspiracy theorists' nightmares. There is actually great promise in this technology, such as the eradication of all DNA-based disease. But of course, there are many dangers as well. Advancing technologies are both a valley of trouble and a door of hope. Our real problem is that *nēpios* children cannot handle the weight of what is on the technological horizon. God has hidden powerful tools and abilities within creation that can only be stewarded by mature sons. (A steering wheel in the hand of a three-year-old is much different than one in the hand of a healthy thirty-year-old.)

Thankfully, nothing catches the Lord by surprise. He remains sovereign and good upon the throne of His grace. God could have easily hidden or disrupted technological discoveries if they were out of sync with His plans of hope. He's done this before (Gen. 11). The fact that these things are being discovered, or perhaps

Transfiguration of the Cosmos Pt. 2

rediscovered, is one of the many signs that a time of spiritual maturity is at hand. The true Spirit of adoption is stirring in the hearts of humanity like never before. History, as told by Enoch, will not repeat itself—for the One Enoch longed for has redeemed the race of Adam. Now, within our very reach, is the true Mount of Transfiguration—the power and coming of our Lord.

A Final Flash of Hindsight

And that brings us to the punchline. There is one more bit of hindsight here; an extraordinary clue we can now look back upon from our long journey with the Shulammite. This is another element from the Song we didn't point out initially because we would not have been able to appreciate it as much as we can now.

Think back to the fourth chapter of the Song of Songs where we reached the beautiful heights of love within the heart of God; where the Maker of heaven and earth declared that *we ravish His heart*. In that poetic declaration, the Shepherd brought the Shulammite up to the high mountain that gave us the name for the first volume of this study—*The Summit of Truth*. The Shulammite was brought to the high peaks of Amana, a mountain in the northern reaches of Israel with a name that can be translated as "truth." It's where we get the word "amen" and can also be rendered as "agreement." Very simply, the name of this mountain speaks of faith. We saw how the stunning revelation of God's vulnerable and passionate love is the ultimate truth, and our high calling is to learn to say "amen" to it. We are to live life from that glorious place of agreement with God's everlasting love.

Now, in that high place in the middle of Solomon's Song, we did not deal with the fact that Solomon mentioned another mountain right alongside Amana. Take another look:

> *Come with me from Lebanon, my spouse,*
> *With me from Lebanon.*

The Song of the Ages: Part III

*Look from the top of **Amana**,*
*From the top of Senir and **Hermon**...*
(Sgs. 4:8)

The Bridegroom is speaking of two mountains here: Amana and Hermon. Senir is just another name for Mount Hermon (Deut 3:9). So, the Song of Solomon connects the summit of Amana with the summit of Hermon.

In other words, the Summit of Truth *is* the Mount of Transfiguration. The two places are one.

Putting these two mountains together speaks of the finished work of Christ and the journey of the human soul as it awakens to that truth in time and space. When we take our stand upon the truth of the Transfigured One, we find ourselves staring in a mirror. We then experience the same transfiguration ourselves. This is why the Bride was called to "look" from this place and see all of life from its perspective.

When Peter confessed Jesus as the Messiah and Son of God, he was taking his stand upon on the summit of Amana. This then led into a corresponding experience on the literal summit of Hermon. What had been confessed by faith in the sinful city below was made visible on the heights of Hermon above. And that was the purpose of their steep hike upward. In many ways, that hike points to the entire journey of humanity. Perhaps this is why it took *six days* before they arrived there.

Six days later Jesus took with Him Peter and James
and John his brother, and led them up on a high
mountain by themselves.
(Matt. 17:1)

What was revealed to Peter on Hermon was already true in the city below, but it took a confession of faith and a following after Jesus to see it appear. This is the journey of *mankind*. It is

Transfiguration of the Cosmos Pt. 2

an adventure of faith, leading to the full manifestation of God's Word. Even the creation account prophesied this aspect of reality, because after God's initial Word of transfiguring "light," it took six days before His image and likeness would manifest in humanity.

Each of us now find ourselves in the space in-between—the hike from Caesarea Philippi to Mount Hermon. Such is the reason perseverance and patience are so integral to the adventure. John writes of "the tribulation and kingdom and *patience* of Jesus Christ" (Rev. 1:9 NKJV). Within space and time, evil so often appears to have the upper hand—but in clinging to the Word of promise through patient discipleship, we rise above that lie. And this is exactly what happened in the lives of Peter, James, John, and Ezekiel.

Think again about each of those mountainous encounters. For Ezekiel, his vision came while he was specifically locked up in Babylonian exile. He was right in the center of the very representation of human harlotry when a "hope of glory" flooded his vision. It was the same with the apostle John. He received his revelation during a time when the church seemed weak and defeated under increasing Roman persecution. In the same manner, Jesus's own transfiguration came during a time when persecution was closing in on Him. It actually took place right on the heels of His first disclosure about the crucifixion; the moment when man's wicked prostitution would be unleashed in all of its ugliness (Matt. 16:21). But when Jesus took Peter, James, and John up on that high mountain, He was showing them the greater reality. He was doing the same thing He did for Ezekiel and the same thing He would do for John years later. He was showing them the great harlot was defeated and a new Kingdom had come.

The Rise of the Morning Star

In conclusion, this is what Peter says will happen as we, God's Bride and helper, stay focused on Jesus's transfiguration and all that it conveys for the entire world:

The Song of the Ages: Part III

And so we have been given the prophetic word—
the written message of the prophets, made more reliable and
fully validated by the confirming voice of God on the Mount
of Transfiguration. And you will continue to do well if
you stay focused on it. For this prophetic message is like a
piercing light shining in a gloomy place until the dawning of
a new day, when the Morning Star rises in your hearts.
(2 Pet. 1:19 TPT)

All around us is darkness that seems to contradict the lyrics of the Song of the Lamb. But we are learning to sing in the dark. As we do this, our lamps shine and soon enough the "day" begins to dawn. The power and coming of our Lord Jesus manifests through us. This is what it means when it says the morning star will arise in "your heart."

The morning star is actually the planet Venus. From earth's perspective, it is the brightest point of light in the sky before the sun emerges. Like a bridal companion to its star, Venus closely orbits the sun and heralds the coming of a new day for the onlooking earth. And so it is with the church. On the throne of our own awakened hearts—having been washed in blood like the Mercy Seat of old—the light of the Messiah's reign breaks forth. The One who has come, comes again.

Soon, this will be seen and recognized by all. Perfect love will be fully blossomed within the soil of space and time. But in the "mean-time," we are to stay focused on this reality and promise, our feet planted like roots in the high ground of Amana and Hermon, twin mountains of identity and destiny.

20
The Lake of Fire

———•◆•———

Put me like a seal over your heart,
Like a seal on your arm.
For love is as strong as death,
Jealousy is as severe as Sheol;
Its flashes are flashes of fire,
The very flame of the Lord.
Many waters cannot quench love,
Nor will rivers overflow it;
If a man were to give all the riches of his house for love,
It would be utterly despised
(8:6-7)

Our souls were destined to hold the eternal flame. And not only to hold it, but to *be* it. And whether its poetry or prose, human words bear an impossible task in their attempt to express the magnitude of this destiny. Gratefully, what is impossible with man is possible with God. The Song of the Ages is the divine endeavor to communicate this union with Fire through parable and lyric. It is our highest calling to hold the tune of this Song close to our hearts, until its melody blazes out of us like a singing torch.

The Song of the Ages: Part III

Of course, this Song is not limited to the Song of Solomon, though that is where its notes are perhaps communicated the most clearly. We have surveyed the prophetic Scriptures and found that its brilliant rhythm beats through many other parables and historical accounts. But there is one story we have not yet brought into this divine orchestra, and it is perhaps the best story to summarize the entirety of every note we've heard thus far. On top of that, this story also addresses a remaining issue of great controversy; something we cannot bypass as this part of the Song comes to a close. The story is from the gospel of Luke, immediately following the resurrection of our Beloved.

A Long Road

One Sunday afternoon, two friends walked and talked along a lengthy road from the city of Jerusalem to a small village in Israel. The focus of their conversation was the recent crucifixion of Jesus of Nazareth. Like Ezekiel in Babylon or John on Patmos, these men had just experienced a type of exile, having witnessed all of their hopes and dreams crushed under the weight of a foreign empire. They had been disciples of Jesus, having seen His miracles, heard His teachings, and encountered the beauty of grace in human form. Yet three days prior to this long walk, their teacher was put to death in the same way every other so-called messiah and prophet had experienced before then. Such was the sad and anticlimactic ending to a few years filled with undeniable awe. Death appeared to once more have the final word as the age-old beast manifested through religion and politics, seemingly quenching all light of hope. Now they were walking back to their hometown like exiles, downcast and defeated.

One of these men was named Cleopas and some scholars believe his wife was at the foot of the cross during Jesus's death (see Jn. 19:25). If that's true, then Cleopas was missing in action

The Lake of Fire

that day, much like the other disciples. While his wife stood and witnessed the bloody execution of Jesus, Cleopas was presumably hiding in fear. Therefore, the past three days would not only have been filled with unimaginable disappointment, but also with a suffocating sense of guilt. Such an experience would have stitched a tighter layer of dark threads into the already thick veil of death hanging over his heart—the same veil that hangs over the entire earth.

But if truth be told, something much bigger was going on that day. Even though a great sadness overshadowed Cleopas and his friend, hope was actually nearer to them than they could imagine. As the two discussed these events, a stranger joined them in their walk and entered into their heavy conversation. Though initially unknown to Cleopas and his friend, this stranger was the resurrected Jesus who had come to pierce through that veil of confusion and discouragement. After listening to their own take on what had transpired over the weekend, the Lord began to walk them down the long road of Scripture. He showed them a hidden melody flowing through the law and the prophets:

> *Then beginning with Moses and with all the prophets,*
> *He explained to them the things concerning Himself in*
> *all the Scriptures.*
> *(Lk. 24:27)*

As Jesus spoke of these things, the two disciples would later recall a deep "burning" in their hearts throughout this mobile Bible study (Lk. 24:32). Something began to stir within them, but in spite of this, they were still unable to understand the fullness of what was happening. A revelation was knocking on the door of their hearts. The resurrected King of glory was standing in their midst, but their waking minds had not yet realized it. The account goes on to say that as they approached their village, the stranger

The Song of the Ages: Part III

"acted as though He was going further" (Lk. 24:58). Though Jesus was knocking, He was not looking to force Himself upon them. Nonetheless, the men were drawn to something beautiful, and perhaps they were also just practicing good hospitality, for it was dangerous to continue walking those roads at night. So, as the shadows of the day grew long and night settled in, the Light of the world was invited into their home and bread was brought out. It was during this meal that a full revelation began to dawn:

> *When He had reclined at the table with them, He took the bread and blessed it, and breaking it, He began giving it to them. Then their eyes were opened and they recognized Him; and He vanished from their sight.*
> *(Lk. 24:30-21)*

What had been true in their deepest hearts became clear to their physical eyes. Up to this moment, Cleopas and the other disciple were experiencing a progressive unveiling. Initially, in the beginning of their walk, their eyes were covered by the shroud of death. Even though there were some reports of a missing body, the two men walked home in a state of hopelessness. Yet when Jesus entered the conversation and opened the Scriptures to them, things began to shift. A flicker from the flame inside of them began to stir. Like the instructions found in Peter's second letter, these disciples were paying close attention to this Word, and it was leading them to the full breakout of dawn. Through a time of fellowship, Jesus went from breaking open the Bible to breaking open a loaf of bread. And that was the point of no return. What was already true and present became fully known and understood by these two men. That moment led to a wellspring of joy and celebration opening up within their hearts as they realized who had been with them all along.

With this realization came a renewed burst of energy as they immediately ran all the way back to Jerusalem to speak to the

The Lake of Fire

other apostles about what happened. This was a true renewing of strength, for they would have been very weary from their previous travels to and from Jerusalem—not only physically, but emotionally as well. There was also a renewed boldness here, for going back to Jerusalem on that particular Sunday night was dangerous. Doubtless there were people looking for the disciples of the convicted Rabbi named Jesus. Besides that, the road held many dangers of its own, as just mentioned. Thieves and muggers set up shop on those roads and their hours of operation were after sunset. But this is what a revelation of Christ does to the human soul. It washes away exhaustion and replaces it with courage. Such an unveiling puts a fresh spring in your step and a clearer vision in your heart. It wipes away tears from your eyes and gives you true perspective (Rev. 21:4). And just as these men went to tell others about who they'd seen, this kind of unveiling awakens the evangelist inside of you.

This short but beautiful story captures just about everything we've seen in the timeless ballad of Solomon's bride. Ever since the sixth chapter of the Song, when the Shulammite awoke to the One who was already standing in the garden of her soul, things began to rapidly shift. This is what led to her wanting to go back to her mother's house with the good news of the triumphant Christ. Now we've already covered how the "mother's house" symbolizes the city of Jerusalem—that is the same place these two awakened disciples ran back to in order to share their own amazing news.

But there are many other parallels between this story and the many gems buried in the Song of Songs. In the Song, the Bride is progressively fellowshipping with Christ, but in the midst of this she falls in and out of her veiled sleep. Through a good part of the Song, the Shulammite is unaware of the glory she already possesses. In Luke's story, the same goes with Cleopas and his friend. When they first started on their journey, they were completely burnt out

The Song of the Ages: Part III

and hopeless, and yet all their hopes and dreams were already true. They were just unaware of it. The beautiful truths at the top of Amana and Hermon were hidden by the clouds of circumstances. Because of this, they remained overcome by what recent events conveyed. But as in the case of the Shulammite, all of it was a matter of perspective. In reality, the entire world changed that Sunday morning and they were being invited to wake up and stand upon a glorious mountain of truth.

It was that particular Sunday this stranger led the two disciples into an experience that would become the seed for every future gathering of believers. Luke wrote that "while they communed together and reasoned, Jesus Himself drew near, and went with them" (v. 15 KJV). Jesus entered the scene through their fellowship. This was a prototype of what "church" would entail whenever two or three gathered in His name, even in the midst of seeming persecution and defeat. This first Sunday foreshadowed 2000 years of future Sundays, all of which would exist in that "in-between" space between faith and manifestation. Church history itself would become a progressive unveiling—a coming of the One who has already come. Through fellowship, through the Word, through the breaking of bread, the church would be called to experience the presence of Christ now. But this is all leading to a full and complete unveiling, much like what happened at the end of the road when they finally came to their destination.

And this destination is very important. It was a village by the name of *Emmaus*.

Those Who Refuse

There is a great mystery hidden within Luke's account of these events that we will explore shortly. But before we go there, we have to shift our focus toward something that has been building like a plume of smoke as we've made our slow ascent up the

The Lake of Fire

fiery revelations hidden in the Song. We've seen how the fires of Solomon's Song and the fires of Peter's cosmic prophecy are one in the same. It is at this point we come to a simple but controversial question:

What then of the fires of hell?

Is hellfire divorced from the flame of the One who is perfect Love?

The pinnacle of the Song has brought us into apocalyptic territory, and thus into questions such as these. The Shulammite's journey requires we wrestle through this, especially as we reach the culmination of her poetry. Remember, she is the one who has risen from the mouth of God to become Christ's kiss to the nations. Through her words and deeds, Jesus is proclaiming His eternal Gospel to the world. This glorious melody declares *all* have died under the apple tree of grace. There is now a worldwide invitation to "wake up" to this truth, and to receive the fires of the Spirit as the seal that empowers our true selves, transfiguring us into the mature sons and daughters of God. This is the destiny we carried even before the first flames of atomic fire flickered into existence.

But what of those who refuse to wake up?

What of those who stay upon a bed of slumber?

We have climbed the mountainous staircase of fire and learned so much about the grace-filled melody God sings over creation. Now we must inquire about the nature and reality of what the Scriptures call *the lake of fire*...

The Burning Lake

Please know this is not a theological tangent. Hell is uniquely hidden in Solomon's text. It can be found when you once again compare insights between the book of Revelation and the lyrics of the Song—specifically these:

"Love is as strong as death; jealousy is as severe as Sheol."

The Song of the Ages: Part III

Both terms Solomon contrasts with love—*death* and *Sheol*—show up in the Song's apocalyptic sister book. Sheol is the Hebraic term for the realm of the dead. It is what the Greeks and New Testament authors refer to as *Hades*. Look then at how these two words come out in Revelation:

> *Then death and Hades (Sheol) were thrown into the lake of fire. This is the second death, the lake of fire.*
> (Rev. 20:14)

Now before we jump ahead with our many presuppositions about this text, let's pull back and reflect on one of the core things we've learned so far. According to the concluding thoughts of Solomon's Song, love is the very flame of God. This is the same love from 1 Corinthians 13, the love promised to one day fill the cosmos. It is a love that hopes all things, believes all things, and overcomes all things. If Scripture is one interconnected tapestry, then "death and Hades" being thrown into a lake of fire would be nothing less than a picture of death being fully conquered by love. This is another dynamic of what the cross accomplished through the power of the Spirit.

Did you know that the first time the image of fire shows up in Revelation is in the eyes of Jesus (Rev. 1:14)? Meanwhile, in the Song of Songs, Jesus's eyes are described as gentle doves sitting by streams of water (Sgs. 5:12). These are not two different Christs. The same reality is being expressed in different forms. The burning flames and the gentle doves both speak of the Holy Spirit, the One who washes the world in a fiery baptism. In the *lake of fire*, this dual image of water and flame comes together as one. It tells of the intense mercy that will consume everything that opposes the truth. In other words, it is the burning away of the harlot and the ungodly beast, which goes hand in hand with the false name plastered over the face of humanity. The enemy of our souls—along with the

The Lake of Fire

powers, principalities, and the elements of this age—have worked hard to establish the world in the grip of this false name. But John's vision is the assurance of what the Father will accomplish through His Son Jesus and His precious Holy Spirit.

Spiritual Limnology

There's another story from the gospel of Luke that gives us a prophetic confirmation of these things. It's about one of Jesus's miracles. But before we look at it, let's first remember the works of Christ on earth usually spoke to things much bigger than the miracles in and of themselves. They were not just miracles, but "signs" pointing to greater realities. For instance, consider the multiplication of the fishes and loaves and the twelve baskets of leftover bread. That was more than just a miracle of provision. That event also showed how Jesus would eventually break His own body in order to share it with the world. This would be a multiplication of His life that would start with *twelve* disciples (as well as the entire nation of Israel represented by twelve tribes).

The miracle and sign from Luke that is relevant to our present discussion is from one of the few times the word "lake" shows up in the Bible outside of Revelation. The Greek word for "lake" is *limne*. This is where we get the word limnologist, which is someone who studies lakes. Luke is the only other New Testament author to use this particular word, specifically in reference to the Lake of Galilee (which all other authors refer to as a "sea"—though it's really a lake). Interestingly enough, Luke uses the word *limne* when telling the story of a bunch of demons being thrown into it.

This is the account of the possessed man who dwelled in a cemetery close to shore. Naked and violent, this man was living the life of a wild beast. His true genesis in Christ was veiled under the weight of demonic oppression. Yet Jesus went through a nasty storm to come to this man; a storm in which He fell asleep and

The Song of the Ages: Part III

arose in authority. That was another "sign" pointing to His death and resurrection and the overcoming of sin's storm. But after this wild storm was calmed, the signs continued. Jesus made it to shore and found this man, looking at him with eyes like doves and fire. His vision cut right through the thick veil blocking the Holy of holies within the man's heart—the veil keeping him from being in his "right mind" (see Lk. 8:35). The Lord went on to deliver him from an entire legion of demons by casting them into a nearby herd of pigs. Luke then writes, "The herd rushed down a steep bank *into the lake* and was drowned" (Lk. 8:33).

Just like the bread in other miracle stories, pigs also have a spiritual connotation. They represent that which is unclean. It's the same as uncircumcision, or the mark of the beast, or the name of the harlot. It speaks to that same broken issue of identity within mankind that has produced nothing but death. This reality also comes through the story by the simple fact that this man dwelled in a cemetery. But the Lord Jesus came and brought salvation to this individual, calling him to leave the place of death and go home. This miracle was a prophetic sermon speaking of the day when all that is unclean, all that leads to death, would be drowned in a lake. This would be a lake burning with the same fires that brought forth the universe; flames that would reach their highest temperatures in the kindling wood of Calvary. It is the unchanging, all-consuming fire that stops at nothing to restore the original intent of creation.

Now it's amazing when we add in the meaning of the lake's name in Aramaic—the language everyone was speaking during this pig incident. The meaning of "Galilee" in Aramaic is *revelation*. So, in Jesus's own language, these pigs were cast into the Lake of Revelation! This was truly a prophetic act; one the apostle John would see unfold in a symbolic vision many years later.

The Lake of Fire

Burning Down a Village

Because of our warped and guilt-ridden minds, mankind has collectively twisted the intentions and heart of God. This distortion of God's nature is arguably the most tragic part of human history (Rom. 1:23). But in light of this, we can assume that if God is a consuming fire, the historical distortion of His character has also included a distorted understanding of His fire.

A case study of man's incorrect view of fire can be found in yet another story from the writings of Luke. In fact, this is from the chapter immediately following the story of the demoniac cemetery dweller. Sometime after their encounter with the possessed man, Jesus wanted to travel through a Samaritan village (Lk. 9:51-56). Unfortunately, the people of that community refused to let Him enter their town. They had chosen to reject Love itself. Upon hearing this, John and James were deeply offended on behalf of Jesus and offered a solution, a plan that by all accounts seemed biblical and appropriate: "Lord, should we command fire to come down and consume them?"

This question was posed by the same person who would one day behold the fire of God on the island of Patmos. But judging by Jesus's reaction, young John had much to learn. "You do not know what kind of spirit you are of," the Lord spoke in a sharp rebuke.

Now we shouldn't be too quick to judge John and his brother, the "sons of thunders" as they were called. The two of them were only trying to mimic what many of their forefathers had demonstrated *in the name of God*. Like countless other well-intentioned disciples, their understanding of the Scriptures was not yet baptized by the Spirit of holiness and grace. It wasn't until after the resurrection that the true meaning of the Scriptures was opened up to the disciples—not only for John and James, but for the two men on the road to Emmaus, and each of the other apostles as

The Song of the Ages: Part III

well. In this case, Jesus saw right through their unenlightened zeal and religious pride and prejudice. There was a deep dislike—in the name of God—toward the Samaritan heretics who had liberalized the Scriptures and embraced all kinds of idolatry. This is the same thinking often hidden behind many modern sons of thunder who, on behalf of God, speak of hellfire with a similar "spirit."

But Jesus knew something that John didn't. There *was* a fire coming to Samaria. Yet this would be unlike the one conjured up out of their own limited, religious framework. This fire would start as a spark when Jesus touched the life of a broken woman at Jacob's well. This was the Samaritan woman; someone who embodied the life of the striving harlot after a string of broken relationships and failed marriages (Jn. 4). But there at Jacob's well she would meet the same person who had wrestled with Jacob and changed his name. Remember, "Jacob" can be translated as *deceiver*. So, this woman was experiencing the same God who continually comes to burn away our deceptive names with the fire and water of His Spirit.

Now it's important to quickly point out that in the chapter preceding this encounter with the Samaritan woman, John the Baptist is seen announcing Jesus as the true Bridegroom (Jn. 3:29). The immediate next story is where Jesus goes to meet the Samaritan woman. Just like the patriarchs went to a well to find a beloved wife (Gen. 24 & 29), Jesus comes for His beloved Bride in the same exact way! At this well, he finds a woman who had experienced all the false forms of love—and He looks at her with those same eyes of the Spirit. Church tradition tells us this woman's name was Photini and she became a luminous flame throughout the world, reaching countless people for Christ. But this all started with her encounter at the well where she went on to tell her entire village about her new Bridegroom. This is how the true fire of God began to break out in Samaria.

The Lake of Fire

Now it was not long after this when an evangelist named Philip went to that same region and brought them more of the fiery kiss of God. That event would lead to the apostle John finally getting his opportunity to visit Samaria and call down fire from heaven. This time, however, it would be done in the right Spirit:

> *Now when the apostles in Jerusalem heard that Samaria had received the word of God, they sent them Peter and John, who came down and prayed for them that they might receive the Holy Spirit...Then they began laying their hands on them, and they were receiving the Holy Spirit.*
> *(Acts 8:14-15, 17)*

The Trampling of Death

This idea of the lake of fire being the conquering love of God may be difficult for some to swallow, but it will become easier as we continue to allow Scripture to interpret Scripture (in contrast to relying solely upon opinionated commentary that often arises from religious traditions). With that, we'll attempt to connect even more dots and hopefully see that this isn't a push to make the Bible say what we want it to say. The hope, rather, is that this will be a Spirit-led discovery of what the Word is speaking on its own accord.

First, consider the book of 1 Corinthians and what Paul says two chapters after his description of the enduring nature of love. He writes that the "last enemy" to be destroyed is death (1 Cor. 15:26). Revelation declares that death will be cast into a burning lake. Yet this Scripture and others suggest that death will be crushed under the feet of Jesus—for He is the One sitting at the right hand of God waiting for His "enemies" to be made a footstool under His feet (Heb. 10:13). This shows that there is more to the fiery lake of hell than meets the eye.

The Song of the Ages: Part III

Now even further insight emerges when we go back to the Song of Songs. When Solomon wrote the phrase "utterly despised," he was using a word that is almost identical to a Hebrew term meaning "to trample on by foot." In apocalyptic fashion, Solomon is showing us that all forms of false love—all things leading to death—will be *trampled by foot*. And with this, there's something else in the New Testament that needs to be taken into account as well. The Scriptures tell us that the one who holds the power of death, Satan, will soon be crushed under *our feet* (see Heb. 2:14 & Rom. 16:20).

So, this brings up a few questions. Is it a burning lake or is it someone's feet that ultimately destroys the power of death?

And furthermore, do those feet belong to Jesus or us?

Well, if Christ is a consuming fire of love—and if we are His Body—then the answer to each question is…*yes*. Jesus is the One with the keys to death and Sheol, and He told Peter He was giving those keys to us (Rev. 1:18 & Matt. 16:19). So the lake of fire, traditionally known as hell, is love's victory over death, and this gets manifested through the church. By the Spirit, we become the instruments through which He reveals His victory on earth. In other words, God has already judged and defeated sin and death; however, this appears in space and time when people believe and are baptized in the Spirit. This is why the Spirit and Bride say, "Come!" They call for everyone outside the Kingdom of grace to come and wash their robes in holy fire (Rev. 22:14). And with that in mind, think about the church's mission to go and *baptize the nations* into the *name* of the Father, Son, and Spirit (Matt. 28:19). As you ponder that, also recall what gets thrown into the lake of fire…

> *And if anyone's* **name** *was not found written in the book*
> *of life, he was thrown into the lake of fire.*
> *(Rev. 20:15)*

The Lake of Fire

The lake burns away the false name! It's a baptism of transfiguring fire. And perhaps this is why the vision immediately following the burning lake in Revelation 20 is the Bride of Christ coming down upon the earth in Revelation 21. There, John was seeing the feet of Jesus—the full stature of His body—stamping down upon the planet!

These are just more facets of the same glorious promises we've been surveying ever since we saw the Bride rising from the wilderness. All of it has been speaking to one revelation of the Gospel unfolding throughout time. Remember, John's book is called Revelation—not *revelations*—because it is really one truth being dispensed in different forms and facets. Right before his vision of the lake, John was told, "The testimony of Jesus *is* the spirit of prophecy" (Rev. 19:10). Everything in his book, including the lake chapter, is pointing to Jesus's personhood as well as the "testimony" of His accomplishments. They are all different colors of thread in the great tapestry of God's Word. Some thread is just a lot more intense and vibrant than others. And this goes hand in hand with the Song of Solomon—for it is not the *Songs* of Solomon, but the Song. It is one message of union between Christ and His Bride, and the expansion of their glorious Kingdom of love upon the earth.

Redeeming Man's Lowest Point

We mentioned earlier that the word "fire" in Revelation first shows up in the eyes of Jesus. The last place it appears is in a final description about this infamous lake. It says the lake burns with fire *and brimstone* (Rev. 21:8). Now this is where we come back to the power of homonyms—words that can mean multiple things. It's incredibly clear that God used Hebrew homonyms in the Old Testament to speak to people at different levels. It should come as no surprise that the Author of the Old Testament would do

The Song of the Ages: Part III

the same thing with the Greek and Aramaic languages in the New. This word for "brimstone" is one such homonym in the Greek. It's a word that can actually be translated as *divinity*. The term is *theion* and it is the nominalized version of *theios,* an adjective usually translated as "divine." The adjective form is used twice by Peter (in his second letter no less). He says this:

> *His **divine power** has granted to us everything pertaining to life and godliness… He has granted to us His precious and magnificent promises, so that by them you may become partakers of **the divine nature**, having escaped the corruption that is in the world by lust.*
> (2 Pet. 1:3, 4)

So, the same word behind the substance found in the lake of fire is used by Peter in these two instances to describe how someone comes into true life and godliness! It is through divine power—*theios*—that we come into godliness and escape "the corruption that is in the world by lust." Or you could say that it is through God's fierce brimstone—*theion*—that we escape the way of the harlot. All this ties back into what we've learned of transfiguration.

And with that in mind, did you know that one of the transfiguration encounters we mentioned earlier had to do with a lake? It was with Ezekiel and his vision of the Dead Sea—which, like Galilee, is not actually a sea but a lake. It is in fact the lowest lake on the entire planet. At over a thousand feet below sea level, the area has the lowest land elevation on earth. That's very fitting when you consider how this lake happens to be named after the place of man's lowest point. Man has fallen to the dust and death has been the result. But in his encounter, Ezekiel was given a prophetic picture of this geologically significant body of water, which in Arabic is called the Sea of Death. After he saw the temple of God opened up and a river flowing out of the Holy of holies, Ezekiel

The Lake of Fire

witnessed the river eventually hitting this lake named Death. And that is where it was transformed into a place of life!

We've already looked at this vision, but now we see another connecting layer of its truths. Ezekiel was seeing the death of the Dead Sea. He saw *the death of death,* which is really what Revelation 20 is about. Whereas before no fish, not even algae, could exist in that lake, Ezekiel saw it transfigured by the Holy Spirit into a place of abundance. He beheld this transforming work happening through water, but we've made it clear that this is the same reality Peter and John saw as fire.

The End of the Road

It's time to come back to the story of the two men walking down a long road with a humble stranger. The mystery mentioned earlier has to do with the name of their destination. This famous Sunday stroll, which began from a place of brokenness and sadness, and turned brighter and brighter with a progressive unveiling of Jesus, all culminated at a place called Emmaus. Names and words continue to be so vital in capturing God's heart within His Word, and this particular name is no exception. The word Emmaus comes from a Hebrew root term meaning *the Burning Place.*

We've already seen how much this account parallels the journey of the Shulammite and the entire message of the prophetic Scriptures. This aspect of the story confirms this even further. But before we give this a closer look, it's first important to know why this village was given this particular name. Emmaus was located in a certain area in Israel known for hot underground springs that provided the water for warm outdoor baths. These types of places were like ancient spas people would travel to from all over the Roman Empire to find relaxation and healing. The reason for the existence of these hot springs is equally important. In Emmaus's case, the village happened to be geographically located in an area

The Song of the Ages: Part III

known as the Syrian-African rift. This great tear in the earth's crust is one of the world's largest rifts. It extends from the mountains of Lebanon—the location of Amana and Hermon—and goes all the way down to Mozambique, Africa. (Ironically, the geological name for one of the fault lines in this rift is the "Dead Sea Transform.") As with similar rifts, there are an abundance of volcanoes and earthquakes found along its pathways. Volcanic activity and violent movements deep within the earth are the forces that give way to the unleashing of these hot springs on the earth's surface. An unimaginable force of fire and lava is what creates the heat for the baths found in Emmaus, the Burning Place. These are fires hidden in the depths of the earth, the same place the ancient writers of Scripture viewed as the "underworld" and usually associated with Hades and Sheol (Num. 16:33, Job 17:13-16, Ps. 88:6-11). Yet these fires enabled towns like Emmaus to become places for healing and cleansing.

Like so many other stories in the gospel accounts, the road to Emmaus is much bigger than the personal testimony of those involved. It speaks to the larger story of God's redemptive plans for the world. Just as these two men walked in a slow but growing revelation of Jesus—which pinnacled at the Burning Place—such is the case with humanity. There is One who is yet a stranger to many, who is actually our Deliverer from all the heartbreak, disappointment, and regret that fills our conversations as we walk through this age. And so, we are invited to enter into fellowship with this Deliver, though it is a fellowship that is often veiled and requires the eyes of our hearts instead of the eyes in our heads. But through this, there's a slow and growing invasion of Jesus's Kingdom into the world. This will culminate with the burning fires Peter and others prophesied about. Soon enough, the One who erupted from the tomb like a spring of life rising from the tectonic underworld will be revealed in a complete apocalypse of glory. The

The Lake of Fire

Burning Place speaks of this final destination where all of man's elements and works will be cleansed and burned away. Thus, the road to Emmaus is the road of humanity.

The length of this walk confirms this mystery further. Most of our Greek manuscripts state the journey was "sixty stadia" (a unit of measurement that happens to be about 600 feet—so the length would be 600 feet times 60). Now what's interesting is that modern scholarship has shown the distance from Jerusalem to Emmaus was probably much longer. Yet there was most likely an inspired reason behind the distance given in the text. Again, the Bible is not meant to be a literal textbook, but an adventure into the heart of God through mystery and parable. We know very well by now that the number six points to humanity. And so, this *sixty* stadia journey is truly the journey of humanity reaching the unveiling of Jesus. It's similar to the *sixty-six* books of the Bible that crescendo with a fiery book literally called the Unveiling of Jesus Christ. It also connects back to the *six-day* journey between Caesarea Philippi and Hermon. All of it is about our final destination of transfiguring fire!

This is the core message behind the prophetic Scripture that Peter told us to focus upon, just as we would with a lamp in a gloomy place. This apocalyptic fire is our great future hope; yet we've also recognized that this fire has already been released upon the earth. The fires of Jesus's Spirit are all around us, even though we haven't realized their fullness yet. And this lines up incredibly with the Emmaus story as well. For when the two disciples reflected back on their journey down the road, they asked this question:

"Were not our hearts *burning* within us?" (Lk. 24:32)

They were headed to the Burning Place, but the Burning One was already with them!

Indeed, the glory of God covers the entire earth right now, even as you read this, but one day this glory will be manifested for all to see. Nevertheless, the fiery realm of eternity is within reach.

The Song of the Ages: Part III

At any moment, we can allow the Lord to break in and "come." Cleopas's sadness and defeat were only illusions. When he and his friend entered into fellowship with one another—when they opened the Bible and broke the bread—their perspectives became filled with more and more light. And so it is with us. Through communion with the Word and one another, we are invited to taste the powers of the age to come *now*. It's through our personal participation in these things that the realities of the cross penetrate life here on earth. For as we've seen, the judgment of the cross has already been fully established in heaven. Yet God's will is that it would be *on earth* (in space and time) as it is there.

With that said, there's another element hidden within the word Emmaus that brings all of these truths together. The Hebrew root word behind Emmaus, which opened up all this discussion, is the word *yowm*. While this word literally has to do with burning heat, it's also the main Hebrew term for *time*. It most likely got used for both concepts because as the sun rises, the day grows hotter. In the Hebrew mind, a new day starts in the cooler evening. The day therefore reaches its pinnacle as the sun ascends and its heat grows into the late afternoon. So, a revelation of time itself is hidden within the Hebraic understanding of fire! This unlocks another level of the mystery at hand. It shows us that time itself is headed toward the Burning Place—toward the great Unveiling!

The Mystery of Time

What a beautiful and vibrant confidence we have in Christ! And with this confidence, we also see how exceedingly precious this present age is to the Lord. To ignore or deny the importance of physical space-time is a form of Gnosticism; a super-spirituality disconnected from the sacredness of flesh-and-blood realities. The apostles suffered and gave their lives so that people might experience the finished work of Christ within time. Though there is

The Lake of Fire

a victorious fire ahead, there are real consequences to the decisions made within this age. This is because this current epoch is where the choice and will of beings made in the image of God play an important role. Not the only role—but a very significant one that goes back to the continual theme of the Song: *Do not awaken my love until she pleases.*

Because of this, let's recall one final part of the Emmaus story. When the two men arrived at their village, Jesus pretended like He was going to walk ahead of them. It says, "And they approached the village where they were going, and *He acted as though* He were going farther" (v. 28). There is a sense here that Jesus *wanted* to be invited in by these disciples. He was not looking to impose upon their household. We can see here that the full unveiling somehow, mysteriously, dovetails with a true awakening of love. God is not interested in slaves. That false form of love is actually the very thing needing judgment and cleansing. Therefore, we can't demand Jesus to force everyone to wake up from their sleep. To wake up from harlotry is to embrace true trust, the very thing that *cannot* be forced!

But this brings us back to the question we began addressing in the beginning. What of those who still refuse to wake up? What does the end of the road look like for them? It seems we need one more chapter to finish answering this.

21
The Cross Versus the Wand

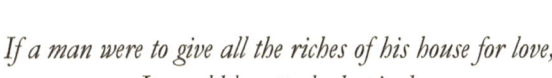

If a man were to give all the riches of his house for love,
It would be utterly despised.
(8:7b)

Fire is an extraordinary substance. It can be used to heat homes, cook food, and launch lightshows of celebration in the sky. Yet it can also be turned into a tool for arson and warfare. Harnessed with reverence, the good it can accomplish is almost limitless. Harnessed with malice and it can release untold destruction. It all depends on who's holding the flame. In the hands of an immature child, fire is certainly dangerous, but in the hands of the mature—especially a maturity marked by love's wisdom—its power is lifegiving and celebratory.

In like manner, it takes a mature pair of hands to handle the fires of Scripture. If not, it can become a tool of arson on the household of people's faith, and of warfare against the knowledge of God. As such, it is the mature Bride of Christ, rooted and grounded in the true nature of the Father, who will have the greatest handle on the lifegiving message behind biblical fire. It should come as no surprise that the wilderness seasons of Christendom have produced highly destructive misconceptions about the fires of hell. But as the Bride rises out of religion, she will carry a much healthier and more beautiful way of understanding its reviving nature.

Still, we are left with the question as to what happens to those who resist love's call. What of those who seem to refuse the invitation of the Spirit and the Bride, and remain outside the gates? And what about the "weeping and gnashing of teeth" and the terrifying "penalty of eternal destruction" for those who reject the truth? It has been important to regain a healthy view of the essence of fire before specifically addressing these questions. A proper understanding of the heart of God is the foundation that can rightly divide these issues. So, having regained that foundation, we can now move forward. And we will say very clearly right from the onset, that even though the whole world is headed for a fiery baptism of love, there is a difference between those who embrace that fire and those who run from it.

The following is sure to offend the mind—both the theologically conservative mind as well the theologically liberal. But I pray you're able to stick through the following section with an open heart, asking the Holy Spirit (with a true embrace of childlike teachability) to lead you and guide you. You may even want to pause now for that purpose…

One in the Same

We are in a day when God is restoring ancient wisdom to the church, much of which goes further back than the theology many of us inherited from a relatively small portion of church history. Accordingly, there's a perspective from some of the ancient church fathers specifically dealing with this issue; a view still held by the Eastern Orthodox church to this day. This is the view that *the fires of heaven and hell are one in the same.*

The Cross Versus the Wand

Eternity is not spatial in the way we understand space and distance. This is hard for us to grasp, but let's just try and catch the main point. In eternity, God's love fills all things. For those who embrace love, this will be pure paradise. But for those who reject love and cling to deception, this fire will be terribly painful. A glimmer of this reality can be seen when you take a set of apocalyptic prophecies from the book of Daniel and compare them with Revelation. In Daniel, we see the throne of God and from it proceeds a river of blazing fire:

> *I kept looking*
> *Until thrones were set up,*
> *And the Ancient of Days took His seat;*
> *His vesture was like white snow*
> *And the hair of His head like pure wool.*
> *His throne was ablaze with flames,*
> *Its wheels were a burning fire.*
> *A river of fire was flowing*
> *And coming out from before Him...*
> *(Dan. 9:9-10a)*

In the Bible's final book, we see the same exact throne. Yet this time there's a river of lifegiving water coming from it.

> *Then he showed me **a river of the water of life**,*
> *clear as crystal, coming from the throne of God and of*
> *the Lamb.*
> *(Rev. 22:1)*

This is reminiscent of the two different ways of seeing the eyes of Jesus. It is two sides of the same coin. The river that Daniel sees is the same as John's river, but it is a different manifestation. To the person who has embraced their true identity in Christ—who has said *yes* and *"I do"* to the Gospel of grace—this river is nothing but

The Song of the Ages: Part III

enlivening water. But for those who choose to cling to false gods and to the elements of this age, there is destruction and loss.

Many of us, especially those in the west, have inherited a flawed belief that hell is an "eternal separation" from God. This is a dogma handed down for generations that has been parroted by well-meaning teachers but is not at all rooted in the ancient texts. In actuality, there's no place separate from the One who fills all in all. "If I make my bed in hell," David said, "behold, thou art there" (Ps. 139:8 KJV). There cannot be a fire where God is not present. This idea of an eternal separation comes particularly from a misreading of 2 Thessalonians where Paul writes the following:

> *These will pay the penalty of eternal destruction,*
> **away from** *the presence of the Lord and from the*
> *glory of His power.*
> *(2 Thess. 1:9)*

This verse involves the translation of the singular Greek term behind *"away from."* Though this is one way to interpret this word, the King James Version happens to get it much better. It says that people will "be punished with everlasting destruction *from* the presence of the Lord." This opens up a completely different perspective on the verse. It suggests there will be an eternal fire of glory that will *come from* God Himself. In other words, it is Daniel's river of fire proceeding from the throne. This is what judges and destroys all that is false. In fact, the verse in Daniel that comes right after the "river of fire" describes the destruction of an evil beast! Thus, for those who cling to the lie of the beast and harlot, they put themselves right in the line of this fire.

The idea of people experiencing the fire of hell in the very presence of God becomes unarguable when you look at the fourteenth chapter of Revelation. There it speaks of those who worship the beast and take on his false name. It says such people

The Cross Versus the Wand

will be "tormented with fire and brimstone in the presence of the holy angels and *in the presence of the Lamb*" (Rev. 14:10). It's hard to get away from a statement as clear as that. The painful burning happens in Jesus's presence—*because He is the fire and brimstone.* This fiery encounter does not happen in some separate torture chamber. Such things were dreamed up in the musty basement of medieval theology. Our Hebrew ancestors knew nothing of such strange notions.

So, in 2 Thessalonians, Paul is not saying people will be put *away from* God. Rather, they will eventually have to come face to face with the burning love that issues from His presence. But this experience will be very different for those who have embraced love and those who haven't. And this is where we need a high dose of humility, for we do not know the details of how this will play out. When Jesus spoke of Gehenna—the burning garbage dump in Israel that gets translated as "hell" in the gospel accounts—He used highly symbolic terminology. Sometimes He referred to it as a place of utter darkness, and other times as that of burning flames. Flames and darkness do not go together, as one produces light while the other is an absence of light. But that's because the metaphor is just that—a metaphor. It's not to be taken literally.

Yet just because we don't take something literally doesn't mean we don't take it seriously.

The most legalistic person in the world wouldn't take out a spoon to gouge out their eye in response to the Sermon on the Mount; yet we should all heed the call to guard our eyes, as things that get through its gates will rape and pillage the beauty of our souls if left unchecked. We never want to minimize the intensity of Jesus's words, for they were intense for a reason. All we know is that if someone has chosen to remain in darkness, there will be a loss so unthinkable it requires multiple metaphors with drastic language to describe it.

The Song of the Ages: Part III

But let's bring this back to our main focus. We're winding down three volumes on an ancient love story expressing the heart of God. The "Song of Songs" *is* the Gospel. It's a revelation of the nature of God and His beautiful plan of salvation, all wrapped up in the person and work of Christ. It's also the revelation of a mature Bride who is promised to arise with the full kiss of His Word. As those who are part of this rising Bride, we are called to be messengers of this Gospel kiss—the Song of the Ages—and so it is imperative we learn to play *all* its notes, even those that seem difficult. Now that we've reached the issue of heaven and hell, and the unity of its fires, we're still in need of more clarity and wisdom. Thankfully, in the Song's apocalyptic finale about death, Sheol, and love, there is one line from this Gospel song sheet that helps us tremendously:

If a man were to give all the riches of his house for love, it would be utterly despised.

Though we've already examined these words, we need to look at them one last time, for they hold the essence of what we're discovering. They also speak to some of the greatest controversies in church history, including the dynamics of sovereignty and freewill. Let us then go a little deeper down the rabbit hole of this verse. We will do that by looking at another story chronicled by Luke where someone made an attempt to "buy" the seal of love. Did you know that someone literally tried to do that? This one story opens up a world of insight into Solomon's apocalyptic text—as well as the destiny of humankind.

Sorcery and Fire

As it happens, the person who attempted this abhorrent act was from Samaria. The account is found in the book of Acts, when a man attempted to buy the seal of God from the apostle Peter not long after the fires of Pentecost fell.

The Cross Versus the Wand

When John and Peter traveled to this region to pray for people to receive the Spirit's seal, a man named Simon offered Peter money to purchase this incredible gift. He wanted to buy the fire. Now remember, the Holy Spirit *is Love*. So, Simon of Samaria was actually offering "the riches of his house" for the gift of Love. This was spiritual harlotry through and through, and thus his offer was met with one of the sharpest rebukes in the entire New Testament: "May your silver perish with you, because you thought you could obtain the gift of God with money," Peter snapped back (Acts 8:20). Simon's request met the harsh truth of Solomon's Song. It was *utterly despised*.

Now Simon's background was very telling. He was a former sorcerer who had encountered the power of the Gospel through the ministry of the evangelist Phillip. Apparently, he had believed in Jesus and been baptized, receiving to some degree the revelation of God's seal, yet it was obvious he had not yet embraced the full reality of the message. Simon still had serious issues with his way of thinking and had not left his old name behind. This brings us back to the book of Revelation. At the end of the great harlot's judgment, John writes of her: "All the nations were deceived by your sorcery" (Rev. 18:23). Isaiah says something similar about Babylon after mentioning her face-covering *tsammah* (see Isa. 47:9). There's something about sorcery that connects to the same underlying meaning of spiritual prostitution—which we are attributing to the very essence of what is being judged throughout humanity.

Sorcery is the practice of gaining access to spiritual realities through different means and methods. At the end of the day, sorcery is just another system of legalism, the real root of mankind's problems. (And this is ironic considering how quick Christians are to condemn the practices of witchcraft and prostitution when the real underlying sin gets dished out at legalistic pulpits. Such an irony makes one think of Jesus's words to the Pharisees in Matthew 21 when He said, *"Prostitutes will get into the Kingdom before you."*)

The Song of the Ages: Part III

So, in his own pagan way, Simon of Samaria was going back to the elemental works of the law in order to gain Holy Spirit. It's amazing how much this ties in with other teachings in the New Testament:

> *You foolish Galatians, who has **bewitched** you, before whose eyes Jesus Christ was publicly portrayed as crucified? This is the only thing I want to find out from you: did you receive **the Spirit** by the works of the Law, or by hearing with faith?*
> *(Gal. 3:1-2)*

Paul was rebuking an entire church community seeking to buy or earn the gift of love through obedience to Jewish law. Because of his former unveiled life, Paul could spot this kind of legalism from hundreds of miles away—literally. He had been rebuked by the Lord Himself with the fiery light of grace and now he was a messenger of the same burning rebuke to the people of Galatia.

Of course, a few years before Peter rebuked the sorcerer of Samaria, he had received his own rebuke from Jesus. This was right before the transfiguration story while they were still at their base camp in Caesarea Philippi. Ironically, this was a time in Peter's life when he shared the same name as the sorcerer…

A New Maccabean Revolt

Simon Peter was a follower of Jesus, but like Simon of Samaria, his old identity still crept into his thinking at times. When Jesus told him and the other disciples about His impending death on a cross, Simon rebuked the Lord:

> *Peter took Him aside and began to rebuke Him, saying, "God forbid it, Lord! This shall never happen to You." But He turned and said to Peter, "Get behind Me, Satan!*

The Cross Versus the Wand

You are a stumbling block to Me; for you are not setting your mind on God's interests, but man's."
(Matt. 16:22-23)

One could argue that this response from Jesus was even harsher than Paul's words to the Galatians or Peter's own warning to the sorcerer. Jesus was calling Simon Peter *satanic*. But this was not a rebuke on Simon himself. Instead, this was a fiery reprimand on his way of thinking—a way he'd grown up with his entire life. Jesus was insinuating that Peter's words were aligned with the very origins of evil itself. Thus, the Lord told Peter he was "setting" his "mind" on the wrong thing. Jesus was coming against a *mindset* here. He was actually dealing with the mind of the harlot—exposing it right within the thinking of His lead apostle. As we've seen, this connects to the mark of the beast and the number of man; the ancient mindset that became the progenitor of all sorcery and harlotry. And this boils down to something very simple...*earning and forcing love*. This mindset is what leads man to death, for Romans says, "The mind set on the flesh is death, but the mind set on the Spirit is life and peace" (Rom. 8:6).

Now if you're wondering how Simon Peter's apprehensive words to Jesus embodied this root-of-all-death mindset, consider the following. As a first century Jew, Simon lived under his community's expectations for a divine military leader who would destroy Rome and instill Jewish law throughout the world. If you read the Old Testament in a purely literal fashion, you can understand why they had this belief since many of its prophets spoke of a coming king who would slay the enemies of Israel and establish Jerusalem as the place from which the law would go forth (see Mic. 4:1-3 & 5:5-6). This connects to the age-old problem of forcing love, because the Jewish law can be summed up with the words, *"Love the Lord your God...and love your neighbor as yourself"* (Matt. 22:36-40). Thus, the very hope for this military leader

The Song of the Ages: Part III

enforcing this law on the world was truly a satanic mindset wanting to force love! Such thinking might have been well-intentioned, but as the saying goes, the road to hell is paved with good intentions.

Simon had grown up in a community that celebrated violent rebellion against oppressive governments. Only about two centuries before his birth was the Maccabean Revolt, a time when *six* men—a priest and his five sons—stood against the empire that had been oppressing the Jewish people and beating down their culture. The Maccabees rose up in defiance and overthrew their enemies through guerilla warfare, outsmarting foreign soldiers on their own land. In the minds of the people, these were the new Joshuas and Calebs who had defeated the physical enemies of Israel. They restored the hope of a Jewish monarchy and the promise of a king who would one day reign from a real throne in Jerusalem. The world Simon grew up in commemorated this revolution, much like American readers celebrate the guerilla tactics of the Revolutionary War (also only a few centuries ago). In Simon's day, there was a deep pride centered around their Maccabean forefathers, and this was accompanied by national celebrations such as Hanukkah, the holiday that specifically honored the Revolt. This was their Fourth of July, a celebration of independence from an oppressing regime. Interestingly, the last of the Maccabees had been a man named Simon. However, when he died, the family's influence waned and Rome soon came in as the next oppressor.

Now we've mentioned how Simon Peter would have been very familiar with the book of Enoch. In the later parts of Enoch, the Maccabean Revolt gets addressed in apocalyptic form. In 1 Enoch 90, the Maccabees are symbolized by a lamb with horns. The horns represent power and thus the overthrow of the enemy. When Simon Peter was told by his brother that John the Baptist was heralding the "Lamb of God," it was very probable Simon

The Cross Versus the Wand

thought this was a true Maccabee-like Messiah who would grow horns and impale the powers of Rome once and for all.

And so hopefully you can empathize with the internal struggle within Simon when Jesus disclosed He was going to be beaten and killed by the new oppressor of Israel. It made no sense at all. The great "Lamb" would be slaughtered without a fight! Such words were incredibly tough to hear for patriotic wannabe-Maccabees like Simon and the disciples. The plan went directly against their national pride and spiritual expectations. In fact, the disclosure about the cross was so offensive to Simon that Jesus's kingship had to be confirmed with glorious power on the top of Mount Hermon immediately afterwards. There, Jesus subverted the culture of the day and redefined their understanding of spiritual writings like Enoch. God was not only writing a new origin story; He was also declaring the arrival of a new kind of horned Lamb.

The Ancient Hill

When confronted by Simon Peter, the Lord knew He was not wrestling with flesh and blood. This is why He called out the name Satan. Simon's resistance to Christ was an attack from the same enemy who tested Him in the wilderness. The same spirit behind both Simons we're looking at—Peter and the sorcerer— had enticed Jesus to throw Himself off the temple as a way to dazzle and attract the masses. Such an act would have essentially *forced* Jesus's messianic reign. The same thing was happening when Satan asked Jesus to bow before him, promising all the kingdoms of the world if He did that one thing. In that moment, Satan was offering Jesus the opportunity to "buy" the world's love. He was trying to allure Jesus into giving the riches of His house for the very love He desired. The Lord was being tempted to become a spiritual sorcerer who would oversee a world full of prostitutes instead of free sons and daughters.

The Song of the Ages: Part III

Jesus rejected this for the same reason He hid Himself when people tried to force His earthly coronation. Satan and the people wanted the Lord to enter into a form of control, but love refuses to do this. Religious legalism and spiritual witchcraft both deal in this realm of control and manipulation. They are defining qualities of man's spiritual infancy—the elements and works of our *nēpios* way of life, destined for destruction by the flame of mature love. At the end of the temptations, we're told the enemy left Jesus "until an opportune time" (Lk. 4:13). It seems that opportune time came in Caesarea Philippi when the carnal way of thinking rose up in Simon Peter.

Thankfully, the Lord pressed through this again and continued His victorious march toward the hill where He would defeat the gates of death once and for all—a hill known as Golgotha, meaning "the place of the skull." This fits into our discussion more than you can imagine. This famous hill was given this name because, from a distance, the area actually looked like a giant human skull. Therefore, the cross was planted into the ground like a stake, and as such, it would strike and penetrate the soil of this skull-hill. Take a moment and get that image into your mind. What was essentially a giant wooden stake struck through the top of a hill shaped like a human head. *This was the sign God was striking down the death-producing mindset of man!* This event was even foreshadowed in the Old Testament when the shepherd David killed a giant named Goliath by striking his *forehead* with a stone. Incredibly, the name Goliath is taken from the same Hebrew root word as Golgotha!

These things are not coincidences. The real oppressor Jesus came to fight against was the empire of carnal thinking. This is the mindset that embodies the mother of all harlotries; the age-old veil we've been looking at all along. This way of thinking always starts with an appearance of good in its appeal for love and godliness to prevail (...*if you eat the fruit, you will be like God...if you reject the cross and confront Rome, the world will become godly*), but in the end it leads to a false form of love and unity—like the sex between a prostitute and a paying client.

Power and Love

We are inevitably brought back to Jesus's words on how it was to our advantage He physically leave. Sticking around would have only given Him power, not love. That is to say, Jesus would have only gained spiritual prostitutes and not a radiant Bride. And this is the crux of the matter and the finale of the whole Bible. This issue of power and love is at the center of man's deepest questions, encompassing the subject of sovereignty and free-will, and extending even to the critical issue of heaven and hell.

To wrap up these thoughts, we must now go a little further down this rabbit hole. There's a faulty belief we have to confront—the idea that the Creator is "all-powerful" in the sense of some cosmic sorcerer who can do anything He wants. God's power is wrapped up in His perfect love, a love that does not control or manipulate. Consequently, there are certain things God *cannot* do. And this is actually very good news because it leads to a creation marked by pure freedom and true love. However, like the good news announcing a baby's birth, this news comes with intense but temporary birth pangs of suffering—for mankind has the freedom to reject love, and that rejection is at the headwaters of all suffering.

Earlier, we alluded to the well-known analogy of heat and cold as one of the explanations for evil's existence. Just as the cold is a result of withdrawing from a source of heat, evil is a withdrawal from love. The cold does not actually exist in and of itself. It is not a "thing." Rather, heat is a thing. It's a substance that arises from the energy that fills the entire universe. In the same way, evil is not a thing. It's not reality. It's *unreality*. And God is not evil just like heat is *not* the cold. Heat can never be cold, otherwise it would stop

The Song of the Ages: Part III

being heat. Its nature would be lost. Similarly, God would cease being God if He ever engaged in anything evil. And just as heat does not give off cold, God does not produce evil. Evil is simply what happens when *we* withdraw from the flame of His Spirit. It is the coldness of death, and it is utterly despised.

This sheds a great deal of light on Solomon's summarizing poetry and the many warnings of Scripture speaking to what happens when a person or nation chooses the path of evil. It's not that people are punished by God for immorality and rebellion. The problem is that people are punishing themselves by going against the very fabric of reality. Violence, depression, fear, lust—all of it is unreality. In other words, it's like entering into the cold. It's embracing what we traditionally think of as *hell*—the "place" people go to for rejecting God. Such a realm has *nothing* to do with punishment from an angry Deity. Rather, it is the natural consequence of welcoming in deception, and it is absolute foolishness. It's like Esau selling his entire birthright for a temporary bowl of soup, when his birthright would have provided thousands of bowls of soup, and much more (Gen. 25:34).

Jesus Christ completely defeated the power of this unreal, cold existence. But at the end of Solomon's greatest Song we see why people can still experience destruction even after Jesus's victorious work of salvation. This goes back to the original evil in the Garden where man attempted to purchase godlikeness—*Love*—on his own. As we've seen, this made prostitution the most fitting metaphor for humanity's problems (and the image of a Bride as its polar opposite reality). For even though we rejected love, we still longed for it, and searched for it in all the wrong places. This striving after love caused all our rebellion in the first place and it was a path of insanity because it involves searching after something that's already ours. It's devouring a small bowl of soup to satisfy a deceptive sense of longing, when there is a birthright of unbelievable satisfaction at our fingertips.

The Cross Versus the Wand

In this realization of what "sin" actually is, we understand why there are still consequences for rejecting the Gospel. It's not that Jesus only semi-finished His work. He completely removed every hindrance to our union with God. In fact, He restored us to the truth of the union we already have. He revealed that God is *not* counting men's sins against them. Jesus is not "knocking on the door" calling people to be rescued from Himself—when He counts up wicked deeds and burns people according to each one. The truth is that Jesus came to rescue us from the false pursuits of love; from what it is already releasing "hell" upon the earth. He came to *save us from our sins*.

Such is the reason Jesus wept over Jerusalem's rejection of Him (Lk. 19:41). He knew they were putting themselves in a spiritual vulnerability that would open the way for the violent plundering of their city. When Rome came in and raped and pillaged Jerusalem, that was not God the Father (even though the literal text can sometimes make it seem that way). It was sin paying out a horrible form of death (Rom. 6:23). But at the Place of the Skull, Jesus defeated the real evil (which was also the underlying power behind Rome). Then, through His apostles, He called Israel to enter into the true Kingdom. In other words, He called them to wake up and enter Reality. Unfortunately, they resisted this call and continued down the path of self-destruction.

Salvation was and is complete. Forgiveness, love, and union have been revealed both to Jew and Gentile. And yet there is still room to reject this message, for love remains the goal of the cosmos.

Free from Isms

This takes us back to a central revelation we've explored throughout our time with the Shulammite—that the cross of Calvary was a wedding proposal.

To be sure, Jesus stood in humanity's place and said *yes* to the Father on our behalf. Our union with God is a firm and settled reality. But the possibility of staying in "unreality" remains,

The Song of the Ages: Part III

which is why the world still experiences the unreality of evil 2000 years later. This happens because the plan of God still involves the willingness of His children. God has sovereignly chosen all humanity in Christ, and yet He will not have prostitutes coming out of this sovereign choice.

Because of this, the doctrine of *universalism* becomes another well-intentioned philosophy of forcing love. It reintroduces the same mindset of Simon Peter, but in a more cushiony way. We, like Simon, would have God force His Kingdom upon the world and make all the evil go away. But what we'd really be asking is that God take out a magic wand, perhaps like the one the other Simon used. We want God to make our problems vanish and essentially force "the law" onto the planet. But this is the *mind set* on man's interests—not God's. Though it seems right to us, this mind has more in common with the Roman Empire than the Kingdom of heaven. God is not a coming emperor, but a reigning Father. And this is why even in His promise to "return," there are an abundance of Scriptures that hint at people still rejecting Him. As noted by Luke, Jesus declared that even if someone were to rise from the dead, there would still be those who do not believe.

As a matter of fact, Jesus spoke of this in an even more graphic way when He talked about people meeting the fire of God with the "gnashing of teeth." The gnashing of teeth was a phrase in Jesus's day signifying anger and rejection. The same exact words are used by Luke in the book of Acts when Stephen presented the Gospel of grace to the religious leadership of Jerusalem and they "began gnashing their teeth at him" (Acts 7:54). This figure of speech has to do with hostility and resistance. Jesus wasn't speaking of sending people to a torture chamber where they would grind their teeth in pain. He was speaking of those who would continue rejecting the very hand reaching out for salvation (see 2 Sam. 23:6-7 & Isa. 27:4). They would reject the river of water coming from the throne, and

The Cross Versus the Wand

because of this, that river would become a painful fire surrounding their loveless, ice-cold existence.

But here's the difficult part for some of the more conservative readers. The opposing view of *infernalism* is equally dangerous with its connotations of eternal separation and punishing torment. God's mercy does not end at the great white throne judgment of Revelation 20. According to a multitude of Scriptures, the mercy of God *never ceases*. In the life of Stephen, we see this aspect of God's heart manifest when the people gnashed their teeth at him and still, he chose to forgive them. The same will be true in eternity when God continues to exude mercy in the face of those who reject Him. God will never stop pursuing and never stop loving—even to those who have spurned the way of love.

So instead of religious *isms* we are left with tension and mystery. Many have entered into intense theological debates over these things, but they argue from within the limits of time and space. In eternity, there are higher perspectives that envelop things that seem to be in contradiction here on earth. Just as we can't grasp timelessness, we have difficulty grasping these spiritual tensions. This includes the great hope of God's eternal love for *all* humanity, and yet a dire warning about the path of self-destruction. We must learn to embrace both realms, for God has sovereignly chosen all in Christ and yet He leaves us with a sobering picture at the end of the Bible. In Revelation 21 and 22, the Kingdom of God is established on earth and its gates are never shut. The doors are open to all who would wash the robes of their identity in the blood of the Lamb. Yet at the end of the vision, there are still some found standing outside the gates. It's almost like God didn't want His Scriptures to predestine man's choice—even though the victory of His love is predestined and settled. This leaves us with a high view of the eternal love of the Father, but with a severe warning about the way of prostitution, sorcery, and fear.

The Song of the Ages: Part III

Wonderfully blessed are those who wash their robes white so they can access the Tree of Life and enter the city of bliss by its open gates. Those not permitted to enter are outside: the malicious hypocrites, the sexually immoral, **sorcerers***, murderers, idolaters,* **and every lover of lies***.*
(Rev. 22:14-15 TPT)

There are many, who in an overreaction to legalistic presentations of the Gospel, minimize or write off this subject altogether. People do this far too often, dismissing certain Scriptures, many times because of their own hidden insecurity in the Father's heart. Rather than wrestling with the Word like Jacob wrestled with God, some avoid certain Scriptures or pretend like they're not there. Jesus made it very clear that staying in *unreality* has consequences. The cold may not be a "thing," yet it can lead to a real experience of numbing and death. Such warnings are not to be our main focus in speaking with people, but they are included in the great song sheet of the Gospel. As we said before, we cannot write out certain parts of the melody, for they hold eternal revelation into the very nature of God's love.

The other danger, of course, is when someone embraces a difficult note in the Bible but plays it horribly off-key. They read the Gospel from a fearful and hyper-literalistic song sheet and the whole thing gets ruined for everyone listening. This is where Jesus's warnings become twisted medieval threats of torture chambers designed by a violent and vengeful Father. We must avoid both pitfalls. We don't want to minimize the intensity of Jesus's words about hell nor do we want to embrace a demonic distortion of God's heart. Such is the serpent's most ancient trick. That slithering dragon lied about God's character *and* about the consequences that would come by eating from the wrong tree. To preach a God who threatens to kill and burn is to preach a dualistic lie; yet to a preach a Gospel without Jesus's tear-filled warnings of destruction

The Cross Versus the Wand

is to come against the fabric that makes up the nature of God's creation. This is a knife-edge of truth requiring us to trust more in Jesus than our theologies and *isms*.

And this knife-edge leaves us with something else. It gives us a sharp urgency to go out and bring the Gospel to the nations, at any cost. Not to manipulate people into following Jesus, but to articulate the true nature of reality—to awaken people to what is already theirs. With the Spirit's help, we are calling humanity to turn their eyes from the watery bowls of soup in their laps and widen their gaze to the Promised Land all around them. As a royal priesthood, we are summoned to this purpose. And, for the time being, this purpose of ours includes the promise of continued suffering—even as victorious ones.

The Lord desires a Bride, a helper who would be *like Him*, who would not pursue the path of the magic wand. A people would embody His nature, even at moments of rejection—like Stephen. Love requires us to participate in the birth pangs of a free universe, especially as those who have awakened to the light before others and must endure persecution and ridicule as a result. The Lord does not want a bunch of *nēpios* following around an adult. He wants co-heirs, mature sons and daughters, reigning at His side. They follow the One who never power-grabbed, never exploited anybody. God's royal priests follow the way of the cross and move in the true power of the Spirit, which has nothing to do with revenge, threats, or control. In the face of evil, Jesus simply released mercy and truth, and this came either as cool refreshment or a fiery rebuke depending on the heart of the listener.

So we come back to this missional call arising out of Solomon's Song. This is the release of the kiss, which is essentially the call to "preach." And we use that word according to its original meaning: *Announce*. We are announcing Reality. We are proclaiming a Kingdom that already surrounds everyone, and indeed already dwells within everyone. We are also calling out the truth: *All* people are headed toward the Burning Place, even though its fire will be received differently depending on a person's heart.

The Altar That Is and Is to Come

In light of everything we've learned, we'll now close with one final analogy for the human story. Not only is humanity walking down the road to the Burning Place, they are also walking down an aisle—to their Bridegroom.

Human history is the story of a veiled Bride approaching an altar where Jesus stands victorious and the Father is presiding over the ceremony. Because of the eternal work of the cross, the wedding is already here. Christ has come and united Himself to humanity. He has said *yes* to the Father for us, and as us. Again, the fire of the Burning One already surrounds us—but what is true in eternity has not totally filled time and space. Humanity is thus walking down the aisle of space-time with the constant invitation to say *yes* herself. And like an actual bridal procession, there is a veil over the true face of humanity even as she walks toward her Beloved. Therefore, this aisle is also the "cocoon" we've been looking at—the wilderness from which we are rising. The altar up ahead is our destiny of metamorphosis and transfiguration, maturity and unveiling. Our destiny is to come to this altar of the cross where the Bridegroom stands—to look into His face and receive His kiss.

And to receive this kiss is the same as lifting off the veil, for a veiled Bride can't be kissed without doing so. Receiving the kiss is to believe in the great love that is already ours. It's to let go of our striving prostitution and decaying sorcery, and find complete and utter rest. More and more, this is happening in the hearts of God's children and it is reaching a glorious crescendo. There are many within the human race who have already said *yes*. These are ones

The Cross Versus the Wand

who have left the house of their upbringing, that immature season of spiritual childhood. They have departed from the false father Adam and the false address of Babylon. These are the Shulammites, and they are the first-fruits of heaven's fiery wedding celebration. They are the mature ones who are calling to their younger sister ... *on the day she is spoken for* ... to receive this kiss as well.

Ninth Selah

In the first volume of *The Song of the Ages*, we learned how there are nine fruits of the Spirit that correspond to the nine fruits exuding from the garden of the Shulammite (Sgs. 4:12-14). We have since found that this garden is the same one from the book of Genesis. The reality and promise of Eden is revealed in the awakened Bride. We are the fruitful garden destined to come from the soil of this planet. So, in this *ninth selah*, let us pause once again and trust in the reality of this secret garden. There are a few more loose ends to tie up, a beautiful projection of everything we've seen thus far—but for now, let us rest under the weight of this promised fruitfulness. Let this final *selah* fill you with the resolve to pause every day and trust in this garden, even when you do not see it.

Especially when you do not see it.

Now you might have to be like one who stands in front of a barren forest in the midst of winter, trusting that fragrant life will emerge in the spring, even though it seems impossibly incongruent with your vision. Imagine that scene for a moment. Imagine standing there in the cold. Faith looks like someone rising above that cold and remembering the potency underneath the snowy bark. Faith is seeing the potential of seed and sap hidden within a frosted forest.

The Song of the Ages: Part III

Just as wild as that springtime vision might seem in the midst of such a cold scene, so too is the idea of an Edenic world. But again, all the power for such a world is already all around us.

We might also use the analogy of electricity. Black power lines and boxy metallic transformers may look quite bland and unappealing. But what only seems like wire and metal is actually the covering vessel for an immense force that surges into buildings and alters entire civilizations. Homes blossom with light, internet, entertainment, and cooking because of this hidden power that is only waiting to be tapped into. Such things teach us about the reality of the Holy Spirit, the One who is all-present, and ready to flow through the stems and wires of our physical lives.

When things seem dry, gray, and powerless—continue to come away. Pause. Breath. Look beyond the horizon of your physical sight and behold the color and light of God's Spirit. The Holy Spirit of God is your identity, your journey, and your final destination. May every *selah* be a fresh unveiling of this wonderful truth.

22
Bringing the Song to the Nations

———•❖•———

We have a little sister,
And she has no breasts;
What shall we do for our sister
On the day she is spoken for?
If she is a wall,
We will build on her a battlement of silver;
But if she is a door,
We will barricade her with planks of cedar.
(8:8-9)

After a marathon of apocalyptic revelation, we're finally ready to turn the corner and head to the finish line. We've surveyed the transforming wilderness and watched the Bride and Bridegroom rise from its dusty plains. We've looked intently at the bright message they carry, the kiss of the ages, the Word of everlasting life. We've also examined the fiery seal of the Spirit and its many implications for the promised destiny of humanity. All of this has laid the foundation for what the Bride says next. In this passage, the Shulammite speaks of her "little sister who has no breasts." Here, she's referring to *immature humanity*—the *nēpios* world that is still asleep, still wearing the veil over their faces. She speaks of the younger sister of the world—those who have not yet embraced the seal of divine love in order to become mature Shulammites.

We'll first point out that the Bride says, "*We* have a little sister…" Remember, the Shulammite is conversing with the One who is both her Bridegroom and Brother (Sgs. 4:9). This reiterates once again how the mature Bride sees all humanity as fellow sons and daughters of God. With that in mind, this statement in the eighth verse of the eighth chapter might be rendered as follows: *Jesus, our younger brothers and sisters are not yet matured. They are still stuck in the elements and works of this age. They are still living under spiritual prostitution, witchcraft, and fear.*

But there is more to her words. She specifically mentions the day this younger sister is *"spoken for."* This was an old way of describing a marriage proposal. It's the day a man offers his pledge to take a woman as his wife. Of course, with everything we've learned about the seal of the Spirit and God's proposal to humanity through Christ, this statement fits like a glove. The previous three verses have articulated the great message of God's proposal and promise to mankind. This is the kiss the Shulammite received and embodied as she arose from the wilderness. In this final scene, on the heels of a full revelation of the Gospel, the Bride is asking Jesus once more how to tangibly bring this message to the world. Here then is another paraphrase of her words:

Jesus, what do we do for our younger brothers and sisters on this glorious hour of your marriage proposal? How do we bring them into the maturity of love?

Special Gifts to Mankind

At the very beginning of this volume, we looked at the apostolic mission of the church. It's of extreme importance

Bringing the Song to the Nations

we review this mission as we prepare to hear Jesus's answer to this question. The mission, if you remember, is to present every person *complete* in Christ (Col. 1:28). We learned how this word "complete" is the same exact term used for "mature." And so, this is the church's real mandate—to bring every person into spiritual adoption. This is synonymous with bringing people into the reality of transfiguration. Don't forgot that the metamorphosized (transfigured) butterfly is only a *mature* caterpillar. A new creation, yes, but also the full-grown destiny of the original creation. So, the mission is help human beings rise into their full-grown state as awakened sons and daughters of God.

Hopefully, this apostolic commission makes all the more sense now that we've looked so intently at the Spirit's seal and the deeper meaning behind the ancient ceremony of adoption. The Scripture doesn't say our mission is to present every person *in Christ*. Rather, it is to present every person *mature* in Him. A huge portion of Christians believe we are trying to get people to say a prayer so they can be "in Christ" and go to heaven one day. Certainly, there is a call to lead people in the reconciliatory power of surrendered prayer to Jesus. However, the insinuation of this apostolic mission statement is that mankind is already "in Christ" in a hidden way. Yet without relationship and a heart-embrace of that gift, this remains only an earthly possibility. This is why Paul talks of people who were *in Christ* before him (Rom. 16:7) while also stating that he was chosen *in Christ* before foundation of the world (Eph. 1:4). Such statements bring us back to that tension within space and time, where heavenly realities are meant to collide with our temporal lives.

In that glorious opening of Ephesians, Paul wrote of this magnificent plan, and this led to the verse a few chapters later that says the nations of the world are *"fellow members of the body"* (Eph. 3:6). The body of Christ includes all humanity; but the problem is that many of His members are immature. Thus, they are the "little

The Song of the Ages: Part III

sister" at the end of Solomon's Song who have yet to access their full inheritance. They have fallen back into the dust of selfishness and fear, drooling and crawling instead of standing up in the full stature of God's image. They remain in the dark womb of the wilderness instead of the light of manifest truth.

Thankfully, Ephesians goes on to explain God's plan to resolve this issue. This involves special *"gifts"* Jesus gave to mankind after His victorious ascension from the womb of the virgin tomb. After making wild statements like: *"There is one God and Father of all who is over all and through all and in all,"* as well as, *"He ascended far above all the heavens, so that He might fill all things"*—Paul then writes that Christ gave the world five special gifts: apostles, prophets, evangelists, pastors and teachers. These gifts are *"for the equipping of the saints for the work of service."* This is meant to bring about one primary goal: *"The building up of the body of Christ"* (Eph. 4:6-12).

Many people, missing the grand scope of God's plans, limit the meaning of this passage in Ephesians to a focus on Christian development—ministries that help those who already believe to become more mature. But in view of the eternal Song of God and the fire that erupted from His heart in the creation of time and space, there is *so much more* to this statement. These are not gifts given solely to the church, but to the world. The Greek text says that Jesus gave gifts to *anthropos*—mankind (Eph. 4:8). Therefore, these gifts are about bringing the entire body—all humanity and all society—into the place of its destined transfiguration. And this is confirmed when Paul goes on to explain the *"result"* of their work:

"As a result, we are to no longer be *children…*" (Eph. 4:14).

There's that word again. In the Greek, this is saying: "We are to no longer be *nēpios*." Everything ties back to this great destiny of a matured humanity reflecting the full image of her Creator. This is the purpose of these ministry gifts.

Bringing the Song to the Nations

Now the function of these gifts is for another study. Our focus here is to simply understand how all these ministries find their fuel and purpose within the context of the Song of the Ages. This is the eternal sheet music that guides the apostolic, prophetic, evangelistic, pastoral, and teaching dimensions of the Body of Christ. If somebody tries to "play" one of these roles outside the melody of the God's Song, it's like sounding a trumpet in the totally wrong part of a composition. You might be a gifted trumpet player, but all your tooting—wonderful and skillful as it may be—will be annoying and ineffective if it goes off the Conductor's plan.

One thing that does need to be said regarding these gifts is that they are not primarily about individual leaders, but the DNA of the entire church. Though some of us may function in a particular area more than another (and for some of us that may be attached to a calling involving greater influence and leadership), these gifts are resident within every single person. Each gift is simply an aspect of how Christ Himself ministered while on earth. Jesus was an apostle (Heb. 3:1), a prophet (Acts 3:22), an evangelist (Matt. 4:23), a shepherd (Jn. 10:11), and a teacher (Jn. 3:2). These are the different ways He impacted the world around Him. Today, this same Jesus dwells within each one of us, and so every aspect of His giftings are meant to come out of our lives. And they are meant to come out in order to accomplish that one specific purpose:

> *...the building up of the body of Christ, until we all attain to the unity of the faith, and of the knowledge of the Son of God, **to a mature man**, to the measure of the stature which belongs to the fullness of Christ.*
> *(Eph. 4:12-13)*

Notice the word "mature" again. This is truly about bringing the little sister of the world into the fullness of divine love.

The Song of the Ages: Part III

Servants to the Father's Joy

There's a story in the Old Testament that foreshadows our Heavenly Conductor's plans regarding these five gifts. The story is from the life of David during his ongoing conflict with Saul. At one point, David sought support from a wealthy landowner in the region of Carmel. The man was Nabal, a name that means "foolishness." In keeping with his name, Nabal made the stupid decision to reject David's plea for help and, as a result, incurred the wrath of the coming king. Fortunately for Nabal, he had a smart wife named Abigail who interceded on his behalf. David was taken by this woman's wisdom and decided not to retaliate. Instead, much like God has chosen to do with evil, David lets foolishness run its course and Nabal ends up dying on his own. David then does the following:

> *...Then David sent a proposal to Abigail, to take her as his wife. When the servants of David came to Abigail at Carmel, they spoke to her, saying, "David has sent us to you to take you as his wife."*
> *(1 Sam. 25:39-40)*

In the original Hebrew, it says David "sent and *spoke*" to the new widow. This is the same phrase from his son Solomon's poetry when he wrote of the day the little sister was "spoken for." David essentially sent a marriage pledge to Abigail, declaring his desire to be one with her. This pledge came to her when she was at Carmel, a place that showed up earlier in the Song. In the last volume we noted how it means "Garden Land," and it speaks to the fact that we are God's Promised Land, His true Eden. Abigail's name is also significant as it can be translated "the Father's joy" or "the Father's delight."

Already we see another parable of the Gospel here. Though we are the Father's delightful promise, all of us have been married

Bringing the Song to the Nations

to the foolishness of sin. Through our union with sinfulness, we've incurred devastation and destruction. Our foolishness has prevented us from honoring the true King of the earth—the One who (like David in this part of his life) has already been anointed and coronated, but has not manifested His full reign upon earth. Paul tells us that before Christ we were married to the law of sin and death, but now we are free to marry Another (Rom. 7:4). Just like Nabal died and Abigail was free to marry David, the foolishness of sin has died on the cross and we are free to enjoy everlasting union with Jesus. Indeed, we are already united, but this still comes as a proposal we are invited to receive for ourselves. There's much more that can be said about the message of the Gospel hidden in Abigail's life, but we now need to shift our focus to what happens at the end of the story:

> *She arose and bowed with her face to the ground and said, "Behold, your maidservant is a maid to wash the feet of my lord's servants." Then Abigail quickly arose, and rode on a donkey,* **with her five maidens who attended her;** *and she followed the messengers of David* **and became his wife.**
> *(1 Sam. 25:41-42)*

Abigail said *yes* to the proposal. In embracing the marriage, there was then an ensuing journey of coming into full consummation. Abigail needed to get on a donkey, an animal of servanthood, and follow the messengers of David with the assistance of five maidens—five ladies who *attended* the Father's Delight. They were there to meet her needs and support her on the journey. These women were most likely at Abigail's side all the way to the wedding. They represent the work of the fivefold ministry in assisting the Bride as she rises into the full manifestation of union.

The Song of the Ages: Part III

Now with her *yes* to the proposal, Abigail was also accepting the call to "wash the feet" of David's servants. This is another powerful picture of the Bride's mission—to reflect the One who washed the feet of His own disciples. This also confirms that this truly is a foreshadow of the fivefold ministry because those gifts are meant to help the Bride step into servanthood. They're to equip her for "the work of service."

But again, the bridal part of the story is the bigger picture. Abigail was "spoken for" by David. Messengers came and announced this. This is the true meaning of evangelism—the announcement of the divine proposal of God's love. Then, the five maidens attended to her needs on her journey of servanthood into consummated union with the King. And that brings us back to the purpose of all ministry. Each of us are called to be messengers of the proposal and servants to "Abigail"—the Father's Delight. This is why even giving a cup of cold water to someone is rewarded, for we are blessing someone who brings the Father deep joy. It's like blessing the Father (and the Bridegroom) Himself!

Before we move on to Jesus's answer to the Shulammite's question about reaching her little sister, let's quickly return to Ephesians 4. After Paul articulates the purpose of these five gifts, he adds these beautiful words that establish the central theme and lyrics of God's Song:

> *...we are to grow up in all aspects into Him who is the head, even Christ, from whom the whole body, being fitted and held together by what every joint supplies, according to the proper working of each individual part, causes the growth of the body* **for the building up of itself in love.**
> *(Eph. 4:15-16)*

The "building up" of the Body, the maturing and awakening, is all about this end goal of love. As Paul wrote, "The goal of our instruction is love…" (1 Tim. 1:5a). Love is the fulfillment of the childish era of law and fear. The childhood of humanity is one without love. This *is* the wilderness from which we're rising. But the mature human race—the built-up body of Christ—is one of passionate and self-sacrificial grace. Such love is the answer to every problem facing the world, and it is not just a good idea, or a feeling, or a philosophy. It's the living flame of God who longs to burn upon the heart of every single person. Love is the Holy Spirit, the Father, and Jesus Christ. Love is the end result of the universe's unfolding destiny. Just as it is the crescendo of Solomon's Song, love is also the crescendo of the cosmos. It is where everything came from and where everything is headed. And again, all "ministry" is meant to function with this goal in mind.

So, What Shall We Do?

With her apostolic purpose clear and set, the mature Shulammite asks Jesus for more insight on *how* to bring the little sister of humanity into this maturity of love. *"What shall we do,"* she asks.

How do we lead Your promised ones into the maturity of the Spirit?

Jesus responds with this:

> *If she is a wall,*
> *then we will build on her a battlement of silver.*
> *But if she is a door,*
> *we will barricade her with planks of cedar.*

Jesus is showing the awakened church how to respond to the world, whether in their acceptance of the Gospel—*a door*—or their rejection—*a wall*.

Now before we look at His answer, lets recall some more things we've discovered along this lengthy and fiery path of the Song's eighth chapter. We've seen how God will not use a magic wand to reach people. He will not force love. This reality has to be synthesized with our presentation of the Gospel. In view of this immense love and the complete atonement wrought by Christ, we cannot honestly preach a message that says, *"Accept Jesus's wedding proposal or be tortured with eternal fire."* Such an "invitation" sounds more like spiritual rape than unimaginably good news.

Of course, many leaders and Christian communities have gotten rid of this antiquated turn-or-burn lingo, yet it remains the theology hidden underneath their re-packaged Gospel presentations. As a result, a subtle stench of theological rot leaks out from under the well-polished floorboards of friendly messages about God's love. Such is the reason we took several chapters just to address the issue of hell and the all-encompassing implications of Christ's work. But now that we have hopefully gained a more mature understanding of grace and judgment—without watering down either one—we can now move on to unpacking Christ's wisdom here.

The Wall of Rejection

"If she is a wall…"

Jesus first speaks of those who say *no* to the reality of His Kingdom. He's answering the question about what we do when people put up a wall of resistance to the love of God. For whatever the reason, whether it's anger toward God or toward the church, countless people have put up walls between them and heaven. Most often it's because of some kind of pain in their lives or a strand of deception sown into their hearts by the serpent—whether through other people, worldly philosophies, or even by the wilderness-dwelling church. Of course, Jesus absolutely values the will and choice of these individual souls—however, we now come to the fact that He does not tell the Shulammite to just let them be. Jesus respects people's freedom, but His love is not passive or aloof. He

Bringing the Song to the Nations

won't stop pursuing people and offering to break every deceptive chain around their necks. So, He says this:

"We will build on her a battlement of silver."

Notice again that the pronoun "we" is used. Whatever building a battlement entails, it's to be done as a joint collaboration between the Spirit of Jesus and His Bride. The Shulammite has risen from the wilderness of law and is moving in greater synchronicity with the Lord, seen by the fact that she is now leaning on her Beloved. This indicates a new humility in receiving His ways and methods. This is the attitude behind her question to the Beloved.

Now that they are moving together as one, Jesus tells her that even if the world rejects His love, they are still to be about the work of *building*. The word for "build" here could also be translated as "repair." It's the term used in the story of Nehemiah when he went about restoring the torched and broken-down walls of Jerusalem. Indeed, people's lives have been burnt and broken down by sin, and our great calling is to bring them into the redemption and healing of Christ.

It's interesting to point out that the first time this word "build" is used in Scripture is in Genesis 2 when God "fashioned" a woman out of a man's rib (Gen. 2:22). The actual Hebrew translation is, "The Lord God built a woman." God built a wife for Adam. *So, the first thing "built" in Scripture is a Bride.* The "building" of the little sister in the Song is pointing to this same construction! Though she's immature and lost in control and fear, the little sister of humanity is still called to be a radiant Bride. Because of this, Jesus says we are to be about the work of building, and He specifically says to build upon her a battlement of silver.

Now a "battlement" was another type of wall. But in this case, Jesus is talking about a wall *of silver*. In Scripture, silver is a constant image of redemption; a term that is all about restoring something to its original value. Since silver is refined in fire, the metal also

The Song of the Ages: Part III

signifies how the fiery seal of the Spirit comes to reveal the true identity hidden behind the dross of a person's unbelief. Therefore, Jesus is calling His church to turn her littler sister's wall of rejection into a wall of redeemed silver! The broken down and burnt out walls of humanity are to be transformed into something glorious.

This tells us that when people reject the Gospel, we're still to be about the work of bringing reparation to their lives. That should bring to mind any Kingdom initiative seeking to infiltrate a place of corruption with righteousness and light. Even if an individual or an entire city resists the Kingdom of heaven, we can still go about doing extraordinary things that bless people and help the individual or community thrive. Jesus modelled this for us beautifully. He would often heal people without any requirement that they follow and obey Him. Of course, Jesus wanted every person to follow Him—but that didn't stop Him from pouring out healing upon people, whether or not they became His followers.

As Christ's ambassadors, we're to mirror His heart, washing even the feet of our enemies. We're to demonstrate God's kind nature to a world that greatly misunderstands His intentions. This is what builds the Kingdom on earth. As we come against people's rejection with goodness, the apostle Peter wrote, "Because of your good deeds, as they observe them, will glorify God in the day of visitation" (1 Pet. 2:12). Peter was writing about the impact of our love on an unbelieving world, and he wrote these words after mentioning the cornerstone of the Kingdom (2:6). Remember, the cornerstone of the entire Kingdom was laid with the cross—the place where forgiveness and mercy were poured out upon a people who had undeniably thick walls over their hearts. *This shows us that radical forgiveness and even martyrdom are sometimes the only way to start building a "battlement of silver" in the midst of our walled sister of humanity.* This is why after mentioning the cornerstone, Peter goes on to call us the priests and kings of the new Kingdom being built upon the earth (2:9).

Bringing the Song to the Nations

And so, Jesus is giving the wonderfully simple answer of living out the Gospel with intense passion while abstaining from forcing it down people's throats. In the church's wilderness seasons, we have done many horrible things to get people to believe or follow Christ. There's been a lot coercion and force involved in our ministry to the world. But we've seen well enough that this is not the way of Jesus. And you can look no further than the Song of Songs to prove this. In the next verse in particular, we'll see the Shulammite acknowledging she too was once "a wall" (Sgs. 8:10). As we know, Jesus still moved in her life and blessed her with redeeming truth, even in her resistance. This is the call of the church as fellow kings and priests walking in the same mature love as Christ. We're to serve the world and build the Kingdom of grace even in the midst of persecution and opposition.

The Door of Acceptance

While the wall represents a resistance and closeness in people's hearts, the door speaks to the exact opposite. If people are open to the Gospel, then a different response is to be taken.

"If she is a door, we will barricade her with planks of cedar."

The word for "barricade" is an intense term that can be used in a more militant context. Essentially, the idea here is that when someone is open to the Gospel, we need to move in with force and power. And notice the *"we"* again. This is also to be done by the leading and empowerment of Jesus's Spirit. These instructions from the Lord should never become an inflexible formula or routine that we run with on our own.

Now when we talk about force and power, this isn't meant to suddenly insinuate a "bait and switch" approach with people, where we play off our desire to bring them to Jesus and then the moment they show the slightest interest to the things of God, we begin shoving it down their throats. On the contrary,

The Song of the Ages: Part III

this is speaking to how to follow-up with genuine openness to the Holy Spirit's influence as people *yes* to Jesus in their hearts. When a person receives Christ—when they joyfully accept that *He has received them*—the discipleship of that person should be swift. Having awakened to their identity, a person needs to be grounded right away in the truth. In the book of Acts, people were baptized immediately upon their confession. There weren't months of waiting for a special baptismal service. Instead, they were quickly placed under the water and considered a vital part of the Christian community. With this, a person was instantly instilled with the revelation of their co-death and co-resurrection with Christ. They were prayed over to receive the pledge of the Spirit—that spiritual baptism of confirmation and empowerment. This all happened right at the start of their journey with Jesus.

The word "barricade" has to do with a military siege or a hostile takeover of an enemy's stronghold. With New Covenant eyes we can see this as the hostile takeover of everything Satan has set up in a person's life. Once an individual receives the grace of God, they should be prayed over to encounter a full revelation of their healing in Christ. With the help of those fivefold giftings, the truth of their identity should be continually reinforced within their hearts.

The next part of the verse says that a person with an open heart should be barricaded with "planks of cedar." This line doesn't require much more commentary when you look at a parallel verse from Solomon's personal life. Look now at something that happened when Solomon finished the work of the temple:

> *So he built the house and finished it; and he covered the house with beams and **planks of cedar**.*
> *(1 Kgs. 6:9)*

Bringing the Song to the Nations

Just like Solomon built and finished the house of God, our King has truly finished the work of redeeming humanity. However, it is when someone embraces this redemption that we can surround them and cover them with the revelation of the cross. We've addressed several times how the cedar wood from Lebanon was a direct symbol of Christ's cross. This confirms even further that when a person receives the Gospel, they should be immediately baptized and immersed in the truth of Christ's work—*barricaded with planks of cedar*. In other words, they are to go through everything the Shulammite herself went through. Her journey was and is meant to be *multiplied* into the lives of people all around the world.

Again, Jesus modelled these things while ministering on earth as the true apostle, prophet, evangelist, pastor and teacher. We can see some of what we're explaining in the way He directed His followers to reach the villages around them. In terms of actually preaching the Gospel, He called His disciples to focus on those with open hearts. This is why some of the most effective evangelism throughout the ages has been through "persons of peace." As a matter of fact, regions where the global church is thriving the most—even in the midst of intense persecution—are where believers are discovering this reality anew. A person of peace is someone like the Samaritan women who showed an openness to conversing with Jesus. After being impacted by that initial encounter, she then went on to tell many more people about the Lord. Such a person is someone the Holy Spirit directs you to—hence the *"we"* in this work of redeeming humanity. This was a key part of Jesus's strategy to the twelve and the seventy when He sent them out into Israel (Lk. 10:6). He called them to find people who were open before fully proclaiming the Kingdom.

We don't have to strive militantly to get people to believe. Oftentimes, we just need to follow the Spirit toward those who already have hearts that are opening up to the things of heaven. But again, as people do open up, we are to move in with power and truth. We're to boldly proclaim the Kingdom of God and the wonderful victory of Christ, surrounding them with the full knowledge of His grace.

Fully Equipped

For a long time now we've seen the Shulammite's desire to reach both Jew and Gentile with the kiss of the Spirit. Whether it was going back to her mother's house or traversing the villages of humanity, the Shulammite has consistently returned to this calling that is so deeply ingrained within her heart. Now that she is leaning upon her Beloved and relying upon His wisdom, her heart's desire is being met. She's partnering with the Spirit of Christ in releasing the Kingdom on earth. She is engaged in the work of both building and barricading. Now we will see how she advances into all of this with one main piece of equipment—the word of her testimony.

23
The Word of Her Testimony

―――•❖•―――

> *I was a wall, and my breasts were like towers;*
> *Then I became in his eyes as one who finds peace.*
> *Solomon had a vineyard at Baal-hamon;*
> *He entrusted the vineyard to caretakers.*
> *Each one was to bring a thousand shekels of silver for its fruit.*
> *My very own vineyard is at my disposal;*
> *The thousand shekels are for you, Solomon,*
> *And two hundred are for those who take care of its fruit.*
> *(8:10-12)*

Before we continue on, we need to return yet again to the Song's apocalyptic fraternal twin, the book of Revelation. There's a mystery hidden in Revelation 12 that will shine more light on the overall message of Solomon's Song while also providing some context for what is spoken next. Look carefully at the following excerpt from John's vision:

> *A great sign appeared in heaven: a woman clothed with the sun, and the moon under her feet, and on her head a crown*

The Song of the Ages: Part III

of twelve stars; and she was with child; and she cried out, being in labor and in pain to give birth.

Then another sign appeared in heaven: and behold, a great red dragon… And the dragon stood before the woman who was about to give birth, so that when she gave birth he might devour her child.

And she gave birth to a son, a male child, who is to rule all the nations with a rod of iron; and her child was caught up to God and to His throne. Then the woman fled into the wilderness where she had a place prepared by God…
(Rev. 12:1-6)

Just like the "mother" in the Song of Songs, this woman in the book of Revelation can be interpreted in several ways. A woman wearing a crown of twelve stars largely points us to the nation of Israel. Israel was comprised of twelve tribes and was chosen to give birth to the male Child who would rule all the nations—Jesus of Nazareth. He was the One who was "caught up to God and to His throne" in His ascension around 30 A.D.

In this vision, there's also a great dragon of satanic evil trying to stop the birth from happening. We get a little window here into the spiritual warfare that has tried to keep Eve's promised "seed" from coming forth. Obviously, Satan has tried to destroy humanity over and over again; but he has most vehemently attacked the nation of Israel. Nevertheless, God turned these demonic onslaughts into the very labor pains that gave way to a true and redeemed humanity at the cross. The text later says that this woman "fled into the wilderness where she had a place prepared by God." She remained in this wilderness for a period of time and was still pursued by the adversary who then attempted to destroy her with a "flood" of water. But it says, "The earth helped the woman, and the earth

The Word of Her Testimony

opened its mouth and drank up the river which the dragon poured out of his mouth" (Rev. 12:15-16).

We're reminded of a couple things here. First, we have another image showing us that "many waters" cannot overcome the love of God. Secondly, this entire scene forms an accurate picture of what happened after the actual ascension of Jesus. In the decades following His ascent to the right hand of the Father, the enemy intensified his efforts to wipe Mother Israel off the map. The city of Jerusalem was sacked and almost completely swept away in 70 A.D. An overwhelming flood of destruction came upon the Jewish people; however, the earth opened up its mouth to receive the people and a remnant was preserved throughout the four corners of the globe. Just as the text suggests, the earth swallowed up the dragon's destructive river and helped the Jewish nation survive.

The vision then goes on to declare that Satan waged war with "the rest of her children, who keep the testimony of Jesus" (12:17). This is obviously speaking of the enemy targeting not only the Jews, but followers of Christ who are like the spiritual offspring of the Jewish people. After the attempted annihilation of Israel, the enemy brought unparalleled persecution to the church. The two centuries following the sack of Jerusalem were some of the most difficult times the church has ever had to endure. And of course, this persecution has continued even to the present day.

The Church's Coming Child

Now just as it is with the mother in the Song, the mother in Revelation can also represent the church—for the church is the one *clothed with the sun*. She is clothed with the righteousness of the Son of God. The church also has a crown of twelve stars on her head. This could represent the twelve apostles who helped establish the church, but it also speaks to the overall apostolic foundation of the Christian faith.

The Song of the Ages: Part III

Nonetheless, this interpretation is a little trickier because it suggests that the church is the one giving birth to the Child who would ascend and rule the nations. This doesn't make as much sense when you consider the fact that the ascension occurred before the church was established. However, this interpretation fits quite nicely when you recall the church's ultimate destiny—that the reigning Christ would be *birthed within His people* (Gal. 4:19). Out of the loins of Mother Israel and Mother Church will come a triumphant people who will rule and reign *on the earth*. We know this is a viable interpretation because the book of Revelation explicitly says that Jesus Christ is not the only One who will rule the nations with an iron rod. It also says overcoming believers will stand at His side and "rule the nations with a rod of iron" (Rev. 2:26). So, this is speaking of an awakened company of believers, a church moving in unprecedented authority and love. It's revealing the truth that both Jesus and His Bride will rule and reign together as one!

Unfortunately, like Mother Israel before her, the church has fled into the "wilderness" and remained there for a long season of time. The church has fallen into a wilderness of law and has suffered great persecution along the way. Revelation 12 prophesies all of this. And yet the final chapter of the Song of Solomon (and the final chapter of Revelation) gives us the greater picture. It shows us that this is only for a season. The church will rise out of the womb of the wilderness like the dawn. Through it all, the Christ Child will be formed within us and manifested for all to see.

In our own day, this transition is already underway. A little over fifty years before the writing of this book, the city of Jerusalem was reestablished. This was a natural sign of a greater reality. Like Adam preceding Christ, natural realities often precede spiritual breakthroughs. Just as Adam was a pattern of the One to come, the modern re-occupation of the Promised Land is a pattern of the church re-occupying the original promise of redemption.

The Word of Her Testimony

The Jewish people returning to their land in the 20th century was a picture of the church returning to her true identity and calling beginning in the next century. This will happen in the midst of conflict, just as conflict surrounded Israel's reattainment of the land; yet eventually the truth will win out. The Bride will rise, and the kiss of grace will be her only message.

But there is a certain promise in Revelation 12 we really want to focus on. In the middle of John's vision, it says this rising company of believers will overcome, and it gives three different ways this will happen. One of them is the purpose behind this whole excursion back into Revelation:

> *And they overcame him because of the blood of the Lamb and because of the word of their testimony, and they did not love their life even when faced with death.*
> *(Rev. 12:11)*

This sums up the entire lesson of the Shulammite's life; the one who learned to embrace the meaning and power behind the shed blood of the Lamb—the revelation of God's love and the truth of His victory over sin. It also sums up the call to walk out this love, which often means laying down one's life in the midst of resistance. But sandwiched between these two summations is the message of her testimony. This is what connects us back to the eighth chapter of the Song.

The Power of Our Testimony

At the end of the Song, the awakened Bride has been given wisdom on reaching the world—both for those who are open to the Gospel and those who are not. She is now speaking to the nations around her. She's embraced the blood of Jesus, and she has learned what it means to walk in overcoming love. In the midst of this, she gives the word of her testimony:

The Song of the Ages: Part III

"I was a wall."

The Bride acknowledges how she too was once closed off to the truth of Christ, just like everyone else. She then adds, *"And my breasts were like towers."*

Since a wall is on the outermost part of a city or stronghold, the towers would be structures standing behind those walls. The Shulammite is painting an intentional picture here. When we understand that the breasts represent spiritual maturity and fruitfulness, we see that she is describing a time when the mature and fruitful part of her identity was hidden behind the walls of unbelief. And this is the case for every single person who has ever been walled up by that ancient veil of spiritual blindness. Inside every person is the potential for maturity and fruitfulness, even if the walls of their life seem a mile thick.

As we've seen, every "little sister" is already spoken for—already called to enjoy union with Christ. These are just different metaphors describing the same realities. The little sister without breasts speaks to immaturity; so too, the Bride's previous life where her breasts were like the towers behind a wall speaks to the same thing. She is relating to the people of the world and giving the first part of her testimony. In essence, the Shulammite is saying, *"I was closed off and resistant to God. Any promise of fruitfulness seemed blocked off and unrealistic. But then something happened…"*

From here she describes something glorious; something that has taken us three long studies of the Song to come to. It's a beautiful verse describing what spiritual awakening is all about…

She says, *"Then I became in his eyes as one who finds peace."*

In His Eyes

A long time ago, we discovered that the words Solomon and Shulammite come from the same root word; a masculine version

The Word of Her Testimony

and a feminine version. However, we have yet to explore what that root word actually is…

It is the word *shalom*.

Peace.

Wholeness.

Completion.

Perfection.

The Shulammite had put up a wall of resistance to this truth. But when she turned to Jesus, she discovered her true self. Her true name. She looked in His eyes…and found her reflection.

Is this not a stunning way of articulating these timeless words from Paul?

> *But whenever a person turns to the Lord, the veil is taken away. Now the Lord is the Spirit, and where the Spirit of the Lord is, there is liberty. But we all, with unveiled face, beholding as in a mirror the glory of the Lord, are being transformed into the same image from glory to glory, just as from the Lord, the Spirit.*
> *(2 Cor. 3:16-18)*

Notice she says, "I became *in his eyes*…" This whole journey has been about discovering what God sees in us and what He knows to be true about us. From the very start, the Shulammite was drawn on this path of the *knowledge of God*—of coming into agreement with what God knows to be true—the "knowledge" that is destined to cover the earth like the waters cover the sea.

When God looks at us, He sees wholeness. This is because He sees Christ, His perfect image and likeness. We are the feminine reflection of divine glory. God has never forgotten this, and the work of His Son was all about recovering this eternal reality. His blood was shed to reveal the heavenly value within our own blood. The Bride is now declaring the word of her testimony based on the revelation of this precious blood. This is how we overcome the accuser, the one who does not want us to triumph in this message of grace. And this is meant to be our main message to the world. It *is* the kiss rising out of the wilderness.

Lord of the Multitude

"Solomon had a vineyard at Baal-hamon," the Shulammite continues. *"He entrusted the vineyard to caretakers. Each one was to bring a thousand shekels of silver for its fruit."*

With more poetry, the mature Bride goes further into her testimony and starts proclaiming what she ended up doing in response to this amazing love. She first brings up the King's vineyard, which she says was located at a place called Baal-hamon. Now Solomon's vineyard is really about God's vineyard—and God's vineyard is really about His people (Isa. 5:1). But as usual, the meaning of this name is very telling. Baal-hamon translates to "Lord of the Multitude." Of course, Baal was a term often used to describe foreign gods. It was also the word for "lord" or "master."

This title in the Bride's testimony about Solomon's vineyard reminds us that initially the vineyard of God's people was under foreign occupation. There, the people knew God as Baal—not as Father or Bridegroom. Hosea addressed this when he spoke of the day when people would no longer refer to God as *Baali*—"Master"—but as a loving Husband. It's the other side of the Gospel coin; the other purpose behind Jesus's shed blood. It not only redeems our identity; it also redeems mankind's understanding of God's identity. And it leads us out of the vineyard of law into the realm of grace.

So, when the Shulammite says the King had a vineyard at Baal-hamon, she's speaking of the multitudes living under a wrong understanding of the Divine. The way she describes this vineyard does indeed take us back the law, and it goes hand in hand with

The Word of Her Testimony

a pre-Gospel revelation of God—seeing Him as Master and not Husband. We see this when she says the King entrusted this vineyard to caretakers. This points us to two things—the first being Moses who was called to be a steward and caretaker of God's house (Heb. 3:5). It also points to the powers and principalities who reigned over humanity during that season of the law (before Christ took back the keys of authority). This was that cocoon and gestation period when God was leading people toward the eventual birthing of true love and authority.

The Shulammite then mentions how the caretakers of this vineyard would bring a thousand shekels for its fruit. There's a strong element of *works* going on here because it seems the point of this vineyard was the funds it could produce. This gives us another subtle allusion to the image of prostitution—the age-old occupation that turns an act of love into a loveless work. This further emphasizes that she is speaking poetically about living under law and fear. And that brings us back to the beginning of her journey when she was burnt out and tired. In fact, it's very probable that this "vineyard at Baal-hamon" was the same vineyard from the beginning of the Song when the Shulammite's "mother's sons" forced her to be a caretaker.

> *Do not stare at me because I am dark, because I am darkened by the sun. My mother's sons were angry with me and made me take care of the vineyards; my own vineyard I had to neglect.*
> *(Sgs. 1:6 NIV)*

So this is all part of her testimony of how she found freedom from the dry wilderness of distance, striving, and legalism. But it's important to note that this vineyard could also be the place where the young Shulammite first met Solomon—the One whose name would unveil the true meaning of her name. He was the Good Shepherd

The Song of the Ages: Part III

who began leading her away from this vineyard at Baal-hamon into the House of Wine—the place of restored intimacy and identity.

Next, the Bride says, *"My very own vineyard is at my disposal; the thousand shekels are for you, Solomon, and two hundred are for those who take care of its fruit."* Here, we see her describing how she came into the maturity of love. In her journey, the Shulammite found rest in the true knowledge of God. As a result, her focus was no longer about her personal work or efforts. Instead, she discovered the joy of seeing all of life as an expression of her union with Christ. Her "own vineyard" was no longer the focus—she gave it away to God. She then added that He could keep all the silver and the caretakers could have their share as well. She keeps nothing for herself. In other words, she boasts in nothing. To put it differently, the Shulammite learned to lose her life that she might truly gain it. This is a picture of someone who has found rest, and as a result, has surrendered their whole life—indeed, their whole identity—to the Lord.

So, you can see even more why we started with Revelation 12. This entire passage of her testimony is rooted in the truth of Jesus's blood and all that it redeemed. It then shows how she learned to not love her own life. These are the words of the overcoming Bride. It's her wonderful testimony that is now shining out for the whole world to see.

24
Chief of the Mountains

———•❖•———

O you who sit in the gardens,
My companions are listening for your voice—
Let me hear it!
Hurry, my beloved,
And be like a gazelle or a young stag
On the mountains of spices.
(8:13-14)

Harmony is defined as "the combination of simultaneously sounded musical notes to produce chords and chord progressions having a pleasing effect." This definition is a beautiful way to explain what happens when you take different parts of the Bible and line them up next to each other. The secret chord of Christ, the message of His person and work, is unlocked with glorious resonance.

Interestingly, another major definition for the word harmony is the following: "An arrangement of the four Gospels, or of any parallel narratives, which presents a single continuous narrative text."[4] Though this is describing an unrelated method of biblical examination, this definition reminds of that greater narrative of the harmonious Song hidden within the Scriptures. Such has been our discovery through every step of the Bride's songful journey.

The Spirit and the Bride

Now one of the more powerful harmonies of Scriptures is formed when you take the very end of the Song of Songs and put it parallel to the very end of the Bible. When the Shulammite calls out for her Beloved to *"hurry"* and come upon the mountains, you can hear a pleasing sound emerge when you also listen to the closing vocals of John's Apocalypse:

> *He who testifies to these things says, "Yes, I am coming quickly."*
> **Amen. Come, Lord Jesus.**
> *The grace of the Lord Jesus be with all. Amen.*
> *(Rev. 22:20-21)*

These two passages truly flow together. However, this melodious connection is amplified when you realize what this "coming" is all about. We've recently arrived at the stunning realization that the coming of the Lord is a constant reality; one which will reach a crescendo, like the end of an amazing song, and bring with it the complete manifestation of God's glory. This is the end of the Bible, the end of the Song, and the end of the road as we saw in the Emmaus story. The fiery destiny of humanity, forged before time itself and sealed at the cross, is now manifesting all around us. The great prayer of the church is that this would be fully released *on earth as it is heaven.*

---

4. "Definition of harmony". *Oxford University Press*. Lexico.com. 1 November 2020. https://www.lexico.com/definition/harmony.

Chief of the Mountains

We now stand in the twilight hours of this age (the wilderness era of law and fear) and the Shulammite Bride is being birthed as the shoulders of the mature Body of Christ. With this, the false notes of this world are dissipating and the true Song is rising. Harmony is emerging between heaven and earth, though it takes a closely listening ear to pick up the growing music. This issue of harmony is more vital than we can imagine, for it is God's eternal longing that the realities of heaven would be properly mirrored on earth. He created humans to be His windblown instruments, and until we learn to let the Spirit echo through our wooden chambers, the fullness of this plan will not come forth. The Conductor's plan involves an eternal partnership—a *companionship*, as we see in one of the words mentioned at the end of the Song. In the eons to come we will be in awe over the wisdom hidden in this plan; though for now, in these brief closing moments of history, this plan comes with a high price tag of suffering.

We end with this discussion on harmony because the Song closes with the singing Bridegroom calling for the complementary voice of His beloved Bride. She's the one who now "sits" in the garden of union. She has eyes opened to the Burning One who already stands in her midst. She's able to sit down and rest in the reality of Eden's Kingdom as a pioneer for the striving world. Thus, she's the same one who partners with the Spirit at the end of Revelation in calling the whole world to "come." This forms another harmonic connection between the two texts. Let's look at it once more:

> *The Spirit and the bride say, "Come." And let the one who hears say, "Come." And let the one who is thirsty come; let the one who wishes take the water of life without cost.*
> (Rev. 22:17)

Together, the Spirt and the Bride call out to the thirsty of this world; those who desperately need the free and effortless drink of

The Song of the Ages: Part III

the Gospel. This drink is the same thing as the secret chord hidden throughout the Bible. Indeed, a good drink to the parched throat is like a good song to the ear.

But we need to pause here, because we just pointed out how the very end of Revelation reveals the Spirit and the Bride calling for *Jesus to come*. Why then do we find in the same section of Scripture a call for the thirsty to come? Who are they calling—Jesus or the thirsty? Many would say these are two separate invitations with two totally different meanings. One is being addressed to a whole group of people who need to receive Jesus while the other is a call to Jesus Himself as a plea for His return.

But what if these verses are not separate? What if these two texts also form a secret chord that is speaking of the same realities we've been discovering? A look at some of the things Jesus said at the end of His ministry will help clear this up:

> *"For I was hungry, and you gave Me something to eat;* ***I was thirsty****, and you gave Me something to drink; I was a stranger, and you invited Me in; naked, and you clothed Me; I was sick, and you visited Me; I was in prison, and you came to Me."*
> *(Matt. 25:35-36)*

Here, Jesus completely associates Himself with the broken people of this world, going so far as to identify even with those in prison. Taking this text and aligning it with the words of Revelation, we find that the call to the thirsty is actually a call to Jesus Himself! As we've seen, it's when a weary human being awakens to Christ within that He appears on the scene. When Christ is revealed, a person's true life is revealed as well (Col. 3:4).

In other places, Jesus taught that giving a cup of cold water to someone brings great reward. What if this is because ministering to people uncovers their true value? Like the tuning of an old but

Chief of the Mountains

good instrument, it resets them to the music inside. Of course, this would totally change our understanding of "rewards." Instead of doing good things for people so we can get gems and mansion keys one day, our reward in blessing others is *Jesus Himself* emerging from the soil of human souls. This is because Jesus is the true gold of heaven. The more He's revealed, the more reward and glory there is. There's nothing better than Him. Jesus is our exceedingly great prize, and we're called to tap into that eternal trophy even now.

Such a perspective on rewards confirms the deeper meaning behind the age-old prayer and desire for Jesus to "come." The real "desire of the nations" is for the gold and silver of Christ to come into the temple of humanity (see Hag. 2:7). *Therefore, the prayer for Jesus to "come" cannot be answered apart from the hungry and thirsty "coming" as well.* This revelation dovetails with Isaiah 58, where God flipped the script on people's understanding of prayer and fasting, explaining that true fasting is ministering to the poor, naked, and hungry. The same might be said of true eschatology. Jesus Christ is hidden within the lost and broken, and so His "return" hinges upon their awakening. In other words, the full Song can't be released without all of God's instruments playing together—even the ones that seem the most bent and distorted.

Now there may be a lot of Scriptures running through your mind that make these interpretations difficult to swallow. Perhaps certain passages have been berating you during previous chapters where we subverted some traditional ideas about the end-times. The concept of Jesus returning on a literal horse in the sky and burning half of humanity (while crowning the other half) is lodged deeply into our psyche. But this is because we have been taught the Bible like a textbook and not like a song and parable, which is the real language of God. We've missed the harmony that emerges when we combine all the different texts, unveiling that great *sod* mystery of the Word. This is the Emmaus way of interpreting Scripture, as we saw with Jesus and the two traveling disciples with downcast hearts and unenlightened eyes.

This way of interpretation, difficult as it may be to take in, also confirms something else. It leads us back to the overarching idea that Eden is meant to return *through us*. While this comes as a joyful surprise to many, to others it brings deep disappointment. For those who have checked out and embraced an escapist theology that allows for sitting around and waiting for Jesus to appear in the sky and kill all the bad guys, this is a tough pill to swallow. Such disappointment mirrors what happened amongst God's people during Jesus's first coming. That "coming" was just too offensive, especially when it involved Yahweh appearing in human flesh (Galilean flesh nonetheless). But this is the great mystery hidden in the Word for those with eyes to see and ears to hear. And it calls us to a higher level of participation in the Kingdom of God than we've ever imagined.

The Edenic Soul

To say it one last time—the Shulammite represents the human soul. Her journey reveals a soul that has returned to its rest in God. Through growing trust, the soul comes back to intimacy with its Creator; to its true identity and to original blessing. This is precisely what we see at the end of the Shulammite's journey where she is pictured as the one who "sits in the gardens." The Hebrew word for "sit" is a term that has to do with habitation and dwelling. It's often translated as "settling down." The Shulammite has indeed settled down and made her abode in the intimate garden of oneness.

The first time this word for "sit" shows up is important. It's found in Genesis 4 when Cain, the son of Eden's exiles, makes his dwelling outside of Eden's gates:

Chief of the Mountains

Then Cain went out from the presence of the Lord, and
settled *in the land of Nod, east of Eden.*
(Gen. 4:16)

The Shulammite's story is the exact opposite. It's representative of those who have left the land of Nod (a term that means "wandering") and gone west, settling back down into Eden's embrace.

Fittingly, the word for "sit" is also used for marriage throughout the Bible. In fact, the word shows up in the book of Hosea, right in the part where the prophet calls back his prostituting wife:

*Then I said to her, "You shall **stay** with me for many days. You shall not play the harlot, nor shall you have a man; so I will also be toward you."*
(Hos. 3:3)

This word "stay" is the same term for "sit" or "settle down." It's used here (and in other places like Ezra 10:2 and Nehemiah 13:23) to signify settling down into marriage. This parallels the journey of the Bride beautifully, for she has left behind the veil of spiritual prostitution—the Nod of wilderness wandering—and has returned to Edenic intimacy and rest. She is now the redeemed Eve who moves in partnership with her Beloved Bridegroom.

And that brings us back to her call to *hurry and come*. She is calling upon Christ, and she is also calling upon the humanity where Christ is hidden. Therefore, she's still speaking to her younger brothers and sisters, even to those who are naked, hungry, and alone. She calls them to come through the open gates of Eden and partake of the Tree of Life within. In calling them to hurry, she's welcoming the very presence of Jesus Himself, for there is One Spirit and One Father who is over all and through all and in all. As such, there is One Body. Though many members of this Body are wandering in Nod—immature and lost under the weight of a

The Song of the Ages: Part III

lying veil—this does not negate the fact that they are still part of the wonderful Body of Jesus.

Such is the reason the Beloved wants the Shulammite to call out to His "companions." The Hebrew for companions here is *chebar*, which can be literally translated as "united." Think about how well that fits in with what we know of the Gospel. Jesus is the friend of sinners. He is the One who has *united* Himself with sinful humanity, having reconciled *all* by the blood of His cross. All humanity comprises the companions Jesus speaks of at the end of the Song. He now wants these companions to hear the Gospel through the harmonious voice of His redeemed helper—the Shulammite Bride.

The Edenic Voice

"O you who sit in the gardens!" He cries. *"My companions are listening for your voice. Let me hear it!"*

There are three different Hebrew words in this passage that bring us back to Eden and reveal something absolutely marvelous. Obviously, the word behind "gardens" is one of those terms. It's the same word used for the Garden of Eden. However, the two words behind *"hear"* and *"voice"* are also connected to our original home in Genesis. These two words are introduced together for the first time in Genesis 3:

> They **heard** the **sound** of the Lord God walking in the **garden** in the cool of the day...
> (Gen. 3:8a)

The word for "sound" can also be translated as "voice." It gets rendered voice in the Song of Songs, but not here in Genesis. This is because it doesn't seem reasonable to translate the passage as describing a "voice" walking in the Garden. However, it really does make sense when you understand that Jesus *is* the Voice of God. Adam and Eve were actually hearing both Jesus and the Father

Chief of the Mountains

walking together! And in fact, the Holy Spirit is in this passage as well, for it says the voice of the Lord God was walking in the "cool" of the day. The word for "cool" is the Hebrew term *ruach*. This is the word for wind and spirit! Yet the translators don't render it this way either, because it doesn't make as much sense. Nonetheless, a literal rendering of the text might read, "The *Voice* of the *Lord God* was walking in the *Spirit* of the day." Therefore, this is Jesus, the Father, and the Holy Spirit all walking together as one. The entire Trinity is pictured here in the original bliss of Eden. What another beautiful mystery hidden in the text!

Sadly, the next part of this verse is where "the man and his wife hid themselves from the presence of the Lord God." This is the moment where man ran from the wondrous fellowship of the Trinity—the soul's first exit into Nod. But praise God, we hold in our hearts the gift of King Solomon, the Song of the Shulammite who lights the way for every soul to return to this original place of fellowship.

To provide a sweeping recap of this volume, this "return" to Eden happens when human beings come back into union with the Voice—the Word Himself. This is what the Shulammite longed for in the beginning through her request for the "kisses of His mouth." We've now seen how she *became* that kiss. The Shulammite is now one with the Voice of the Lord God, walking in (leaning upon) the Spirit as she moves throughout the unawakened garden of humanity. Accordingly, with these final poetic words, the voice of the Shulammite goes on to echo the Spirit and Bride from Revelation: *"Hurry, my beloved, and be like a gazelle or a young stag on the mountains of spices."*

A New Paradigm for the Seven Mountains

In an earlier chapter we saw how the gazelle and stag are both poignant images of Christ. Therefore, the Spirit and Bride are

The Song of the Ages: Part III

calling upon Christ to hurry, to come swiftly on the "mountains of spices." There's a final mystery hidden in this last part of the Song that we will now attempt to unseal. To do so, we will first turn to something spoken by the prophet Isaiah.

> *Now it will come about that*
> *In the last days*
> *The mountain of the house of the Lord*
> *Will be established as the chief of **the mountains,***
> *And will be raised above the hills;*
> *And all the nations will stream to it.*
> (Isa. 2:2)

For centuries, both Jews and Christians have held this verse close to their chests, teaching it to successive generations and celebrating the hope it conveys. Isaiah's words tell of the wondrous promise of the Kingdom of God reigning over every aspect of society. It speaks of the one mountain of God that will be "chief" over all the other "mountains" of the world.

Now remember that in the Shulammite's closing words, she also mentions "mountains" in the plural. Both the "mountains" found in Isaiah and those in the Shulammite's final verse are speaking of the same thing. They are referring to all different aspects of culture and society. In the last days—which we are in right now—the mountain of God, the culture of heaven, will be established as the chief amongst every other mountain. And all the nations will stream to this one reality.

For a moment, recall the image of the menorah, Moses's prophetic lampstand with its six branches proceeding from a center branch. Out of that center would flow a stream of oil that filled each of the other branches, providing the way for light to ignite (Zech. 4). We looked at this extensively in the second volume of *The Song of the Ages* when we discussed how Jesus compares the entire

Chief of the Mountains

church to the Hebrew menorah. The six branches, we discovered, represent humanity while the seventh branch represents Christ.

Now for the last half century or so there's been a movement within many sectors of the church focusing on the "seven mountains" of culture. Like our discussion on fivefold ministry, we're not going to get into the details and history of this teaching, though it is a fascinating study. Instead, we'll just summarize and say that these seven mountains are usually delineated as the sectors of business, government, education, media, arts, family, and religion. Each of these areas involve the key places where human life plays out. And indeed, they are all places where the culture of heaven needs to be cultivated. This corresponds powerfully with the imagery of the sevenfold lampstand, but it requires one small revision to the seven mountains paradigm.

Jesus said the lampstands *are the churches* (Rev. 1:20). When we merge the seven-branched lampstand with the seven mountains perspective, we realize the whole world is called to be the "church." The church is not on a separate mountain called "religion." Typically, the mountain of religion is equated with places of worship, such as churches, mosques, and synagogues. Of course, proponents of the traditional seven mountains teaching would say that many of these are false systems of religion. But really, all of religion is false. Religion is a lie that was birthed in Eden at the Tree of Knowledge. It is man's efforts to attain union and rest.

The mountain of religion doesn't need reformation—it needs annihilation. In reality, the "church" or *ekklesia* exists wherever there are human souls awakening to the love and light of Christ. Church can happen in any arena. You can gather together in a designated building to worship just as much as you can join up in a living room for a family gathering, or a boardroom for an executive meeting. Now some will point out that there is a "true religion" according to the book of James. This involves caring for

The Song of the Ages: Part III

the orphan and the widow and keeping oneself unstained from the world (Jms. 1:27). But are these not things meant to happen in every sphere, whether business, family, the arts, or government? Are not each of these areas called to be "unstained," demonstrating the purity of God's creativity and love?

Now this is not to neglect the idea of a seventh mountain, but rather to reframe it as the "chief of the mountains" from Isaiah's hopeful prophecy. This is why the image of the lampstand is so helpful. The six pipes of culture—the places where our humanity is expressed and lived out—are all meant to be connected to that center pipe; and that connection is simply an awakened union with Christ. This is not a mountain of religion, but a mountain of awakened life. The Kingdom, the church, the Bride—we can wrestle through the nuances and different aspects that work within each of these terms, but ultimately they speak to the same thing. They are all terms trying to pin down man's renewed fellowship with the Triune God. They are manifestations of the spice-laden Christ living His life through us.

On that note, we come back to the Song and the Shulammite's final burst of poetry. She says that these mountains of the world are filled with "spices," a description that has come up a few times throughout the Song. Not surprisingly, it has been used to describe both Jesus and His Bride (Sgs. 4:10 & 5:13). The word represents the fragrant, resurrected life of Christ. And certainly, this fragrance can be found in every mountain of society. It's the beauty hidden within all things. It's the *sod* mystery hidden within the sod of the earth. The life of Jesus is the fragrant and delicious life waiting to erupt from the soil of every region on the planet. We're not waiting for some ethereal and Platonic city to come down from the sky where we will play harps and sing hymns on a literal walkway of gold. We're waiting on something else; something much richer and much more *real.*

Chief of the Mountains

We're waiting for families all across the earth to mirror the intimate fellowship found within the Triune Family. We're waiting for businesses to model the generous and joyful handiwork of heaven. We're waiting for the arts to exemplify the creativity that spoke the stars into existence and lined up their coordinates with mathematical purpose and aesthetic wonder. We're waiting for the governing work of assembled public life to resemble something greater and more majestic than the hierarchies of angels. We're waiting on the fullness of Christ's incarnation appearing in each and every person in all the ways they go about their day. In that regard, we're waiting on something that is already here, like the fragrance inside of a soon-to-bloom flower, or the song hidden in the throat of a sleeping singer.

The full release of this Song is nearer now than when we first heard the Gospel's melody. It's coming on the mountains and leaping on the hills. A harmony is building and soon it will fill the whole earth like the waters cover the sea. Only then will the great symphony of the cosmos be complete. In the meantime, each of us are an instrument in this wonderful Song. Let us join the chorus and welcome in that great crescendo. And let the grace of our Lord Jesus be with all.

Amen.

About the Author

Nick Padovani is a husband, a father, a social worker, and a friend of Jesus. He is also the pastor of a beautiful and flourishing church community. It is his joy and passion to see God's children awaken to the full inheritance in the love of Christ.

Nick is also the founder of Eyes Open Press. For more books, updates, and speaking opportunities, please visit:

www.eyesopenpress.com

More from Eyes Open Press

Eyes Open Press is a unique publishing house with a vision to sound loud the trumpet of God's all-encompassing grace. If you enjoyed *The Song of the Ages,* check out Dylan DeMarisco's *Made Perfect* and Mo Thomas's *Into the Abyss.* Both are available at Amazon and www.eyesopenpress.com.

To see more of Nick's writings, check out the online magazine *Elisha's Riddle*. This publication is a monthly dose of wonder, revelation, and prophetic hope. Each subscription **supports the work of Eyes Open Press** in helping authors and creators release the Good News!

 Discover more at www.ElishasRiddle.com

www.ingramcontent.com/pod-product-compliance
Lightning Source LLC
Chambersburg PA
CBHW020415010526
44118CB00010B/262